PAST TENSE

Jean Cocteau

PAST TENSE

VOLUME I

DIARIES

Introduction by NED ROREM

Annotations by PIERRE CHANEL

Translation by RICHARD HOWARD

HARCOURT BRACE JOVANOVICH, PUBLISHERS

SAN DIEGO NEW YORK LONDON

HBJ

LIBRARY OF CONGRESS CATALOGING-IN-PUBLICATION DATA

Cocteau, Jean, 1889–1963.
Past tense.

Translation of: Le passé défini.
Includes index.
1. Cocteau, Jean, 1889–1963—Diaries.
2. Authors, French—20th century—Diaries.
3. Artists—France—Diaries.
4. Moving-picture producers and directors—France—Diaries.
I. Chanel, Pierre. II. Title.
PQ2605.015Z473 1987 848'.91203 [B] 86-12060
ISBN 0-15-171289-1 (v. 1)

Designed by Michael Farmer
Printed in the United States of America

B C D E

Contents

Introduction

THE DISTINGUISHING feature of a diary as opposed to a memoir is on-the-spot reaction, the writer's truth as he feels it, not as he felt it. If that truth is no more "truthful" for being in the first person, it does contain the defining character of immediacy. The intimate journal is a literary form used almost solely by the French. They keep it as a sideline—a book about how hard it is to write a book—fragmentary by its nature, forever unfinished. Not only France's authors, from Rousseau, Baudelaire, and Amiel to Charles du Bos, Jules Renard, and Julien Green, but her other artists and even politicians—Berlioz, Delacroix, de Gaulle, Poulenc, Malraux—have made literature of their lives. The genre has never been popular with non-French Continentals, still less with the British who prefer autobiography, and (at least until recently) is virtually unpracticed by Americans, who, with all due emancipation and collective carnality, do retain a decorum toward their personal selves. We know less about the daily grind of such graphic romancers as Philip Roth or Edmund White than we do about that circumspect *littérateur*, André Gide. Gide, the modern world's most famous diarist, was so enmeshed in the genre that he not only published quadriannually throughout his life a journal documenting his existence, but in his only novel allows his alter ego, Édouard, to keep a diary whose entries are interpolated like ballast to stabilize the various frantic plots of *Les Faux-Monnayeurs*; simultaneously with his novel Gide kept a special diary called *Journal des Faux-Monnayeurs* detailing his problems—and Édouard's—in developing the novel; and in his regular journal he detailed the problems of composing the *Journal des Faux-Monnayeurs*. Claude Mauriac, in *his* diary, describes a charmingly strained postprandial hour in the country home of his famous father, François Mauriac, where the two had persuaded Gide to spend a weekend. The trio of authors are clearly anxious to retire to their rooms, ostensibly for a nap, actually to confide to their separate Rashomonian journals the literary lunchtime remarks before they fade from memory.

How is it that Jean Cocteau, of all people, during this long display of intimate self-promotion among his peers, never kept a diary? Was he not the most public, the most spellbinding creature of culture in Paris during the first half century? If Diaghilev's demand to the young poet, "Astound me," had in 1912 unleashed a talent which proceeded to thrill every caste with its ballets, monologues, paintings, drawings, plays, novels, essays, poems, choreography, and even church murals (as a musician Cocteau did lack a voice but compensated by "inventing" Satie and the Groupe des Six), was Jean-the-man any less formidable? Had he not inherited from Wilde the title of world's most dazzling talker and from De Quincey that of the world's most conspicuous *opiomane*? Was he not dogged by the suicides of many whose strength was unequal to his? Had not *Le Livre blanc* pseudonymously described his bouts in the all-male brothels of Toulon, bouts depicted visually a decade later in his melancholy lithographs for the novels of Jean Genet (the Cocteau of the working class)? Had he not attended operas with Barbette, the Texan trapezist in drag, and created (some say destroyed) names now more legendary than his own—Jean Marais, Edith Piaf? Had he not been glorified by Proust as Saint-Loup, by Gide as the comte de Passavant, and by Freud himself in an analysis of *Blood of a Poet*? Was not the sight of those long hands, rebellious hair, and tapering nose an almost daily fact in the press for fifty years? Could it not be argued that insofar as cinema has now become our most expressive, our most *telling* art, and that insofar as his nine films were the most influential in Europe and by extension the world, Jean Cocteau was the most important artist of our time? And finally, was he not infatuated with this very importance?

Yes, why had he never kept a diary?

Well, Jean Cocteau did in fact publish a sort of Journal, *Opium* (1930), albeit on the specific subject of disintoxication, just as the *Journal de la Belle et la Bête* (1946) and *Maalesh* (1949) were day-by-day reportings on the specific subjects of filmmaking and theatrical touring. But he never kept a journal on his more generalized quotidian doings, although he did over the course of the years pen many a retrospective self-portrait as well as historic portraits of famous friends, vignettes which served as the sole quotable matter for his various biographers during the thirteen years after his death.

Now it turns out that for the thirteen years before his death he did keep a diary—a voluminous one at that. This long-secret fact, now revealed, has caused a resurgence of all his work in France. The opening pages would seem to coincide with Cocteau's permanent removal from Paris to the Midi, where, in the lavish Villa Santo Sospir at Cap-Ferrat, he passed his remaining days with two friends, the actor Édouard Dermit and the wealthy Francine Weisweiller. The book cannot be said to be any more or any less a bid for immortality than the bulk of Cocteau's earlier vast and varied oeuvre, and its inception predates by four years his official "immortality"—the 1955 reception into the Académie Française.

This first volume came out in Paris in the early fall of 1983, twenty years to the day after the poet's death. Surely his will would have stipulated the discreet period so as to impose a proper distance and to avoid problems with living persons, yet not so discreet (like Mark Twain's fifty-year stipulation) as to divest his papers of gossip value and to allow the chief actors to dissolve into limbo. Cocteau himself chose the name *Le Passé défini* (how prettily the grammar balances with Noel Coward's *Present Indicative*), suggesting he did intend publication posthumously, the title is so clearly *après coup*; the book's not about the definite past at all but, like every diary, about the present. Given his flamboyant reputation (one can't help but take lightly Cocteau's contention that reputations of public figures are made by their public more than by themselves), the book promised to be succulent, especially since Cocteau himself had once said—and this, despite the ongoing appearances of the diaries of so many of his quick and sober colleagues—"A diary should appear only after our death. Who cares about entries like, 'Reread *Andromache*. Lunched at Madame So-&-so's'?"

I devoured *Le Passé défini* on the spot and made entries in my own diary:

27 DECEMBER 1983. Went to bed with Cocteau, vaguely disappointing, except for the close (to me) vitality: the journal covers eighteen months, beginning in July 1951 (six more volumes are promised by Gallimard during the next years), in which nearly every entry brings home an event at which I was present. But the fragmented philosophical gems were all later polished and reset more tellingly elsewhere. What blinded me yesterday is frayed today—the constant harping on being read and then forgotten by those few who read. "*On peut dire à n'importe qui et n'importe où une chose qu'on a déjâ écrite. Elle est neuve. Il n'est pas rare qu'on nous conseille de l'écrire. Même ceux qui nous lisent ne se souviennent de rien.*" Maybe those readers are too polite to say that his conversation seems a replay of what they've already read. Or maybe, in different contexts, an old *tournure* takes on new light, even new sense. Don't I reread my own diaries, having forgotten that I used a charmed phrase here, then reused it there? Cocteau was too quick to accuse his public.

In passing, he writes of me in an episode which I too have described: our visit, with Marie-Laure de Noailles, to her mother's at the Villa Croisset in Grasse. I noted: "On arriving, Cocteau announced to Madame de Croisset, 'It seems like yesterday that I was bringing Marie-Laure back from our outings.' (He'd not been in this house since the summers of World War One when the adolescent Marie-Laure began nursing the love-hate she never forsook.)" *His* entry, though, wilts when he tells us that "*Comme je n'ai aucun sens du temps, j'ai l'impression d'y revenir après une promenade.*" He forever states that he has "no sense of time," yet isn't it precisely because he does have a sense of time that he has the *impression d'y revenir*? Again he tells wrong (wrong theatrically) an anecdote—retold in my *Paris Diary*—about Garbo at the Véfour where clients mistook her for Madeleine Sologne. Isn't that irony sufficient? But Cocteau adds what musn't be added: "*Le sens du légendaire est perdu.*" Never apologize, never explain.

His pro-Stalin leanings seem naïve even for then, as do his generalities about Americans: Americans hate Negroes, yet they all do their best to acquire a suntan.

Around that same season Boulez proclaimed: "Every musician who has not felt the necessity of the serial language is useless." (Omit the word *not*, and I would agree.) Cocteau, who for the first time had no bandwagon of his own, jumped on that of Boulez, with statements like: "It is understandable that young musicians today take their stand on Schoenberg and find in him an arm against works which fear his science of numbers." But the "countercharm," of which he was approving, was himself; nor is it probable that he would have recognized any work of Schoenberg.

Dalton Baldwin recently told me that after a recital of French songs which he gave with Souzay around 1960, Cocteau backstage dismissed every work on the program—Ravel, Poulenc, Debussy—except Gounod, whom he claimed the master of French song.

28 DECEMBER. Cocteau's diary is hard to put down, not least because I'm continually comparing his version of this or that event with my version. For example, in December of 1951, the notorious debacle at the *Bacchus* gala when Mauriac, a few seats down from us, arose at the final curtain and fled, amidst a battery of flash bulbs and shocked gasps; and Mauriac's vitriolic attack on Cocteau in *Figaro littéraire* on the twenty-ninth, followed by Cocteau's open reply, "Je t'accuse," next day in *France-Soir* (which Cocteau admits to having written *before* Mauriac's article appeared), both men tutoyering each other like beloved enemies. Indeed, I seem to recall—but where's the fact? I've searched everywhere—that he signed his public letter "*Ton ennemi qui t'aime.*" This sort of front-page squabble between renowned intellectuals about religious morality versus artistic prerogative, though seemingly petty at the moment, is majestically stimulating on rereading, especially in the light of America's know-nothing journalism and a government that eschews literary argument.

Yet who will find himself now in the grip of such reading where Mauriac is unknown and Cocteau but a onetime moviemaker? If the diary were translated, would I myself feel uncomfortable at others reading this mess by an idol? Cocteau's need for love and acceptance is touching, and what I personally owe him is incalculable. Yet what once passed for insight now seems specious. At the very outset, look at this false analogy as he chides so-called existentialists: "*Ne rien faire et boire dans des petites caves, c'est existentialiste. C'est comme s'il existait à New York des 'relativistes' qui dansent dans des caves et qu'on croie qu'Einstein danse avec eux.*" But there *aren't* any "relativists" dancing in "caves" in New York. Existentialism is a philosophy, and Einstein was a physicist, and physics, though open to misuse, cannot be misinterpreted and cultified in the same sense that a philosophy can. In this chaotic journal Cocteau resembles his Sphinx—"I secrete my thread, let it out, wind it back and spin it in"; most of those threads were deknotted into smooth essays the following year, notably in the *Journal d'un inconnu*. As with my unimpeachable Ravel, who dimly showed clay feet a few years back when Orenstein published a batch of his juvenilia, so Jean Cocteau changes—perhaps evolves, and for the better—to my ken.

His words on Proust (on "re-rereading" Proust, as he puts it) do ring with the authority of One Who Was There. No such demystification exists in any other article on Proust. . . .

29 December. Finished Cocteau. The man and his work will remain always among those three or four most influential upheavals to blind me against other aesthetics, other voices. But if childhood loves can never be dislodged like wisdom teeth, they can still grow loose in their sockets in our old age. Cocteau, in repeating to exhaustion his every *bon mot* lest we may never have heard it, weakens, by revealing his tricks, the very foundation of his structure. Even Debussy, the nonpareil, when I examined the war-mongering text for his very last work, *Noël des enfants qui n'ont plus de maisons*, became an average vengeful creature subverting his own art.

That was then. Today, nearly three years older, I'm also wiser for having read the vast second volume, and admit to an impatient thirst for the third. It is wrong to read Cocteau's diary for its art, for art is by definition sculptured, economical, with a planned ending, while this vulnerable and open-ended affair is a continually backtracking blueprint, as removed from the finished products being polished simultaneously as, say, Baudelaire's loose letters from his tight verse. *Le Passé défini* exudes the utter authority and utter insecurity combined in all true artists; indeed, it could only have been composed by a true artist although it is not itself art. By its nature it lacks the tailored care of the formal journals. It contrasts to the body of Cocteau's poetry, from the perfumed perfection of *Le Prince frivole* in 1909 (*Au revoir! il le faut, pour désunir les couples / Que je longe en glissant sur mes pieds bleus et souples . . .*), through the touching honesty of the still-uncollected love poems slipped nightly under the door of Jean Marais in 1939 (*Ah! je chante, je chante / Pour t'avoir le même demain / Car la vie a l'air trop méchante / Sans la caresse de ta main*), to the crystalline sadness of the hundred alexandrine quatrains in *Le Chiffre sept* (1952) which begin:

Voici que presque rien de ce fil ne me reste.
Sa pelote était lourde et me bondait le coeur.
Et le coeur si souvent a retourné sa veste
Qu'il croyait ne jamais perdre de sa douleur.

If the poems, and thus the whole catalog (for Cocteau referred to himself as solely a poet, whether concocting a libretto, a film script, a pornographic story, or a woven rug), are as much style as content, the diary is mainly content with only passing stabs at style.

What is the tone of this content? Cocteau's diary is not what the French call a *journal intime* in the sense that it limns sensual or carnal reaction. Discretion reigns. The book seems out of the eighteenth century, like Mozart or the philosophes, in that there's little talk of food or of birds & bees, much less of romance or raw sex; and, despite the author's most frequent residence in the south of France, his subject is urban. Mentions of nice weather are rare, succinct, never descriptive, while mentions of work, friendship and social life (the index contains close to two thousand names, half of them "dear friends") are the core of Cocteau's concern. Already in 1932 on the first page of *Essai de critique indirecte* he had noted, "*Je me réserve de vivre et de faire l'amitié (plus difficile à faire que l'amour)*. . . . " The mood is warm, sincere, tactful, thoroughly unbitchy even when directed toward François Mauriac, whose mean and nagging assessment of Cocteau is a thorny refrain throughout these pages. ("*Pauvre Mauriac. À sa mort il aura tout eu, sauf tout*" "Poor Mauriac. At his death he will have had it all, except it".)

Cocteau's homosexuality is often mentioned by others, and not rarely with miscomprehension, as by his biographers Steegmuller or Brown, or with a sneer, as by such "friends" as Igor Stravinsky or Coco Chanel, but it may surprise readers that it is never mentioned by himself. Whatever his public odor as a citizen, it was never abetted—as was Gide's or Jean Genet's—by his own writings or movies, and whatever his private leanings as an author, his diary is not a confessional. So his motive for caution, for posthumous publication, seems unclear. "The Gidean method consists of pretending to say all in order to hide all; a diary exists so that its writer can enter into it without reserve anything that goes through his head." So writes Cocteau in *Le Passé défini*, without reserve, but not divulging much either. Still, a diary is the sole literary form *sans* form—the one literary genre without guidelines. If, as I claimed earlier, a diary is a book before it becomes a book, to some extent all art is a diary in that it reflects its maker's hidden nature despite itself. (A symphony is a diary in a code so abstruse that even its composer cannot decipher it. Unlike painters or writers, composers are seldom jailed for subversion.)

Cocteau all through this book seems anxious to be thought a Thinker. He did indeed have an original, active, and fabulous mind, but a Thinker he was not—not in the sense of being (like, for example, Auden—is there any other among poets?) an intellectual, an analyst. His long speculations on Time, on Distance, or on other such scientific matters as the absolute reality of flying saucers can be savored without embarrassment only if savored as fantasy, just as Freud today can no longer be read except as poetry. On the other hand, Cocteau's flair for the character sketch (of Picasso and his family, of Chaplin and his, or of the temperamental comparison between Spain and France) is as canny in words as on the drawing board. No less spirited is the description, unselfpitying, of his own ill health. How, during seizures of violent illness, he is able to *write* about them, as well as to write twenty letters a day and then to write about writing the letters, can be explained only by an indefatigable craving not to be forgotten. (On his tombstone in Milly: *Je reste avec vous.*) Glory, not power, guided him. Which explains the absence of malice, even when faced with huge disappointments, in all those longing to be loved.

When people ask me, "What was Cocteau like?," I'm always inclined to forget that I was with him only six or eight times during the thirteen years of our acquaintance. True, we corresponded regularly during these years; he designed covers for my music; I composed a ballet with Jean Marais in 1952 and thus was in steady contact with the poet by proxy. True again, to reside in France as I did during the 1950s when Cocteau was in daily evidence—pronouncing from the screen, over the air, and from bookstore *vitrines*—was to be, even for the peasants of Oléron, in his inescapable presence. And true, Cocteau had a habit of collective *tutoiement* so that in a room packed with people each soul felt singled out. To meet him once was to know him. His need to be liked made him give all, disseminating himself indiscriminately throughout the globe; yet while you were with him you were seemingly the sole beneficiary of his charitable flood of fire. I've known few people in my life with such infectious charm; it may be affectation or opportunism, but it can't be bought, and it can't be faked.

Jean Cocteau's diary mirrors this personality so contagiously that twenty-two years after his death he, like Whitman, risks "springing from the pages into your arms." But does culture ever cross borders intact? Not even music is a universal language. Cocteau, who, despite his contention (contradicting Frost's "poetry is that which can't be translated") that "*La langue d'un poète ne pouvant qu'être traduite*," never, except for his films, quite "took" in the United States. Neither did Gide, until his diaries were translated here in the early forties. As with Gide—indeed, as with every French nonfiction writer—99 percent of Cocteau's literary and social references are French (with occasional exceptions like Shakespeare, Hemingway, Gershwin, and Garbo), yet Gide's dramatis personae have come to be familiar to two generations of international readers.

Will Cocteau's diaries, now that they are in English, help to make his entire catalog a success over here? I do and don't hope so. Because I love the work of this wildly controlled, snobbish, adorable, frightening, irritating, unusual, haunting, and generous genius, I want to share it with America. And because I love his work, I want to keep it to myself.

—*Ned Rorem*

Note

FROM 1951 TO 1963, the year of his death, Cocteau kept this journal in spiral-bound sketchbooks, 10 by 16 inches. Here, among passing references to events of the day, are true journal entries, in a mixture intended to serve Cocteau as a biographical memento as well as to record the movement of his critical reflection.

Cocteau anticipated the eventual publication of the text, and its title—*Le Passé défini*—is his, as well as this advice to future editors: "Omit what is no more than memoranda, as well as repetitions caused by my forgetting I have already told what I am telling" (August 17, 1953).

Thirty-two years after this journal was begun, its literary value and its documentary usefulness can no longer be dissociated, except by an altogether arbitrary choice. Except for the repetitions, then, and the excisions which Cocteau's heir, Édouard Dermit, has considered indispensable (in each case indicated by the sign [. . .]) the text is uncut, so that—according to one of the possible meanings of Cocteau's adjective—this past is henceforth determined.

The editor wishes to express his gratitude to Louis Évrard for his help throughout; he also thanks Édouard Dermit, Laurent Boyer, André Fraigneau, Boris Kochno, and Jean Marais for information they so kindly provided.

—PIERRE CHANEL

PAST TENSE

The Diaries:

July 16, 1951 – December 28, 1952

*July 16 · 1951**

Existentialists. Never has a word diverged so far from what it means! As if drinking your life away in one little hole after another is being *existentialist*. As if there were *relativists* in New York who dance in bars and imagine that Einstein is dancing there with them. [Jean-Paul] Sartre has nothing to do with this phenomenon. He has the best manners, the warmest heart, the noblest soul of anyone I know. He loathes laziness. We often marvel together over the strange path his school has taken.

---

*The journal begins *ex abrupto*. However, this is not the first time Cocteau kept a journal; there exists, in a private Parisian collection, a journal from Cocteau's youth (June 28, 1911–April 1912), several fragments of which were published in *La Revue des lettres modernes*, nos. 298–303, 1972. Besides the forthcoming *Journal sous l'Occupation* (March 1942–April 1945), *Opium, Journal d'une désintoxication* (1930), *La Belle et la Bête, Journal d'un film* (1946), and *Maalesh, Journal d'une tournée de théâtre* (1940), are journals, as well as *Retrouvons notre enfance* (1935), and *Mon Premier Voyage. Tour du monde en 80 jours* (1937).

In Sicily, on a mountainside called the Plain of the Greeks, where people speak some kind of Albanian incomprehensible to the Italians, I was told (through an interpreter) that they were about to open an existentialist club.

People separate mystery from reality. Yet reality *is* mystery (there is no such thing as reality). Those who know this are poets or apt to understand poets. Everything else is aestheticism.

In painting, what I like is the act itself.* What comes of it doesn't matter to me. To paint is to work alone, without intermediaries: to put *your* night into *their* daylight, and not to bother about anything but work.

Odd that Americans, who despise "people of color," should be so eager to let the sun bake them as black as possible.

Francine† has extinguished in me any notion of *thine* and *mine*, that melodrama of bourgeois education.

A friendship without duties and without gratitude is true friendship. Otherwise it is an *ersatz* love (as people understand love). A craving to add more drama to the drama of existence, a drama which friendship alone makes acceptable.

I am often criticized for not writing my memoirs, for not having written a daily account. Aside from the fact that I have no memory for dates, so that it is impossible for me to tell things chronologically, I have seen too much and heard incredible things. People would think I make them up.

Without my realizing it, painting has completely changed the

---

*Cocteau had taken up easel painting in 1950.

†Mme Alec Weisweiller, *née* Francine Worms, became one of Cocteau's close friends in 1950, during the shooting of *Les Enfants terribles*, Jean-Pierre Melville's film drawn from Cocteau's novel. She was related to Nicole Stéphane (pseudonym of Nicole de Rothschild), who played the part of Élisabeth, and several sequences of the film were shot in Alec and Francine Weisweiller's Paris town house, 4 Place des États-Unis. On Easter Day 1950, Cocteau became Francine Weisweiller's guest in her villa on Cap-Ferrat, the Villa Santo Sospir (on the southeast tip of the cape); he undertook to decorate the interior walls throughout.

way I work *as a writer*. Instead of writing *Bacchus** from the beginning, I work on scenes scattered all through, as if I had to cover a canvas. I keep retouching them, constantly "re-covering." In other words, I proceed by "values" rather than by "lines." Gradually the *whole thing* is taking shape, acquiring a contour. Still prone, the play is beginning to stretch its limbs. Once it is alive, I'll nurse it until it can stand up and walk on its own.

A play is not a sermon. The ideas cannot be mine—they must be the characters'. As soon as I express my own ideas, the mechanism jams. I have to cut and wait till the seam forms. If I did the stitching on the spot, the seam would show.

There can be a lot of talk in a play if the dialogue moves toward action or toward a speech that supersedes action—toward a development that helps the action mount up, move toward its goal. *Active speech* is the secret of theater. Otherwise everything stagnates, and the audience stops listening—waiting for something to happen and tired of waiting for something that doesn't happen. The chalk line in front of a chicken: if this line isn't there under the words, the spell is broken and the audience refuses to follow to the end.

For example, in the scene between Hans and the Cardinal [act II, scene vi], the dialogue must move toward "Are you truly innocent?" and then toward "You don't believe in God." Without these developments, the contradictions indispensable to the psychology of Hans's character would confuse the audience.

Besides, if there must be contradictions, a character should be conscious of them and mention them—should tell the audience about them before the audience realizes that the dialogue swarms

---

*A play in three acts. Sets, costumes, and direction by the author. Created by the Compagnie Madeleine Renaud–Jean-Louis Barrault, at the Théâtre Marigny, on December 20, 1951, published in 1952.

The reader should note that, in general, titles of Cocteau's works are given in English when they have been translated in current editions, otherwise they have been left in French.

with contradictions, regards them as mistakes, and uses them as a weapon against the author.

. . . .

JULY 27 · 1951

My dreams are so complicated, so real—so close to a real life which they invent down to the last detail—that I could keep a diary of them without ever revealing they were dreams. But I wonder if that strange life wouldn't hinder me and wouldn't lose its luster once it was written down (like certain plants that turn dull as soon as you take them out of the water). It must be the fear of this that keeps me from transcribing anything, that makes me scour my mind when I wake up, scraping off that creeping inner grime.

Gradually, and almost without my realizing it, my play has come together out of its own shards. One day I discovered that these shards constituted a dense sequence and that all I needed to do was rework the details. From which has emerged a play about that *hard* virtue I set in opposition to the soft kind. This was the misunderstood theme of the *Lettre à [Jacques] Maritain* [1926]. To restore to God the intelligence transferred to the devil's account, especially in the sixteenth century, when the devil took the leading role.

Hans is good. The Duke is good. The Cardinal is good. Lothar is good. Christine is good. This is what seems new to me in this play, since we usually look for strength in a principle of wickedness. Hans is an intelligence in chaos; he flies into the flame without thinking what he is doing. The Cardinal wants to save him and, of course, restore him to the church. The Duke admires the young man's freedom of mind and has doubts about his inclination toward the Reformation. Lothar espoused the Reformation in rebellion against a narrow-minded community. Hans shows him a truant path, a free school which delights his youth. Christine falls in love with Hans, who is unlike the young men of her world.

The other characters, the Bishop, the Provost, the Syndic, serve their own interests, and to them Hans represents only a dangerous anarchy.

Gradually I discovered the resemblance between this historical period and our own: both in the grip of wars of religion, sects, and schisms. (Communism as a religion, a fanatic ideology, confronting the reign of gold, the golden calf.) Did not Luther say, after accepting money from the feudal lords: "If the people had their way, we would be ruled by the dregs"? A remark I put in the Duke's mouth, since he has just clandestinely met Luther at the elector of Saxony's house, in Thuringia.

The Cardinal is a Roman and broad-minded; he astounds the Bishop; he accepts Hans's extravagances because he sees in them that primitive mysticism which true princes of the church prefer to piety.

The play may scandalize—my critics, unfortunately, taking the characters' words for my own and making no effort to understand the meaning of the whole (hypnotized by individual arguments). The play has no cause to plead. It merely shows the terrible solitude of individuals committed only to themselves who refuse to espouse the directives of any particular political faction. "If you would only acknowledge order," the Cardinal says to Hans, and Hans corrects him: "Take orders!" The Bacchus story, on which the action turns, is an old Byzantine custom. But in Byzantium, the victor of the ordeal consented to be its victim. He was sacrificed on the seventh day. I don't know if he was really a Dionysus. The significance, it seems to me, is that of a kingdom in miniature. The Bacchus custom, much diminished, still existed in Switzerland not so long ago—in Vevey if I'm not mistaken, during the grape harvest festival. Ramuz told me how disastrous it used to be when the victors lost their heads and afterward refused to return to their ordinary lives; they broke their engagements, dreamed of movie careers or of getting rich no matter how.

Of course, I envisaged the custom in its extreme form, when the consequences might exceed the limits of a masquerade.

P.S.: It is crucial to realize that the characters of *Bacchus* are living through events which we see stripped of detail and in perspective. The characters inhabited just one site within a total environment we can consider from a bird's-eye view. They guess; they speculate; they err. No science, no method guide them. Christine can suppose that Luther is not responsible for the threats imputed to him, whereas the true adherents of the Reformation know that Luther made them and that the church is only too happy to circulate the fact. Hans has been educated by a dangerously lucid abbé, but he has no foundation. He is the victim of a very pure disorder of mind.

There are two journalists who make it possible to imagine what journalism could be if France had not adopted a style which consists of covering herself with mud, gloating over her scandals, delighting in what goes on backstage, creating that "backstage" in order to divert the world instead of informing it. These two journalists are Thierry Maulnier and Georges Briquet. Georges Briquet is a radio sports reporter. Listening to him is an admirable experience. He has the precision of numbers. If he makes a mistake in his French—he is improvising at top speed, amid the din of the crowd—he immediately corrects it. Thierry Maulnier's articles are published in *Nice-Matin*. I happen to see them because I'm staying on the Riviera, but these articles, which are frequently masterpieces, should be published in Paris, on the front page of some major paper. (Though I doubt if a paper worthy of them exists.) Extraordinary article on the Tour de France yesterday morning. (The only classic of great journalism: Hugo's *Choses vues*.)

For three days now I've let *Bacchus* rest. (*Drop* would be more like it.) I force myself to think about other things. Preparing a canvas. Documenting sets and costumes in Holbein. Answering a pile of letters. Swimming in the Mediterranean. Trying to write the presidential message to the Fédération nationale du spectacle. In short, I'm making every effort to gain some perspective. I was looking for a secretary to whom I could dictate my hieroglyphics sentence by sentence, so that afterward I would have a clean text to work on. The director of the École Pigier in Nice sent me his son, who is preparing for his law exams and would like a job during his vacation. I shall begin this first cleanup operation on Monday. In a play, the whole problem is to portray ordinary speech, avoiding the highfalutin and not falling into platitudes. Virtually no one is interested in the French language anymore. Translations from American English are to blame, and the confusion between journalism and literature. In the theater, language is respected only if it is *a* language, specific to one author, difficult to follow, and making all the characters in a play express themselves in the same way. Recent popular successes may seem surprising. They involve complex works written in an obviously refined language. I wonder if the snobbery now extinct in an elite which has become too individualistic to obey orders hasn't emigrated to a public scared of seeming stupid and reassured when it doesn't quite understand what's going on, what's being said. This is the only possible explanation of the successes I see around me, which certainly are amazing. Today's public despises the mediocre comedies that used to make up the programs of road company tours. What it wants and applauds is what once seemed the property of that famous elite, which avoids serious work in order to take in any spectacle at all, armed to the teeth with defensive and offensive weapons. (For example, I hear of [Paul] Claudel's triumphs among the miners in the east of France, presumably Communists and dead set against a man of the church.) There is also a vague aspiration toward grandeur, toward nobility, toward lyricism, toward everything that used to be rejected by a public which symbolized *the least possible effort* and which now acclaims *L'Annonce faite à Marie* and *Le Soulier de satin*.

I should add that I've always acknowledged the popular success of *Phèdre*, *Britannicus*, or *Andromaque*. But nothing is more direct, more theatrical than Racine, when approached without the absurd reputation for boredom he gains in our schools and without the learned grime that dims his luster.

Fashion. Never lose sight of the fact that fashion becomes costume, that a theater costume must regain the vitality of fashion, that historic events were drowned in the torment of the quotidian, that heroes eat, digest, and shit.

The Tour de France. A phenomenon observed by Thierry Maulnier: all rebellions, all arguments, all factions give way to the bike. The Tour de France cannot be a visual spectacle; it goes by too fast. It is a *narrated* spectacle (told by the radio, the newspapers). It is a *chanson de geste* whose troubadours are the reporters.

The older I get, the more I realize that I am not read. My fame consists of rumors. Gossip. I can say to anyone, and anywhere, something I've already written, and it will be new. Quite often I'll be advised to write it down. Even those who read me remember nothing.

Admirable that so many strive to perpetuate an art which interests no one, and admirable that this art which interests no one preoccupies everyone and remains a nation's sole privilege.

Pétain dead. His death is an apotheosis. Pétain is dead, long live Pétain. His mediocrity overcomes all criticism. Everyone presents him the arms and excuses of France for having condemned a marshal to death. Messages from archbishops, high mass in the cathedrals—in Notre-Dame. They ought to canonize him. "You cannonaded, now be canonized." An age of speed: never have we seen a man move faster from disgrace to glorification.

JULY 29 · 1951

I was sixty-two on July 5. Hard for me to believe, probably because everyone, one way or another, still treats me as if I were nineteen. Besides, my mind and my figure remain the same and deceive me.

At Milly,* when I was dictating the *Entretiens autour du cinématographe* [1951] to [André] Fraigneau, I sincerely believed I was through, but since then I've completed the Villa Sospir decorations, painted twenty canvases, and now I'm finishing a play. Which proves that the poet obeys the commands of his own night, about which he knows absolutely nothing.

Almost every sentence of *Bacchus* is a historical quotation. My main sources were [Frantz] Funck-Brentano's *Luther* [1934] and Renan's *Vie de Jésus* [1853]. But I take them out of their context. I shift sentences so that they change lighting and help advance an imaginary action. Because these remarks are no longer found scattered in books but come out of the mouths of Hans, the Cardinal, the Bishop, the Duke, they take on a contemporaneity which scrapes off their patina and gives them the vitality of the new. Most likely they will scandalize and be attributed to me. This happened to me already, in *Antigone* [1922], when my foreshortenings of Sophocles had the same effect. People took the most famous arguments in the scene between Antigone and Creon to be my own declarations: insolent and internationalist. "Who knows if your frontiers have a meaning for the dead?" was hissed, to my astonishment, by half the house.

It has not occurred to a single newspaper that Rimbaud would be Pétain's age.† But that would be to set true glory against false. Rimbaud and Pétain were contemporaries; it takes all kinds.

The Frenchman pays his taxes and knows nothing of the wealth of French soil. He remains ignorant of his own resources, his own values. He imagines he is ruined, insults his true glories, imitates the nations arming and contending because they cannot live on their own resources, as France could if she wanted to and understood her own desire. But for centuries France has been committing

*Cocteau's country house in Milly-la-Forêt (Essonne) since 1947.

†Arthur Rimbaud was born in 1854, two years before Philippe Pétain.

suicide not quite successfully. Her strength lies too deep, and her disorder is what saves her from monologue; France always dialogues. Disputes and debates which astonish the world *keep her from being taken seriously*, which is the beginning of the end. (Which leads to imperialism.)

Between Nice and Monaco, every house is for sale. And more are being built. Indispensable deals. This is how the disequilibrium starts.

Need for heroes. Before movies, before the Tour de France, young people had *Les trois Mousquetaires*. D'Artagnan, Athos, Porthos, Aramis were the big stars—d'Artagnan biggest of all, and rightly so. Now Jean Marais* always polls first. I approve his joining the Comédie Française, which decimates his income but allows him to give a real meaning to the cinema's phantasmal and superficial glory. [Marcel] Pagnol tells me: "He doesn't have the voice of his own chest. He'll be a fine Néron, a fine Polyeucte. If he avoids Hugo's tirades and tantrums, he'll have a triumph in the Rue de Richelieu."

Luther used to be called the *Reichsführer*. Odd to realize how much Hitler was inspired by his methods. Hitler treated the Jews the way Luther treated the peasants. He preached their massacre, their tortures.

Speed of the Age. How could I have believed during the Occupation, when my work and my person were covered with mud and mockery, that huge demonstrations in my honor would be held in Munich and in Berlin.

Our age is academic and uneducated; everyone is a professor who knows nothing and is eager to teach it to everyone else.

---

*Jean Marais was born on December 11, 1913, in Cherbourg. An actor and painter, he met Cocteau in 1937 and played the part of the Chorus in the latter's adaptation of *Oedipus Rex*. Poet and actor became close friends, and Marais was Cocteau's preferred interpreter in both theater and cinema. See Cocteau's *Jean Marais* (1951) and *Jean Marais, l'acteur-poète* (1959); Jean Marais, *Mes quatre vérités* (1957) and *Histoire de ma vie*, with 117 poems by Cocteau (1975).

. . . .

JULY 30 · 1951

Wonderful giant Virgin at Saint-Hospice.* Higher than the chapel, not quite so high as the steeple, easy to confuse, from out at sea, with a tree. It dominates the Bay of Saint-Jean. They keep trying to hide her away. Everyone thinks she's ugly. She dates from 1903—a beauty. An extraordinary object of nobility and grace.

As an individualist, [Maurice] Barrès lost his standing by going into politics, and since his politics were bogus, he lost his seat as well. It will be a long time before *Les Déracinés* and *La Colline inspirée* can redeem him.

Judas, a dealer in rabbis.

The trouble started with the Encyclopedists. They told everyone to think. As a result, stupidity thinks—something which had never been seen before.

People always talk about climate, about good air. It's what's underground that counts, that influences us. Paris had good foundations: sand. New York has metal underpinnings. Pagnol says Americans try to get off the ground—they invent crepe soles and jump up on tables; they build skyscrapers. I work much more easily out at sea. In our villages, disease and madness come from underground. There are villages in the east of France (iron mines) where cases of insanity are past counting. In Milly, the subsoil is sand and water. It is important to be aware of the foundations where you live.

Bacchus is just about ready. I'm starting to dictate, to disentangle my text. The hard thing is to make the period's very complex

---

*The point of Saint-Hospice, east of Cap-Ferrat, where the Niçois hermit Hospice, or Auspice, died ("Santo Sospir," the name of Francine Weisweiller's villa, is a dialect form of "Saint Hospice"). This bronze-plated statue of the Virgin, 375 feet high, is the work of the Milanese sculptor Tranquillo Galbusieri, commissioned by a local donor who had planned to place it on top of the steeple. The plan was abandoned, and the statue stands on the ground next to the chapel.

atmosphere simple and understandable: don't overload the lines of action; never lose sight of the fact that the characters can't see things from our perspective—they misinterpret. For instance, Christine still believes it's a lie that Luther started the peasant revolt, whereas the reformers know it's true. Christine thinks it's a rumor started by the church.

I must show, *without saying so*, that Luther's new position inclines the Duke's family toward Hans and detaches them from the Reformation.

Of course, my play, which has more than one meaning, will disturb and displease. But a one-meaning play robs the theater of that accidental quality which generates its power. Our modern terminology is very dangerous; if people can no longer use words like "message" and "commitment," they doubt their own intelligence; they reach a point where they claim that the refusal of political commitment is a negative commitment. Commitment to neutrality readily passes for opportunism.

What movie people don't know: nothing less "facile" to make than a *difficult* film and nothing more difficult to make than a "facile" one.

. . . .

AUGUST 1 · 1951

My tapestry* has arrived from Aubusson. The workmanship is masterful—especially since the Aubusson workshops had given up "modulating" (Matisse's word), fashion now calling for flat colors juxtaposed. I had had the foresight to give the cartoon to Atelier Bouret, which specializes in copies of seventeenth- and eighteenth-century work. It is all the more amazing to see how faithfully the

**Judith et Holoferne.* 10′ x 11′6″. Collection Francine Weisweiller. Figures in Cocteau's film *Le Testament d'Orphée* (1959).

pastel tones* are reproduced, and my tiniest scribbles and hesitations transcribed, since the women are working a few inches away from an approximate tracing and not following the work itself, which is some distance behind them. The intensity and diversity of the yarns are incredible. The various combinations melt into each other.

The tapestry represents Judith leaving Holofernes's camp. Her deed is behind her. Holofernes's head, which she is carrying, is disfigured by death. Judith is no longer a woman but the pen to write her story, the sarcophagus to preserve it. Like a Jewish ghost, she passes through the groups of guards, who are sleeping in the moonlight. On the upper right, her servant, like some sort of insect, casts a last glance into the room where the beheading took place.

. . . .

AUGUST 2 · 1951

A characteristic of our times: the terminology people use, misapplied and drained of its meaning. The words *commitment* and *message* turn up in salon conversations like the disputes of casuists incapable of following a single idea. Nothing stranger than these pedal-boat excursions on deep seas by ignorant intellectuals who take themselves for divers.

Preface (June) for the Munich Pinakothek†

Since I am not a painter and have no right to paint, save insofar as I consider myself free to use any expressive vehicle, I have had to confront certain problems and to solve them in my fashion.

---

*Cocteau had completed the cartoon of *Judith* at Milly-la-Forêt in the autumn of 1948, in pastel on three wood panels, "underpainted black like slates."

†The exhibition of Cocteau's paintings, tapestries, and drawings in the Haus der Kunst, Munich, on January 18, 1952.

Consequently, these canvases are balanced between drawing and painting, between abstract and representational forms.

Above all, my investigations have been concerned with light, the light proper to the picture, to the characters and places I conceive, with no other source than the mind.

I do not possess, alas, the knowledge which permits me to follow methods, however disobediently, as in the case of a Picasso, whose unreal "realism" is prodigious.

I exhibit these canvases only because I am reluctant to undertake the work without running the risks involved.

Second preface (August). I am neither a draftsman nor a painter. My drawings are a kind of writing—loosened and relooped. As for painting, it is the act of painting itself which delights me; it requires no intermediaries but the hand and the eye.

What results from the act of painting concerns me no more than how the colors and forms of plants are organized.

Only my instinct guides me here, and the necessity of not claiming the prerogatives which belong to the born painter.

I conceive of a picture, and I try to copy that conception as faithfully as possible. I work at it until it separates itself from me and lives a life of its own.

That is the mechanism and the meaning of the canvases I am showing. I observe in them, as any outsider might, a certain balance between abstract and concrete, between my darkness and the light.

. . . That truth, perhaps, which Goethe set against reality. More truth rather than mere truth.

We're going to begin work on the film.* Frédéric† is coming here this morning with the cameraman. He's bringing the Kodachrome

---

**La Villa Santo Sospir*, 16 mm Kodachrome film on the poet's activities, his paintings and frescoes in the villa.

†Frédéric Rossif, Cocteau's assistant for the film.

film. While I'm getting the texts of *Bacchus* ready, I'll ask Frédéric to get the equipment set up—tracks and lights.

In most cases, a poet is treated as if he were dead. Posthumously, as it were. Letters from Germany inform me I have won the Victory Prize. Where? Why? The young people who are writing me seem to attach the greatest importance to it. Odd I haven't been informed.

The Saint-Jean-Cap-Ferrat Chamber of Commerce asks me to become an honorary citizen, for life. I answer that I had adopted the cape and would be proud to have the cape adopt me.

The Riviera was Russian, once upon a time. Then it became British. Now it's Belgian. Money changes place.

. . . .

AUGUST 5 · 1951

Finished disentangling the first two acts. Soon I'll begin to dictate the last act.

Inaccuracy of journalists. For all his ridicule of the article reporting that Sartre and I were writing a play about Werther, Claude Brûlé reports in *Paris-Presse* that my *Judith and Holofernes* tapestry represents the life of Medea. Why Medea? He saw the tapestry only on the floor and never in its entirety. I never told him what it represented. So he had to make up something. The same thing goes for the frescoes, in which, according to him, I am illustrating the story of Orpheus, whereas Orpheus plays no part in them whatever.

The typewriter is dangerous; it depersonalizes texts that come from your hand, empties them out, makes them look dead.

A play's contour must be simple. How hard it is, getting rid of whatever is superfluous without losing the weight of the whole or the intensity of the details. I have a closetful of notes and books, themselves filled with marginal notes. And out of that full closet, all that's left are a few bits of dialogue and the red thread that runs through the action. Sometimes I'm tempted by a note I've never used. But I resist; it's just that note which would be superfluous.

The villa is an anthill. *Film* is the magic word. Gardeners and decorators are working like crazy. They've already changed the furniture and the blinds in the *grand-salle*. The tapestry is being hung. They're planting portulacas, for color.

. . . .

AUGUST 6 · 1951

Yesterday, testing for color and for the canvases outdoors.

For Auric* and Toumanova, I'd like to do a last *Orpheus* (after my play and my film). Title: *Fin d'Orphée.*†

I've worked out the sequence of dances and the set. My painting *Tête d'Orphée mort*‡ will be the curtain. But the costumes—I'll find something after the work on *Bacchus* in September.

. . . .

AUGUST 15 · 1951

Picasso's genius serves as his intelligence. And his intelligence as his genius. A fact. Make of it what you will.

Let's finish the film. Have taken 4,600 feet of film, out of which I'll probably keep 2,000. The work was pleasant because this house makes everything pleasant, but difficult, too, because of the lack of perspective, the corridors, and our pick-me-up apparatus. What

---

*Georges Auric (1899–1983), friend of Cocteau's and composer of music for his films and his ballet *Phèdre* (1950). In 1919 he had composed a song cycle, *Huit poèmes de Jean Cocteau*, and in 1921 the overture and interludes for *Les Mariés de la tour Eiffel*.

†This projected ballet was never created.

‡1951. 54 x 65 cm. Collection Édouard Dermit.

will come of it remains a riddle. Color and its whims. Ivanov comes tonight for the reels. The rest is in the lab.

Our times. The Lettrists need money; they ask me for help. Being fond of Isou, I do what I can. I was supposed to meet one of his young friends,* who telephoned this morning, when I wasn't at the villa. Instead of asking when I would be back, he insults Francine and says my absence is inexcusable. Vulgarity is a style, but stupidity is inexcusable.

We'll go for a sail on the *Orphée II* Sunday.† I'll edit the film at sea. At my age, there's no time for vacations. Vacation = work.

Telephone call: Jouvet died at eight o'clock. Giraudoux, Bérard,‡ Jouvet, one after the next. They're gathering to collaborate on some new play: a ghost sonata!

. . . .

AUGUST 16 · 1951

Style of the times. This morning I was in Nice, in a little gallery where a young Hindu was showing his work. Some journalists

---

*The young friend in question is Marc Guillaumin. Isadore Isou, founder of the Lettrist movement, writes to Cocteau on August 30 to explain the search for money as the consequence of a *wager* made by Marc Guillaumin: "We all still believe in millionaires who show their money if we know how to *talk* to them, or *smile* at them." This involves "a total conquest . . . which is not only *practical* but *spiritual*," etc., a struggle of solitaries "against a machinery of anonymity." He also asks Cocteau to introduce him to people in film distribution circles. See below, August 31, 1951, and October 11, 1952.

†Francine Weisweiller's yacht.

‡Christian Bérard (1920–1949), painter and designer. Studied with Vuillard and Denis; first exhibited with NeoHumanist group (Berman, Tchelitchew); his friendship with Cocteau dated from 1925; designed sets for several of his plays, including: *La Machine infernale* (1934), *Les Monstres sacrés* (1940), *Renaud et Armide* (1943), *L'Aigle à deux têtes (gowns)* (1946); and his films: *La Belle et la Bête* (1945), *L'Aigle à deux têtes* (1947), *Les Parents terribles* (1948); illustrated several of his books, including: *Opéra* (1927), *Reines de France* (1949). Cocteau writes in the catalog of Bérard's retrospective exhibition in Paris, April 1950: "Christian Bérard was my right hand. Since he was left-handed, I had an astonishing right hand, learned, delicate, light: an enchanted hand."

were there. When I leaned down to take a cigarette out of my rolled-up trouser cuff, where it's simpler to keep them in the car, one reporter exclaimed: "Now that's marvelous!" Another asks: "Why have you given up?" Which means: "Why are you working on the Riviera instead of hanging around bars in Paris?" For these young men, that's work. Real work is time wasted. Another said: "We want to make it right away." "To make what?" "Just making it . . ."

Ivanov has left with the reels. The end of a film is always sad.

. . . .

AUGUST 23 · 1951

On board the *Orphée II*. Lunch with Jean Guérin at Bordighera, where he is staying. We leave for Genoa. Engine trouble. We drift all night. Return to Genoa delayed because of bad gasoline. Genoa. Filthy harbor. We leave Genoa for Portofino, a marvel. Houses painted in *trompe-l'oeil* in a pocket of sea flanked by dark hills covered with trees and flowers. Too many yachts. Mussel poisoning. We leave Portofino for Portovenere, where we are now. How much I prefer this almost tragic Portovenere with its tall houses squeezed against each other, its walls, its caverns, its towers, its forts. Portofino can protect itself against cars, radios, guitarists, and accordionists—they don't get in—and no new buildings can go up. But Portofino cannot protect itself against royal highnesses and against fashion. The fishermen have stopped fishing. Their skiffs have Vespa motors and are used for excursions. About a hundred restaurants form a half circle around the harbor. The yachts tangle anchor chains. Floating garbage. Stagnant water. In Portovenere, nothing but fishermen. From a distance, it looks like a ruin, a city dead of leprosy. Close up, it reveals great nobility, a proud and very simple grace.

. . . .

AUGUST 24 · 1951

We leave Portovenere after trying to take a few shots that may be useful for the film. Back to Portofino. We anchor in the harbor, and tomorrow morning we'll go to Recco, which I glimpsed in passing; it looked as if it had a splendid jetty, laundry hung out between the houses. Wind too high to use the sails. Eight hours to make the trip.

Written the texts for the film. As simple as possible. I find 116 shots usable (with luck). I'm afraid we're short.

Seen from the sea, the Italian coast is incomparably lovelier than from the road. The stupidity of our architects has not penetrated the villages and the harbors wedged between the rocks. An incredible tangle of houses, all enchanting in shape and color. There was a bit of this charm in (wrecked) Toulon, in (rebuilt) Saint-Tropez. There was a different charm in that corruption of baroque and perverted orientalism in Nice and Monaco. Of which we are ashamed. We let them fall to pieces. We replace them by white barracks. Always a great traveler, beauty was in the habit of visiting Italy. Now ugliness is taking up residence in Milan. It may well triumph there, before settling in everywhere else. What is left for us to do but follow her to some Greek island or else smoke opium with her in a remote province of China. By *beauty* I mean not the picturesque but the sense of proportions.

Reread Swift (*Gulliver's Travels*). I find this superior to *Candide*. Swift's noble soul is antipodal to Voltaire's (ignoble soul). Laputa is a very good account of what is happening right now in America and Europe.

People express surprise that I avoid society, but I'm lucky enough, at Santo Sospir, to inhabit the island of the Houyhnhnms—share Swift's disgust for the Yahoos.

High sea. Banging into everything.

I believe that each of my works is capable of making the reputation of a single writer. Yet my fame derives not from them but from a few films and drawings around the edges of what I've made, from a legend consisting of gossip and carelessness. No author is so known, so unknown, so misunderstood as I am. This is probably a lucky thing, for authors about whom everything is known leave nothing to learn. When they die, only bones remain—the marrow has been sucked out. Bad translations, productions altered by foreign censorship and the whims of actresses, bad prints of films, a few misleading anecdotes—such things account for the glory of a poet who can be maddened by a misplaced comma.

Impossible to anchor off Recco at night—we know neither the depth nor the jetty. We anchor around nine in a creek near Portofino, where we will eat (the *Orphée* is pitching too much for Le Frisé* to cook), sleep, and sail tomorrow morning.

. . . .

AUGUST 25 · 1951

Back to Portofino. We wanted to anchor in the channel outside the red and green lights. But aside from the danger of the site, the water is too deep. We enter the harbor, less crowded with yachts this time. Sun this morning; we shoot a panorama of the harbor and part of the sun-dappled hull (to link with the connecting shots). We sail at eleven, toward the channel off Recco. I've forgotten the name of that town that looks like Toulon before it was destroyed. Swim and lunch. We're heading for the Riviera now, avoiding Genoa, which would lengthen our route.

Reread *The Three Musketeers* and *Twenty Years After*. I wonder whether Dumas isn't the only real historian. What he invents always

*Crewman of the *Orphée II*.

seems true. Others' truth seems false, and surely is. While there's every chance that Dumas hits the nail on the head.

Will the monstrous stupidity of Gide's *Journal* ever be discovered? What a mountain of hypocrisy and lies concealed by the pretense of telling a truth limited to the picturesque. During the Gide-Ghéon quarrel, Ghéon told me: "He owns up to the little black boys, but not to the policemen." He had asked me to take care of Marc Allégret and show him something of Montparnasse, the Cubists, *les Six*,* etc. I saw little enough of Marc, but Marc convinced Gide that he was spending all his time with me. He drove Gide crazy and turned him against me without my suspecting a thing. Gide (confessing this to me just before I left for Egypt†) added: "I didn't know Marc's true nature yet, and I offer my apologies."

Last week, Christian M., who is shooting a film with Marc in Nice, told me a similar (and recent) story about him. Which has reminded me to write down the conversation with Gide which explains why he speaks so ill of me in his *Journal*.

Of course, it's not because he speaks ill of me and lies about me that I find Gide's *Journal* ridiculous. It is the dreariest herbarium, that *Journal*, the most trivial collection of dried plants, for all the Latin labels. I've met Protestant pastors in Switzerland who spend their vacations on such tasks: filling herbariums with perfectly familiar plants and labeling them with unknown names.

Gide has never experienced the discomfort of infinity. Not infinity even—merely the sense of the loss of proportional values. All discomforts came from petty sources, nothing but pettiness. No kindness. A botanist's curiosity. Under the magnifying glass.

"We distributed coins"—"Trees forming a vault." One day I

---

*A group of six composers Cocteau frequented in 1920: Georges Auric, Louis Durey, Arthur Honegger, Darius Milhaud, Francis Poulenc, and Germaine Tailleferre.

†For a tour of his theatrical company. See above: *Maalesh*, note for July 16, 1951.

remarked to Gide: "Your *Voyage au Congo* is modeled on Loti." He confessed with one of those sniffling giggles that made him hunch his shoulders: "I discovered Loti in the dentist's waiting room. You've solved the mystery." *Mystery* in Gide turned into a kind of plaint, a recitative, an excuse for *vocalise* performed on some word through clenched teeth as if he were drawing the vowels and consonants up out of a well. I remember, the day of his last visit to Milly, in the vestibule, how he must have quoted M. Jourdain's little phrase twenty times: "Teach me the almanac"; he so loved saying the word *almanac*.

It was the child in Gide that I liked. His immoralism seems to me a lot of nonsense. And his Nobel is a hoot. After refusing to greet Gide in the Café Lipp one day, Jean Genet told me: "I find his immorality quite suspect." Gide wanted to meet him. "I don't like," Genet observed, "judges who lean so amorously over the accused."

11:00 P.M.

How sickening to be on this old catastrophe the sea, far from that old catastrophe the coast, under that old catastrophe the stars. And how sickening to realize that to all these catastrophes, men add their own.

The wind drops. No engines, no sails. Sailboats always have the wrong winds or no wind at all. And when there are engines, they break down. So here we are, flung about like a can of worms.

The engine has been started (working poorly).

If the youth of 1951 were to realize the absurdity of the translations of American books that Americans themselves despise, if they were to read *The Three Musketeers* (which they consider absurd), they would be saved from absurdity. Alas, they sink deeper and deeper into it. (Aggressive—pedantic—ignorant.)

. . . .

AUGUST 28 · 1951

Society expels every element alien to its mechanisms. (The theme of *Bacchus*.)

Intelligence has been granted me in the form of intuition and sudden flashes. Which makes me seem highly intelligent, though I am no such thing. Which gives me the disadvantages of intelligence without the advantages. I am not bright enough, and I have the reputation of being too bright.

I do not believe in this earth. But I believe in the feelings experienced here, and in the pastimes created.

It is my turn. Claudel's. Colette's. So I've sent my will to Bucaille, the attorney.

The journalists are talking about Doudou's adoption.* Which risks antagonizing the court.

It would be madness to paint or to write for people, since people want to paint or write for themselves, and since even if they can't, they think differently from us, and since they can't think beyond themselves, they think we're wrong. But sometimes our works encounter people who would have liked to write them or paint them, and this creates a kind of family for us out there in the world. Art's only excuse is that it makes friends for us.

. . . .

AUGUST 30 · 1951

B.'s ball in Venice.† Monday. I must be the only one who's not using his invitation. The ball is costing five hundred million francs.

---

*Édouard Dermit was born in 1925 near Pola, of Slovenian parents who emigrated to France the same year. In 1947 he met Cocteau, who was soon to consider him as his adoptive son and to make him his heir.

†A costume ball given by Carlos Beistegui, at the Palazzo Labia, September 3, 1951.

Two hundred million to the Communist party and for "popular entertainments." It costs about as much as a warplane, and I prefer a ball (provided I don't have to go).

Venice. The story of *Othello* concerned one Signor Mauro, a Venetian merchant. Whom Shakespeare made into a Moor.

Keep braiding one's wavelengths back into oneself. That way they gain all the more external power and surround us with a huge affective and protective zone. Don't talk about this. Never talk about our secret methods. If we talk about them, they stop working.

Time does not exist. It is a phenomenon of perspective. So we always have time. Impatience is stupidity. Hard for youth to struggle against it. Then, "the less time one has," the more one knows the feeling of having time. Picasso was right. *It takes a man a very long time to grow young.* I feel younger than when I was young. Freer, less greedy, less hurried.

The Lettrists ask me: "How did you manage to be part of four avant-gardes?" Answer: "I adhered not to the school but to the movement."

Only intensity matters. Talent—you have it or you don't. Intensity must be our one study. It is what keeps the work from being *à la mode*, from being *démodé*.

. . . .

AUGUST 31 · 1951

When I asked one of the Lettrists why they grant so much importance to the world and to the successes to be won there, he answered that science would eventually permit the resurrection of the earth and that it could not take place without something that contains us, without a living work. This was the first time I ever heard something intelligent and valid about the possibilities of the future.

Difficulty of a will. Make it as simple as possible. Find someone reliable who will find someone reliable to make arrangements which, written out in detail, seem to me full of legal traps. Bourdet wanted to make a will that would omit nothing and would protect Denise, with the result that he dispossessed Denise on account of one or two clumsy little sentences.

Reread *Twenty Years After* and *The Viscount de Bragelonne*. What charm Dumas has, what nobility; never have imagination and history been braided together so well. Athos dies *an old man* at my age. D'Artagnan dies *an old man* before he is my age. Don't forget I am an old man. Even if my mind and body do.

Fortune. Jeannot,* who earns fortunes, hasn't a sou left. The income tax people are after him. Suppose I buy back his shares of Milly, which would allow him to pay his taxes and still leave him Milly, since what's mine is his—more than if he owned a cash share.

Here, sun and sea bathing. In Paris and in Deauville, where Alec Weisweiller is, rain and hail. Cold weather. Yet the distance between Paris and the Riviera isn't as great as the distance between New York and Hollywood.

Depending on the altitude, all the plants of China and Africa can be found here on the Riviera. At the source of the Var, they've just discovered a species of dwarf willow that grows only in China. In Antibes, they've found mandrakes. The antiques dealer in the covered market has dug up one. As if the Riviera's climate were brought here by invasions, like everything else.

. . . .

SEPTEMBER 2 · 1951

Whenever Picasso is interested in something, he denigrates it. This he has in common with Goethe. Whatever does not disturb him he praises to the skies.

---

*Jean Marais.

Sun here at the cape. Rain and cold at Port-Cros.

Lunch at the Altana.* The luxury and the scale of it all overwhelm me *on sight*. No use walking through the grounds. One glance, and I'm exhausted.

Cricket opposite my room. He chirps *day and night*, never stops for a minute.

Pathos of the times. The reason one is accused of being "inhuman" in 1950 is the care one takes with one's work. Only the rough sketch is human now. Whatever is botched and perfunctory is called "human." *The profession, the craft*, which consists in fabricating the vehicle by which the human is expressed, passes for an intellectual task from which humanism is excluded. The well-written, well-painted work is "cold." Whereas what's written or painted anyhow is "human." This is the defense of the mediocre. It has the superiority of numbers on its side.

. . . .

September 8 · 1951

Incredible death of Maria Montez—heart attack in her bath, drowns. Jean-Pierre† was out with the little girl.

La Villa Santo Sospir. The reels have arrived. Projection this evening. Disaster—either something wrong with the negative or a problem with the ultraviolet filter. The good things are very good; they disturb the substance in a rough and solid way. Outdoor shots to be retaken. Out of six reels, I can keep only very little. By montage I'll be able to recover the style. The first projection always rivets you to your mistakes. I'll look at the whole thing more calmly later.

---

*The Antibes villa of Guy Weisweiller, Alec's brother.

†The actor Jean-Pierre Aumont, who had created the part of Oedipus in *La Machine infernale* (1934), husband of the actress Maria Montez.

. . . .

SEPTEMBER 10 · 1951

I had expected to redo my prints in London, but Frédéric says on the telephone that the values correct themselves after the first print. Fine, in any case I'll introduce some original takes into five copies. I'll shoot each take five times. Then the negative will be satisfactory. But how odd to have five extra copies (like a special edition). To introduce luxury into film, the antiluxury enterprise *par excellence*. (Mass-production enterprise.)

Sent Georges Auric the sequence of scenes for the ballet *Orphée* so he can begin the music.

I dare not even telephone Milly, I'm afraid to learn that Martin* is dead. Minguet's letter holds out little hope.

Tonight we projected the six reels again for separations. Completely different impression. The first day's surprise no longer existed, and everything gained in strength. What disappointed us then was the distance between what we had imagined (expected) and what was happening in front of our eyes. Tonight our impression was based on what we were seeing. Disappointment no longer being the basis of our experience, the film's qualities won out over its defects. Be on guard against the mind's mechanism, to habit, expectations, and first contacts.

Ball in Venice. Beistegui hadn't invited the wicked fairy: journalism. Consequence: his ball was a disaster, and it rained. The truth is that it did not rain and the ball was a success. The Venetians adore parties and applauded the costumes; López,† who had spent several million francs on his, looked like the old lady at a wedding.

Every tiny detail of his costume had to be historically accurate. The whole thing produced no effect whatever. These society people

---

*Cocteau's dog.

†Arturo López-Willshaw came to the ball as a mandarin.

know nothing of the secret of the theater. What works and what doesn't. According to the magazines, it looks to me as if Diana, Élisabeth, and Daisy* wore their costumes properly. You could tell—they worked. Fath reeked of the music hall. Beistegui had turned down an offer of eight million francs (from the Americans) to film the ball.

. . . .

SEPTEMBER 11 · 1951

Martin is dead. Juliette and Louis† in tears on the phone. I told them to take him back to Milly and bury him in the woods where he used to follow Louis everywhere.

I should have reshot my direct takes this morning. Wrong colors. Overcast sun. It's the same thing each time. First clouds after five days without a single one.

The paper says that Jeannot will adopt my mask formula in *Nez de cuir*.‡ A false nose was absurd. A leather half mask sets off the face and frames the eyes. What is stationary makes the rest even more mobile, more alive.

Lunch here with Delannoy. Dinner at the Hôtel du Cap with Christian-Jaque. We talk about the—alas, all too unmysterious—mystery of film financing. Granted, everything costs too much. But our films make money. For whom? Not for us. The figures are in order when they are shown to us. What do these figures represent? What manipulations? What receipts? Here begins the mystery of that ruin which seems to affect neither producers nor distributors. Moreover, these figures never correspond to the obvious facts, to letters from abroad, to personal information. It is certain that the film industry fattens only its industrialists and that

*Diana Duff Cooper, Princess Shashavadze, and Daisy Fellowes.

†Juliette and Louis Biéber, Cocteau's staff at Milly-la-Forêt.

‡A film by Yves Allégret, from the novel by Jean de la Varende.

we are their milk cows. How to change this rhythm? We are up against a wall. So I give up and prefer to use the camera as an amateur. Even on the commercial level, this method is more likely to be profitable.

. . . .

SEPTEMBER 12 · 1951

Telephone call from the Aurics. They're coming to see me Sunday.

I'll probably be going to Paris Monday or Wednesday to meet with [Jean] Vilar and to work on the film.

. . . .

SEPTEMBER 14 · 1951

Varnished the paintings. Pay no attention to what people say. Give myself up to work until this work becomes exactly what I wanted. This method always triumphs. Spiro* asks me: "Why did you do that?" and he adds: "I would have done it differently." Odd. I don't ask him why he wears a Marx Brothers mustache.

No clouds until four. I was able to shoot the house from lighthouse side.

Spiro will come tomorrow to help me varnish the two big canvases. Painted on linoleum.

. . . .

SEPTEMBER 15 · 1951

Our good manners consist in not demoralizing the artist—sparing him our criticisms. But this same artist does not spare us his.

*Painter of Hungarian origin living on the Riviera. See *Spiro*, twenty-one reproductions of paintings with a letter from Jean Cocteau (Nice: 1951).

Enclosed within his own personality, an artist takes other people's personalities for mistakes.

Shot the paintings with Dr. Ricoux.*

Whenever I meet a journalist, he interrogates me, forcing me to a point where it would be pretentious not to answer. Then I say a few words which he makes as much noise out of as he can. Whereupon I am held responsible for the noise. This conspiracy of noise has replaced, in my case the conspiracy of silence. *Moreover, the two get on famously together.* For noise conceals real work and establishes that reputation for *brio* which critics confuse with professional conscience. Picasso's strength is that he circumspectly gives his skill a look of clumsiness which fools the world and preserves an equilibrium for him between racket and reserve. Rebarbative *brio*. Which is why his kindness pretends to be cruel.

The Atelier Bouret in Aubusson writes that they don't have enough work to stay open. I'm going to send them *Ulysses and the Sirens*.† A canvas cannot cost as much as *Judith*.

The doctor raises a new problem: the sound track on the negative and absence of sound on the direct takes. Consequently a machine-gun din. I could say in the text that we're going to switch over to silent filming, hence all the noise. That would be admissible and even funny in an experimental film. Only such texts would mean nothing if the copies are no longer combined with the original.

Sometimes wealth seems to me as amazing as genius.

---

*Cocteau's physician at Beaulieu-sur-Mer and an amateur filmmaker.

†A 1951 painting transposed to tapestry, 6′ 10″ x 4′8″. Collection Édouard Dermit. "Ulysses has himself tied to the mast and his ears stuffed with wax. A sailor lying nearby has pulled his cap down over his ears. The sirens cavort, sing, are amazed at their lack of success." From Cocteau's note in the catalog of his Nice exhibition, 1953.

. . . .

September 16 · 1951

Many kings of France were assassinated. All were assassins. (Except, maybe, François I—and even then.)

The equilibrium I want for *Bacchus*: a play of ideas in which the action (the progress of the action) is interesting. Usually one takes precedence over the other. It seems to me that *Bacchus* offers the interest of a play of action, which nonetheless remains a play of ideas. (The opposite of a *pièce-à-thèse*.) Thesis and symbols are what disgust me most.

Reread *Queen Margot*. Astonishing amalgam of history and *histoires*; Dumas even manages to have a very precise style. It must come from reading so many chronicles of a period when everyone wrote well.

I'm afraid the paint I use is affecting my fingers. My hands hurt a lot during the night. Still, when I get back from Paris I'd like to paint a big canvas: *Jesus Tempted by Lucifer*,* where all the forms would be inscribed within triangles.

. . . .

September 18 · 1951

It's not enough to *stand fast* morally; one must stand fast *physically*.

Did the Virgin for Italy (drawing).

Yesterday saw Alexandre Alexandre† for Munich.

We leave for Paris at four.

The cat-organ of the procession of Philippe II in Belgium: the

---

**The Temptation on the Mountain*, 5′6″ x 6′1″. Collection Édouard Dermit. "Jesus listens to Satan, who offers him the visible world. He barely listens. His gaze is elsewhere." Cocteau's note in the catalog of his Nice exhibition, 1953.

†A journalist moving in film circles.

organ was set on a cart, and cats were attached by their tails to the keys. They played a cacophony as they struggled.

Auric tells me that Stravinsky's new opera,* created in Venice, is his most perfect work, but in a direction which suggests nothing monumental. In the line of *Mavra*. Mozart and wrong notes. Badly rehearsed. Faulty preparation. A work fascinating in the score.

Lulu† says: "In six years the film will earn its money back." Christian-Jaque: "According to my calculations and the evidence of the receipts, the film should earn its money back in a year. A year and a half, to be pessimistic."

Not surprising, given the dog-eat-dog ways of the film industry, that everything eventually collapses. Producers and distributors are eager to fill their pockets before the collapse.

. . . .

SEPTEMBER 28 · 1951

At my age, it's easy. You no longer climb up the slope; enough to let yourself slide down, *with all your weight*. For the young, it's not so easy: you have to climb *up* the slope *with all your weight*.

Between September 15 and 26 I was in Paris and at Milly. Moulouk died.‡ I had lunch with Jeannot, who said nothing about it. He preferred not to mention this death.

Prepared costumes and sets for Auric's ballet.

Redid the outdoor shots, following my experiments in the Kodak labs.

Saw Jean Vilar. I think he is one of those directors who want

---

**The Rake's Progress.*

†Lucienne Watier, impresario at the Ci-Mu-Ra Agency (*Ci*nema-*Mu*sic Hall-*Ra*dio).

‡Jean Marais's dog. In Cocteau's film *The Eternal Return* (1943), Moulouk belongs to Patrice (Jean Marais).

to rewrite the play. Very difficult relations. He promises a certain nobility, but I had supposed him less like his predecessors. Blinders. Unlikely that things will work out. (I hear that actors do not like him.)

Jeannot says to Paulvé,* speaking of Paul Morihien†: "He's a shrewd businessman." Paulvé answers: "Let him offer me a contract—any contract. I'll sign it and still get around him." Later Morihien asks Paulvé if he got around *me* and how he managed to do so with *Orpheus*. Paulvé says: "It's simple. I made Cocteau a producer. *Orpheus* is a very bad production deal. A magnificent distribution deal!" Lulu Watier hasn't a clue to these master plans, these delightful cheats, these gangsters who know the gang will stick together and talk about it without the slightest embarrassment. Ci-Mu-Ra is a small-time agency.

Yesterday I took outdoor shots in reverse, which should be very funny. I shall say: "Picasso made ceramics at Vallauris. I've tried to make flowers. I've managed a few." And I shall be shown fabricating a convolvulus and a hibiscus.

For a very long time painters of the past could not work for themselves. It was understood that there was a master and apprentices. Inadmissible nowadays, when apprentices seek to be master. Chardin was allowed to paint an apple, a few centimeters of tablecloth, a leaf, etc. Rubens's apprentices signed in an eye, in a nostril; we have found their signatures thanks to microscopes. But in those days apprentices were already masters. Today let someone else work on a corner of your canvas, it will look dead.

Everyone thinks he will do better than you. Not better. Different.

Every work is posthumous. Once you write the word *end*, the

---

*André Paulvé, film producer and distributor.

†Friend of Jean Marais, Jean Cocteau's secretary, and, at this time, a bookseller and publisher in Paris.

work is dead and you are dead to this work. To change something in it is to tamper with the work of a dead man—a kind of sacrilege. (Be on guard against retouching.)

The Americans rewrite our plays because they think they know a public that they do not know, that no one knows, since the public does not exist; it is a series of fugitive phenomena of a collective hypnosis. Tallulah* "adapted" *The Eagle Has Two Heads*. She would have had a success with my play. She had a flop with hers. She and her public, of course, hold me responsible for this flop. Especially since Tallulah is taboo in America and since she's always right.

My *Orpheus* [1927] has just been performed in an off-Broadway theater in New York. With considerable success. The play was about to move to Broadway, but after the *Eagle*'s catastrophe, the Broadway producers turned their backs.

Les Parents terribles [1938] is a success in London, *in spite of the translation*. There is enough strength left in the play to succeed. But what a pity one can never prove one's own strength in another language. *The Eagle Has Two Heads* triumphed in London in a preposterous translation by Ronald Duncan. Stanislas *spoke* in the first act. In the last act, the Queen and Stanislas spoke in verse.†

The cover of *Match*: [Pierre] Brasseur in *Bluebeard*, a color film by Christian-Jaque. He has a *blue* beard. This was the first thing not to do. Judging from the sleeves and the legs, I suppose all the rest is in keeping.

When I'm asked if I'm going to make another film, I answer: "I've gone on strike. My bosses didn't pay me."

If you read your play aloud to ears deaf to half of what you say, the play is disturbed, distorted, dislocated, and you read on without

*The American actress Tallulah Bankhead (1903–1968).

†In this prose play, Stanislas remains mute in the first act.

recognizing your own work. Those who look and listen poorly spoil what they see and hear. You have to wait until their dirty water drains away. Sometimes it takes a long time.

My limits.

There is a height I cannot reach, a high note that is not in my range. If I try, I produce a *grimace*. You must make up your mind to acknowledge your limits. This is probably the underlying reason I have changed means of expression. The hope of finding that note *elsewhere*. But the limit remains the same everywhere.

I have had complete moments. "*L'Ange Heurtebise*."* "*La Crucifixion*."† Impossible to will such moments. Moments of acute solitude. Solitudes which will remain solitudes—never to be strewn with candy wrappers.

To admire is to efface yourself. To put yourself in someone else's place. Unfortunately so few people (and so few French people) know how to get outside themselves. In the presence of certain spectacles, I actually no longer *exist*. To be what I see and what I hear.

Paris has become the world's stupidest and most pretentious city. A third-rate provincial capital. [. . .]

The Americans had Poe and Whitman. They couldn't have cared less. All they cared about was their journalists. They didn't even know that Poe had invented mass journalism (Maelzel's chess player).

The Russians no longer want their past, but they have it. It's in their blood. The Americans collect other people's past because they have none. They dream of an instantaneous tradition. A scientific tradition. The immediate museum. You astonish; they consecrate you; they kill you. What matters is to go on to something else.

---

*Poem, with a photograph of the angel by Man Ray (Paris: 1925).

†Poem (Paris: 1946).

Baudelaire has written incomparably of decadence. It is the great moment. The acme of civilizations. *Vive la décadence.*

A few pages by Rilke on the death of Charles the Bold* are among the finest (even in translation) in all writing.

The world is ignoble. What is noble insults the world.

The earth tries to shake off its fleas, to kill them. And is less and less successful in doing so, for we have managed to avoid the great plagues. Hence the earth cunningly employs the learned to discover destructive forces. Men are in terror of them, but they invent them—at any price. And their pride impels them to suppose they have mastered the catastrophes they merely serve.

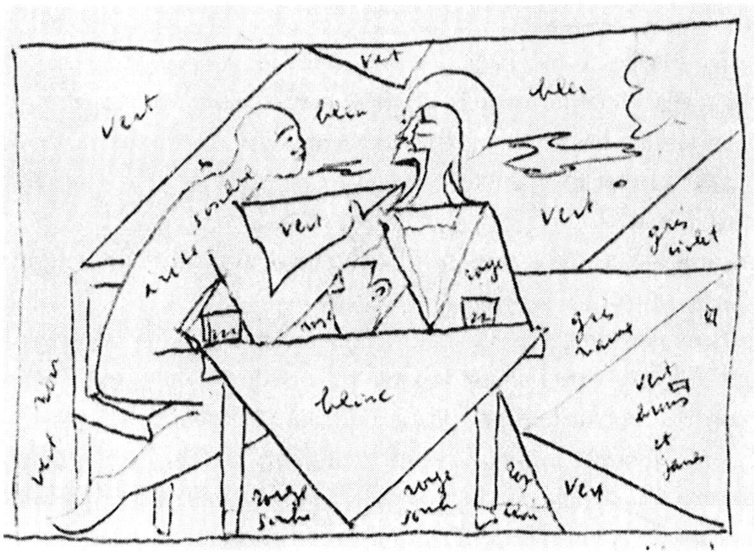

Triangular construction of the painting
The Temptation of Christ on the Mountain

*In *The Notebooks of Malte Laurids Brigge* (1910).

. . . .

SUNDAY

My hands get worse and worse. When I rub, there's an almost voluptuous itching, a kind of terrible pleasure which intensifies and becomes pain. The crises occur chiefly at night. In the morning they calm down, and my fingers are hard, puckered like rind.

I am beginning to do the underpainting on beaverboard for *The Temptation on the Mountain*. The substances have a gasoline base. Then I shall coat the whole thing with retouching varnish. Then I shall paint on it, layer after layer.

Tomorrow (Monday) I'll send the six additional reels to Kodak. Paintings and garden taken in reverse and shots of the walls by floodlights.

Wrote for *Life* magazine on Marlene Dietrich.

Phone call from Jeannot. He says: "A man in mourning for a dog is ridiculous. That's why I didn't tell anyone Moulouk was dead. I called to tell you because Yvonne* had come from Jany Holt's boat and I didn't want to seem to be hiding something from you."

If things don't work out with Vilar for *Bacchus*, I'll take Philipe. Without Jeannot and without Philipe, performance becomes an insoluble problem. An unknown wouldn't be solid enough, and I disapprove of auditions (the disappointments they cause). Penury of actors.

Something very beautiful always begins by surprising, by disturbing, even by *alarming*. The Indian singer Yma Sumac† was not a success. Her voice moves through all ranges. No one knew what

---

*The actress Yvonne de Bray, who appeared in Cocteau's plays (*Les Parents terribles* [1938], *Les Monstres sacrés* [1940]) and films (*The Eternal Return* [1943], *The Eagle Has Two Heads* [1947], *Les Parents terribles* [1948]).

†Peruvian singer whose tessitura was of an exceptional range and who had just appeared in Paris.

to do with it. No one could find the right music. Hearing her sing from soprano to bass, the public fled (*the devil*).

A period eye. Diderot writes that you have to step back from a Chardin to see what it represents. Chardin, who passes now for a *trompe-l'oeil* painter, painted like Manet, like Cézanne: impressionism *avant la lettre*. All you have to do is glance at a book on Chardin to understand how astounding his painting must have been. Today we no longer *see* what is well done. It throws us off. It is in the direction of the *well done* that one must take one's course; those who count on the *ill done* miss the boat.

Telephone call from Christian-Jaque. Tomorrow, lunch between Cannes and Grasse where they're shooting *Fanfan la Tulipe*. I'll see Gérard Philipe. How many trails, how much exhaustion in order to arrive, no doubt, at entirely different goals.

Reread *The Castle*. For us it is the Kremlin.

The Prince is the Nazi regime. For Kafka it is God, the search for grace. Since the dictators make themselves gods, Kafka's books (written much earlier) correspond to the regimes of dictatorship.

Use of retouching-varnish in layers. (Spiro.) Terrible mistake. Smooth painting, but dead. The varnish cancels out what is underneath—the old mixture. A pane of glass separates us from the painter's soul. One is amazed by this slick painting. Nothing touches us. Nothing *lasts*. The secret of glazes (Vermeer) is lost. It was an entirely different science.

Hersent "discovers painters." He buys left and right. Since the word is out, he gets stuck with terrible daubs, cheated. Interesting to follow the story. He can't tell the difference between his Buffets and his Dubuffets. He drags his finds to the bank, opens a door, calls the teller, and asks him what he thinks. The teller admits he doesn't understand a thing. "Painting," Hersent tells him, "requires a great deal of study." He is M. Jourdain.

The Saint-Sauveur family. A Saint-Sauveur is a bookkeeper for the Castaings.* He is ashamed of his job. He appears in the shop in riding breeches and a pink coat. Once at Chanel's I ran into Pauline de Saint-Sauveur, already extremely old, on the stairs. As soon as she caught sight of me, she exclaimed: "*Zut! Zut!* I can't bear it. They're still asking me to do *Venus* at the Beaumont Ball!"†

The magazine *Noir et Blanc* mentions my possible election to the Académie. For once the article is true. "It must be said that Cocteau has done nothing to get himself elected." And it also points out that I have turned down the Académie Goncourt.

The members of the Goncourt put Colette up to asking me to join them. I told her that Pierre Benoît had undertaken to deal with my election to the Académie Française and that I could not show him such tactlessness. At first glance, the Académie Française seems to be anything but my style. But [Paul] Éluard says: "Your election would still cause a scandal. So it's in your line." Naturally I'll go only if I'm asked. No question of offering my candidacy.

A little later. When the minister of education asked: "Why don't you wear your ribbon of the Legion of Honor?" I answered: "Unfortunately I'm no longer of an age to wear ribbons."

Jouvet's death is turning into an occasion of national mourning. [. . .]

The journalists are saying that Jouvet "discovered" Bérard. Now I brought Bérard to him for *The Infernal Machine*. Jouvet wanted nothing to do with him. I spent a month persuading him. After that, Jouvet couldn't do without him. Of course, Bérard's sets required a certain kind of direction. The work was ready-made.

---

*Marcellin Castaing and his wife, the decorator Madeleine Castaing.

†Count Étienne de Beaumont (1883–1956), Raymond Radiguet's Count d'Orgel, gave several costume balls between the wars in his Paris mansion in the rue Masseran.

Jouvet's style. Back from South America, after the Liberation, Jouvet wasn't very sure of my standing. Instead, he was making up to Éluard and Aragon. He was sure of theirs. In his lecture at the Athénée he cited many poets' names, but not mine. Four days later he saw me in Éluard and Aragon's box at the Gala-Résistance des Champs-Élysées. When his lecture was published, he had added my name.

These are the terms in which Jouvet refused to stage *Les Parents terribles*: "The play is admirable, but it won't make a sou. I need money."

Not long before he died, Jouvet, who didn't know what play to put on, asked my advice. I asked him what had become of that play of Giraudoux's that takes place in Aix-en-Provence.* This is what he told me: "Suzanne Giraudoux came to dinner at my house. She was delightful. We talked about the play for a long time. Just as she was about to get into her car, she said: 'You'll never have that play. You tortured Jean all his life. You killed him. You are his murderer.' "

Doubtless Suzanne Giraudoux was alluding to the requirements of a director who obliged Giraudoux to rewrite his plays ten times.

Giraudoux's preciosity. The intellectuals' delight: constant comparisons with Racine. Racine was the opposite of a *précieux*: cruel and direct.

What we see is what seems to exist. We do not see what exists. The invisibility of beauty is terrible. We begin noticing the beautiful when its perfection is tarnished. When it is comfortable. When it finally *looks beautiful*.

**Pour Lucrèce [Duel of Angels]*, unpublished at the time. Jean Giraudoux died in 1944. See Cocteau's *Souvenir de Jean Giraudoux* (1946), illustrated by Cocteau's drawing of Giraudoux on his deathbed.

. . . .

MONDAY

Picasso says: "I keep making mistakes, like God."

Nietzsche never makes mistakes, except in *Zarathustra* when he becomes "poetic." To be poetic is the opposite of poetry.

Picasso was told: "In America they would build you a golden bridge," and he answered: "I would sleep under it."

Picasso has inverted the character of the rich *clochard*.

Pierre Benoît: "At the Académie, you will have your friends against you and every honest man for you."

The trouble with art is that you cannot make it by being an "artist."

My 16 mm color film: amateurs are making the films of professionals; I owed it to myself to make the film of an amateur.

. . . .

OCTOBER 2 · 1951

Went to see Gérard Philipe at the Fragonard farm (near Grasse). He is perfectly charming and gives a reality to the character (*Fanfan la Tulipe*).

Gérard's glamour and Jeannot's. They glow, but each one with a very different light. The others don't glow at all. The only point the two have in common is that their charm has nothing sensual about it. It is a charm which derives from childhood. Childhood inhabits them. The beauty of their faces, their expressions, their attitudes come from that. They both have *physical genius*.

An affectionate reunion with the whole crew, friends and colleagues, a thousand memories of our work together. Matras* takes

---

*Christian Matras, Cocteau's cameraman for the film *The Eagle Has Two Heads* (1947).

me into a corner and tells me that technology disgusts him, that he has adopted my system of improvisation. That he has put away his filters and lenses. That he now uses only very little equipment and that if he needs a dissolve, he gets it only by light. He apologizes for having contradicted my decisions in *The Eagle*. I tell him they were made because of Edwige [Feuillère] and her fear of images that would be too distinct. The film was shot only in outdoor locations and in sets knocked together in corners of the farm. It cost a hundred fifty million francs. And what would have been saved by making it in the studio? True, a lot of people have to be fed and housed. I tell Mnouchkhine the result of my investigations. He tells me this film is his last bullet; if it doesn't succeed, they can't produce any more. (And half the film is paid for by Italian money. An Italian actress* is playing opposite Gérard.)

At lunch (under a magnificent tree) I told them about my 16 mm film. I explained why I was not bothering about splices and that I was deliberately flouting "technique." (Like the retouching-varnish which kills the life of the canvases.) Amateurs want to be professionals and fail to profit by their advantages. What I wanted was to make a real amateur film, home movies, a free film. (With no concern for photographic continuity. Images which contradict and upset each other.) I even mixed day shots and night shots. After a general view of a wall by day, I show details of the fresco by artificial light.

Telegram from Marcel Herrand:† "Would like to do radio series (5 broadcasts) *Le Cap de Bonne-Espérance*. Who should do music? Perhaps Darius [Milhaud]. With all my heart."

Herrand performed *L'Ange Heurtebise* incomparably. He will do a splendid job with *Le Cap*. Telegraphed that I advised Poulenc or

---

*Gina Lollobrigida.

†The actor Marcel Herrand performed in Cocteau's plays (*The Wedding on the Eiffel Tower* [1921]; *Roméo et Juliette*, [1924]; *Orpheus* [1926]); and in his film of *Ruy Blas* (1947).

Arthur [Honegger] for the music: Darius is sick, far away, and his music would be too strong, too intractable for a radio text.

Fine article on the villa in *Ce Soir*. They'll still be saying I'm a Communist.

. . . .

OCTOBER 3 · 1951

I began again on *The Temptation on the Mountain*, a much harsher style this time. I had been exploiting the facilities of painting, to which I was not entitled. I must replace the science of painting by another science—a poet's science. The sources of light must be the mind.

In Monte Carlo, Olivier, the prince's right arm, whispered that the prince was *ashamed of the casino*. He asked if I couldn't do something for the principality. A festival where I would speak in public. I answered that the prince was wrong, that the casino was the last temple. The acknowledged Temple of Chance: a god much more powerful than is imagined in our period of economic planning. That I was ready to speak to this point if the prince would make me a Monégasque citizen. For a poor taxpayer rather envies this rock where people live without taxes, like South Seas birds. Unfortunately I think the prince would like to hear the principality's historic role praised to the skies. A desire which oddly matches a falling-off in the casino take.

Lunch at Bordighera. Sea too high, wind too low. Annette* sick. Forced to turn back. Lunch at Villefranche, Chez Germaine.†

To someone who kept talking to him while he was painting, Derain remarked, without turning around: "Do not talk to the pilot while he is on duty."

Francine went to Monte Carlo to buy records. The salesman

*One of Édouard Dermit's sisters.

†Cocteau was a habitué of this restaurant on the quai Courbet.

couldn't get over the fact that she was buying classics. "At your age!" he exclaimed. "Very few people buy them. M. Matisse buys them from us to paint by. He stops at Beethoven."

. . . .

OCTOBER 4 · 1951

The whole inside of my left hand is inflamed. No idea what to do.

Countless letters that must be answered every day, or else I seem pretentious or indifferent to other people's crises. The mail exhausts me and gets in the way of my work. And each correspondent thinks he's the only one who writes me.

. . . .

OCTOBER 6 · 1951

Cut a piece of cigarette paper in half. Put the two pieces on top of each other. Cut them both—and so on, fifty times. What will be the thickness of the pile of superimposed pieces of paper? Twenty-six million kilometers. (Calculations of grains of wheat.) Under the influence of nitrogen protoxide, I experienced this monstrous multiplication, when a second represents several centuries. This phenomenon inspired the time of Orpheus's journey, which occurs while the letter falls into the mailbox.*

Temptation of Christ on the Mountain. Worked this morning on the tree and the sky. I painted the still life (glasses of red wine, apple, jug) in a crude, realistic style to underline the unreality of the rest. (The triangles; Christ's robe, two different reds; Satan iridescent; the halo transparent.) The mad-looking sky is an exact copy of the sky on the Riviera the evening the Castaings came to Santo Sospir, last week.

---

*Cocteau's film *Orpheus* (1949).

That I am envied and misunderstood is a phenomenon I have been used to for a long time. Surprised, then, to receive a manuscript from a young man in Mostaganem (Oran) named Millecam. His book is called *L'Étoile de Jean Cocteau.** I hadn't believed such perspicacity was possible. Sometimes he has Nietzsche's diamond edge. The parallel between Spinoza's work and mine is astonishing. Splendid summary of *Blood of a Poet* [1930]. I wonder if his perspicacity includes the knowledge that his exegesis is correct but that I made the film without thinking of the meaning which he attributes to it and which it has. I suspect the book will provoke amazement.

News of the film. Kodak says the reels are excellent. Possible to edit the film at Santo Sospir. Painting exhausts me. After each day's work, I look like a rag, a corpse. Editing the film will be something of a rest.

The drama of my life results from the fact that my invisibility (the soul's elegance) is turned into a spectacle by journalists. I am a ghost that people see and that everyone sees in chains, armor, and the other conventional attributes of ghosts. There are even people I scare.

What young Millecam wonderfully brings out is the incomprehension of an aesthetic epoch confronted with an ethical work. Claude Mauriac is incapable of understanding my sentence "I am a lie that always tells the truth." He quotes it against my person.† I meant that every man is a lie because social life and the obligation to make contact burden him with masks. But every second I try to contradict this lie and through it to proclaim my truth.

Millecam explains very well that I am looking not for beauty but for truth. That only such truth, my truth, seems beautiful to me, and that I do not bother with any of the drapery aestheticians

---

*Published in 1952, with a letter from Cocteau to the publisher.

†Claude Mauriac, *Jean Cocteau ou La Vérité du mensonge* (Paris: 1945).

hang about me. (*Invenire*. To discover. To take off what covers.)

I have learned, and with some sadness, from Pierre Borel,* that he has discovered the source of *The Wanderer* [*Le Grand Meaulnes*]. It's a tale from *Le Magasin pittoresque* entitled "*Le Grand Klantz.*" Everything is there. Alain Fournier used to devour those old periodicals out in the country. The resemblance to certain passages of *Villette* is flagrant, but remote. Here the tiniest details match up. Alain Fournier adopts even the *title* of the tale from which he takes his "inspiration."

. . . .

SUNDAY · OCTOBER 7 · 1951

Last night was the worst of all; this morning my fingers are as sore as if they had been burned.

Yesterday, in the car, Francine referred to "My boat." And immediately corrected herself: "Our boat." Her whole exquisite nature is there. Afraid someone might think that something she owns doesn't belong as much to her friends as to herself. She has managed to root out my bourgeois inheritance of Mine or Thine; Milly is hers and Édouard's as much as Santo Sospir is ours. Besides, though she doesn't know Jeannot well, she has adopted my attitude toward him. He is one of the powerful members of the family she has created by a kind of solitude within her own family. Which doesn't keep her from being impeccable, tender, dedicated to her own. No doubt it's this perfection of heart and a remarkable elegance of soul which keep her real family from taking umbrage at our friendship and at seeing her treat my adoptive son as a brother. She gives no purchase to spitefulness, except the worldly kind she is quite oblivious of and which takes its course. During

---

*A young poet whose collection *Des Mots* was published in 1955 with a brief letter-preface by Jean Cocteau.

our trips I have never heard anyone call her anything but *mademoiselle*. No one suspects that this little person is a grown-up lady and that she has a daughter nine years old. Her purity glows around her.

At the time of the absurd incident of Antoine's* wife—when the Paris newspapers were saying that she was *my* gardener's wife and that the drama had occurred in *my* house—Alec might have resented the whole business, and with some reason. But he did nothing of the kind, despite the nastiness of the gossip.

People cannot realize what Francine is for me, aside from my affections for her: *i.e., an example.*

To become a secular saint.

To look like . . . A saint that looked like a saint wouldn't be one. Not to look like a poet. Scandal and legend save us from such *looking like* . . . We are protected by an armor, by a carapace of mistakes.

Only one valid law: Never hurt others. Never diminish others. Never answer insults.

To acknowledge a favorable power is to lose it. When Jean Marais speaks of his luck, he is entitled to do so, for such luck does not exist. He produces it. He baptizes misfortune luck. If this luck had really ever existed, he would have nipped it in the bud.

Just finished working on the painting. This craft—this craft I lack! Facing this picture, you feel what I was trying for and what I was unable to achieve. I'll work harder. Since I have no professional skill, I shall find other means. Extreme exhaustion of indirect means.

Doudou puts it this way: "You don't know the city and you wander through the streets. Picasso has a map. He knows where he's going."

Why am I said to be a Communist? Because I once said that

---

*Francine Weisweiller's gardener.

there is only one great politician in our time: Stalin. This has nothing to do with the system. Stalin refuses all dialogue because he knows that a conversation with fools always degenerates into a dispute.

An age of aesthetes who claim they detest aestheticism and of fools who regard themselves as sages. Keep in the shadows. Watch: consider the disorder of these aesthetes, these fools. Have nothing to do with their intrigues.

Sign of our times: uneducated learning. Irreligious spirit: no sense of human religion.

People would like to believe hell exists. There the duchesse d'Uzès and Père Gibier would be eternally devoured by an infernal pack. Absurd blessing of the dogs. The ceremonies in Notre-Dame, attended by the parliamentarians, heirs of the Separation. I prefer the Borgias. God means nothing to them, only power.

Savonarola, worse than the Borgias. The real criminal. His poisons: he burns Leonardo's *Leda*. Read Maria Bellonci's book on Lucrezia Borgia: somewhat jumbled, but accurate.

. . . .

Monday · October 8 · 1951

[. . .] When one of our works doesn't suggest any of the others, we are disturbed, as is the public. A resemblance reassures and permits us to lean on something. The new is the void, for the time being. (Until the poor imitation comes along.)

Lunch yesterday with Coco Chanel at Roquebrune. She is writing her memoirs. She has that extremely incisive style of the true memorialist.* Her fashion (her reign) was a reformation, with all

---

*Begun with André Fraigneau's help, the writing of her memoirs was soon abandoned by Gabrielle Chanel.

the austerity that implies. It was a revolt against frills and furbelows. If I didn't know she had been brought up a Catholic, I would imagine she was a Protestant. She protests inveterately and against everything. Her little black swan's head. One of those Auvergnats with Romany grandparents. Her gypsy style. Laval had that look of an Auvergnat gypsy.

Fernay writes that my speech to the unions produced a huge impression. Of course, no one dares say a thing. People are dying of fear.

The Liberation, the shame of France, has been the Saint Bartholomew's Massacre of values. They had to be destroyed, slain at all costs. Dishonor anything out of the ordinary. Save the rich. Shoot the poor. The builders of the Atlantic wall are acquitted, and a poor woman who washed dishes for the Germans in order to steal food for her family is sentenced to fifteen years in prison. And to think that young men have loyally participated in this masquerade. That Jean Desbordes lost his life in it.*

My own destruction had been arranged. I was saved by Éluard and by Aragon. I was blamed for my friendship with Arno Breker, and tomorrow Arno Breker moves to Paris. The Germans poisoned the wells behind their retreat; they left us the plague. Hatred,

---

*Jean Desbordes, born 1906, met Cocteau at Christmas 1926: "He brought me a manuscript, a typewritten bundle of shapeless cries. Suddenly he fell asleep, spoke of another world, flew, walked on water. I lost no time: I devoted myself to teaching him how to sleep—how to install that sleep of chance and to become aware of himself without losing his freshness" (from Cocteau's preface to *J'adore* [1928]). *J'adore*, by its sensuality, scandalized the Catholic circles Cocteau had been moving in since 1925. He broke with them and continued to support the young writer's work: *Les Tragédiens* (1931), *La Mûe* (1936), a play performed at the Comédie Française in 1938 under the title *L'Âge ingrat*. In 1930, in *Blood of a Poet*, Jean Desbordes played the part of Louis XV. He went on to publish: *Les Forcenés* (1937), *Le Crime de la rue Royale* (1938), and *Le Vrai Visage du Marquis de Sade* (1939). Working in the Resistance and arrested by the Gestapo, he was tortured to death in Paris on July 5, 1944. See Cocteau's articles on *Les Tragédiens* in the *Nouvelle Revue française*, May 1931, and on *L'Âge ingrat* in *Le Foyer des artistes*.

discord. The fake tribunals. The hurly-burly for booty. "That delicious moment when you can take revenge without risk" (*Bacchus*). . . .

And my poor Jean Desbordes tortured, killed, in the rue de la Pompe. Not a word has been said about it. He belonged to the Polish Resistance. The first chance that came along. *His death was for nothing.*

Read the book: *Le Système*—by Jean Maze (?)* An edition of a hundred copies. Cannot be sold. (Especially the texts he quotes.)

Poor Maritain, so naïve, so pure. Emoting on the radio from New York, during this disgusting business. (What Saint-Exupéry calls the Party of One.) I didn't belong to it, he says,† because, at a distance, I wanted to be a witness for France and not a witness against her.

Telegram from *Life* thanking me for the "magnificent text on Marlene." I rarely get thanked, and in such terms. Usually I receive letter after letter, phone call after phone call. I send the article or the drawing. The article is published with misprints, the drawing badly reproduced.

I can see perfectly well in what direction a real painter would take the picture I'm exhausting myself over. But one retouch would involve another, and so on. My only hope is to succeed at the first go. (The apple on the table.) A little bright yellow was enough for it to live. I would have liked to be born a painter. Writing is not authentic work.

The problem is to achieve a relief, a depth with this determination of flat triangles. I may have to put lighter areas inside the flat surfaces. (The two reds of Christ's robe.)

---

*Jean Maze, *Le Système* (1943–1951) (1951).

†He: Saint-Exupéry. In New York in 1941 and 1942, he opposed the Gaullists ("the Party of One") provoking between Maritain and himself a polite but unresolved controversy.

. . . .

TUESDAY · OCTOBER 9 · 1951

It would be interesting for a memorialist to know what kind of life the Turkish hostage Prince Djem lived at the Vatican. Cesare Borgia adopted his style. Dressed as a Turk. Djem and he headed the papal procession, on horseback and covered with jewels. Women of the people crossed themselves as they passed. I seem to remember that Prince Djem was handed over to the king of France. The private life of this prince must be very curious.

The periodical *Neuf* thanks me for the piece on Al Brown.* Are we acquiring the habit of thanking?

The author of *Le Système* says that I put on plays during the German Occupation (which Anouilh is never reproached for doing). He fails to say that those plays were interrupted by tear-gas bombs, that my actors were beaten up, and that I almost lost an eye on the Champs-Élysées to the fists of the men of the PPF. Every day *Je suis partout* and other collaborationist journals demanded that the Occupation authorities have me shot. The day after the incident on the Champs-Élysées, the headline was: "M. Cocteau Salutes Only the Jewish Flag." I suppose I owe my "laundering" (that was the word) to the fact that Éluard and Aragon knew I had refused to salute the flag of the Anti-Bolshevik Legion. On the other hand, the Americans would not thank me for that. That's politics.

Of course, I have secrets. If I told them, they wouldn't be secrets anymore; they would become ineffectual. A secret once told evaporates.

Annulment of Lucrezia Borgia's marriage. Pregnant by a papal

---

*"*L'Affaire Al Brown*," 1951. On Al Brown, whom Jean Cocteau helped in 1937 and 1938 to regain his status as the "black wonder" of boxing, see Jean Cocteau, *Poésie de journalisme* (Paris: 1973).

nuncio, she comes to testify that she is a virgin. Her husband, who had slept with her, was obliged to sign an avowal of impotence. In exchange, Allessandro Borgia grants her a dowry.

The studio at Santo Sospir and the studio at Milly are finished. At Milly, I turned the attic between the turrets into a studio.

Every theater in Paris has sent me a letter asking for *Bacchus*, and I'm faced with the same problem as if I had no theater at all. Because I have no actor. Jeannot is at the Comédie Française where he's rehearsing *Britannicus*. Gérard Philipe is hand in glove with Vilar, whose projects and contexts seem to me too big and too chaotic for my play. Which leaves Simone Berriau (with what actor?) or Jean-Louis Barrault. I'm not pleased with the choice, but the Barrault productions attract the young and attentive public I need for a work which requires real listening.

London asks to read *Bacchus*. I'll have a manuscript sent, though the play seems to me dangerous in England. As Van Loewen* says: "The British wouldn't dare write such a play, but they're glad to have a foreigner do it."

France is at present the country richest in dead (concealed) money. If this money appears, the state confiscates it. The state is turning into a great feudal lord. No difference between the French system and a despotic one. Look for investments, you will find no such thing. Look for money for any shady deal, no trouble at all. The state forces us to commit fraud. The state declares that we must seem poor, and if we admit we are rich, other countries will ruin us. Inextricable.

Egypt is forcing the English to clear out. It was long ago that I first saw the American industrial occupation of Egypt. Egypt cannot support herself. It's clear that it is the Americans who are taking action. The undeclared war we are watching is a war between

---

*Literary agent.

America and England. The Russians are much less involved than we suppose.

To extinguish craftsmanship in France is to destroy what stimulates foreign demand. Once craftsmanship is done away with, we shall be a very minor industrial power. I was able to order my second tapestry from Aubusson because the shop had just received a small American commission (one that has nothing to do with the genius of the Atelier Bouret). If the commission had been a big one, Bouret would have told me he wasn't free to take on my tapestry.

I have just reread some chapters of the book *Le Système*. I was wrong. The author deceives us by a seeming intelligence, a show of justice. He is an idiot and an embittered one. The book must have been written in a spirit of revenge.

That he is wrong about me doesn't matter. But I realize: if he is wrong about me, who is to say he isn't wrong about the others?

. . . .

WEDNESDAY · OCTOBER 10 · 1951

It is likely I would not have devoted myself to poetry in this world, which remains insensitive to it, if poetry were not a morality. If it did not require a style of the soul and if it did not become, in the long run, our very soul. Poetry compels us, at every moment, to a nobility and a love which keep us from distractions, which save us from hesitation. Poetry is a kind of open cloister whose extremely severe discipline dwells within us. If poetry were not an ethic, if it proceeded from aesthetics, I should avoid it like the plague. I discovered this cloister rather late—in 1913. I thought poetry was within my command. In 1914 I *took orders*. (Poetry's orders.)

If poetry were a trade, a profession, if I expected something from it, if I hoped for some glory, the exercise of this solitude and the stupidity which disturbs it would be intolerable. Yet I accept them without bitterness—with joy, as a monk prays for his fellow men, even if they deride his prayers.

I was thinking about this while I was painting, struggling to paint and no longer even realizing how exhausted I was. I never believe that a picture will be *seen*. I try to get outside myself onto the canvas, to join what I want to be and what I always feel so far from, what I always feel so unworthy of.

We must realize that this religion of poetry is without any hope of recompense.

One very important sentence in Millecam's book: "When the poet says 'I,' he is speaking of the cosmos."

As a matter of fact, there would be a kind of egotism in seeking only one's own equilibrium, if one were not certain that this equilibrium collaborates with a universal equilibrium whose advantages we shall never know. Which comes down to this paradox: acute individualism is the highest form of collaboration with others.

The contrary of the "ivory tower." Everything amuses me; everything interests me. I am the best audience of the free-for-all.

Which accounts for my total indifference to death. I was dead before I was born. I shall be dead after my life. To be afraid to die is as strange as being afraid to be limited in space.

The sea is still too high for sailing. Paul* tells Francine that a fisherman and his son have just been drowned off the island. They had been warned. They insisted on going out for their nets.

Rereading Max Jacob's *Cornet à dés*, I come across: "The honeycombs of the interminable gauze curtain, that is how I imagine the houses of New York"† When I wrote that the skyscrapers were like gauze,‡ I had forgotten that sentence.

---

*Captain of the *Orphée II*.

†In *Le Cornet à dés* (1916), a fragment of *Le Coq et la perle*.

‡In *Letter to the Americans* (1949): "The minute I set foot in the city, I felt that lightness of the air in which skyscrapers hang out their gauze, set up their hives from which a golden honey flows."

That is how we imitate without realizing it. In the same way we come to think the same things at the same time (Sartre and *Bacchus*). Waves. A single wavelength records them at the same moment. People think we inspire each other. A family resemblance.

Being religious, Max Jacob did not have the religion of poetry. That would have been a pleonasm. He enjoyed writing and often sought to amuse others, his young visitors. This gives certain texts of his the strange expression he himself assumed with his monocle. When he composes a true poem (there are splendid ones in *Le Cornet à dés*, the poems without titles), he surpasses Apollinaire. But what a pity some of his poems in prose correspond so little to what he demands of the prose poet in his preface and leave no more residues in us than a dream. Many of the prose poems in *Le Cornet à dés* correspond to the Cubist arsenal of the period, consisting of provincial haberdashery and chalk hopscotch squares on the sidewalks. I'd like to reread the poem on the sardana that opens *Le Laboratoire central*.* I still remember it with amazement. Unfortunately my copy has been swiped because of the dedication. Maurice, no doubt.† Dear Max! He was always on the defensive. Because of those who mocked him, teased him, ran him down, many of his poems have the style of village gossip. Loved, cherished, even feared, he would have avoided this back-room atmosphere. He flies so easily, when he flies. The ease of flight in dreams. After his death the Resistance praised him to the skies. This enthusiasm did not last long. He had ceased to serve.

Max once told me that during Apollinaire's lecture on poets, when he came to Max, Guillaume had burst out laughing, covering his mouth with his hand.‡

**Honneur de la Sardane et de la tenora* is the second poem in *Laboratoire central* (1921).

†Maurice Sachs. See Jean Cocteau, *Journal d'un inconnu* (Grasset, 1953): "One year, when I was staying at Villefranche, Maurice took a wheelbarrow and stripped my room in Paris of all it contained. . . ."

‡In 1908, Apollinaire gave the last in a series of three lectures on poetry, "*La*

I have his last letter. He had written me from the train taking him to Drancy and entrusted his letter to a station guard. A frightened collaborator who wanted to pre-whitewash himself saved it, but too late. He was dead.

. . . .

October 11 · 1951

This world's error is to live on the idea of success. Christ's failure is not the crucifixion. It is the Vatican.

America is buying everything (in order to succeed). Buying China. And will buy the Russians. What will happen? A secret rebellion against such domination. A new resistance. A day will come when America's purchasing power will cost her dear.

In *War and Peace* there is a marvelous chapter. Prince André, wounded, stares up at the clouds. His dream is to know Napoleon, who is his idol. He hears voices. It is Napoleon and his general staff. Prince André doesn't even glance at him. He is watching the clouds.

Tonight I watched the sun setting, fast and red. Poor absurd little earth which turns so fast on its axis. Poor little earth of financiers and murderers. [. . .]

Returned *Le Système* to Chanel. Grim book. A mediocre man accuses mediocre men.

When the work is done, when you have passed within it, it becomes an object which circulates. A rude awakening. A play has to be performed to be a play. A picture must appear on a wall to be a picture. The act of painting, of writing ceases to be a hypnosis. The object which replaces the act tries to provoke a collective

---

Phalange nouvelle," in which a passage concerns Max Jacob; this appears to be the circumstance alluded to here. This lecture was published in *La Poésie symboliste, trois entretiens sur les temps héroïques* (1908).

hypnosis and involves us in the disappointments which the solitude of our work had spared us. Uneasiness of contacts. Picasso's terrible eye, for instance. Necessary to avoid putting him in sudden contact with any confessional object. He is a confessor I avoid because of my fear of my weakness and of my faults. Besides, he possesses a defensive method, the method of his solitude, which expels that of other people, especially if he discovers that you are not lying. His role is that of a despot. He seeks to be the only ruler, and he could adopt Napoleon's terrifying sentence "A man who has an idea is my enemy."

How many letters, how many individual cases where I am absolutely helpless, where it is difficult for a young man to realize how pernicious it is to be in a hurry, how difficult contacts are with others, how help requires the exclusion of everything else, everyone else, how impossible it is to give advice. An honest man who answers letters honestly always seems to be pulling back, refusing to give a hand. (Problem of "success.")

Wrote to Jean-Louis Barrault that perhaps we can do the play together.

Today Spiro came. He made me varnish the still life of the table. The two glasses of red wine. The apple. The jug. I won't varnish the triangular tablecloth, but all the rest. Spiro advises using retouching-varnish, which makes the colors revive as the colors of seashells do in water, and then revarnishing the still life with regular varnish, so that it gets as much depth as possible.

I had worked on the figures of Christ and Satan. The Satan is charming, as he should be. A Satan from Ecbatana. One of those adolescent Satans of Verlaine. He talks, talks, proves, tries to convince. Christ listens, but He listens *elsewhere* and with one ear. I have pondered each millimeter of this canvas so intensely that the canvas itself thinks. This compensates for the painter's craft I lack, whatever Spiro says. Too bad this board is so heavy. I'd like to send it to Munich. It would unify the whole group. This large composition summarizes the investigations of the last six months, and if I am so determined to paint, it is from this work that I shall set out, from it that I shall take my *flight*. It is a huge springboard.

Max Jacob was right to say: "A picture turns, turns. When it stops turning, that's when it's done." My picture stopped turning this morning. I can only reinforce it with little touches, make the surfaces smoother, darken the landscape seen from a bird's-eye view. It's a well-*told* picture. A poet's picture. The only kind I can hope to make. Spiro notices the pale green rifle formed by the sky between Satan's arms. Satan offers charm but aims at Christ with this rifle. No doubt someone will say that this Satan is a "Negro." People take all dark figures for Negroes. I am increasingly aware how badly people see what is shown them, judging it with only one eye and so quickly . . . I pity the painters who look for an understanding audience. I do not show. I show myself. I even show myself up.

. . . .

SATURDAY · OCTOBER 13 · 1951

Letter from Kodak. They're sending one of their specialists, a M. Cox, for the editing. He'll be with us for a week.

Time's little jokes. Man Ray has me bring the photograph he had taken of me in Montparnasse. Francine asks when it was taken. "Fifteen years ago." It was thirty-five years. Last night Jean Guérin had dinner with Walter. I asked for news of little Richard from Villefranche. He's a father and a grandfather.

Worked on the sky of *The Temptation of Christ*.

I have been to see Dr. Cossa in Nice, for my hands. I am not one of his patients, but I have heard he is a wonderful diagnostician. He declares it is an eczema and tells me to bear it, for if he manages to clear it up, he says, it will provoke something worse elsewhere.

Today Spiro is bringing the photographer for the canvases. Alexandre wants them for a number of *Graphik*.

King Farouk at Cannes. A gentleman lays down four jacks. The king lays down three kings and declares four. "I am," he says, "the fourth." And he takes the pot. Another time he doesn't show his cards. "Do you doubt a king's word?"

A lady asks her neighbor for a light. Farouk is opposite her. He tosses her his gold lighter. The lady lights her cigarette and sends the lighter to the croupier, saying: "For the staff."

Apropos of industrial occupations. England should have followed the advice Napoleon gives in the *Mémorial*: England, he said, should have not disastrous colonies but banks all over the world.

America "buying China" seems a huge deal. But only the nerve centers can be bought. In 1936, when I was in China, it virtually belonged to one Englishman, Victor Sassoon.

If England were to do in Egypt something like what America is doing in Korea, we shall have feudal wars among feudal powers. Perhaps this will be the style of the struggles of our times.

. . . .

OCTOBER 14 · 1951

Tonight I painted the crocuses. One under Satan's chair, as if it were growing out of his ankle, the other at the extreme right, between Christ's robe and the landscape. Spiro pointed out during the photograph session that Satan's dark hand looked as if it were touching Christ's right cheek, so I made the hand lighter. It is possible that I will change its angle and show the extended forefinger. On Satan's right hand and on his left wrist and at the crook of his left elbow, I painted veins like the ones on the hand of Michelangelo's *David*. I wanted to make him very human, despite his very earthy, animal coloring. (Prince of this world.) On the other hand, Christ, traversed by the landscape's forms and lights, is half here, half elsewhere.

. . . .

October 16 · 1951

I worked night and day on the big new canvas Édouard bought in Nice. A huge head of a woman draped in white behind a red curtain which takes up the whole left side.* The head is painted in pale blues, whites, and bisters. I took my inspiration from the Medici Madonna. Actually my *tragédienne* looks like the young man in the *Victory*. From which I conclude that the model was the same. Michelangelo's faces all have a fish eye and a big mouth.

The beaverboard of *The Temptation* is beginning to warp. S. thinks it is the wood backing. Once I have varnished it and the doctor has made the film, we shall wet the wood and clamp the board so that it will flatten out. I suspect it is the consequence of moving from an unheated studio to the heated rooms of Santo Sospir.

Letter from Jean-Louis Barrault and one from Jean Vilar. It seems that Vilar is more enthusiastic about me than about the play. Whereas Jean-Louis seems really devoted to the play. I wrote Vilar that his plans and his setup were too big for a play with just one set. After editing the film, I shall go up to Paris to see Barrault and Madeleine.

**Portrait d'une tragédienne*. 146 cm x 114 cm. Collection Édouard Dermit. "This head originated in the model Michelangelo transformed into a man or a woman according to the requirements of his allegories": Cocteau's catalog note for his 1953 Nice exhibition.

. . . .

October 17 · 1951

If Maria Bellonci's book is as accurate as it seems to be, it shows how a terrible reputation can be created and sustained without any real cause. Lucrezia Borgia was a good little girl, rather docile and not at all scandalous except for her clothes.

The Borgia poison (*la cantarella*) appears in Rome only after Lucrezia's marriage to Ferrara. It is possible that she never even knew what it was. Sad to say, but the result of this whitewashing is a rather boring book in which worldliness prevails over intrigue. Where did Hugo get his material? Bellonci has pored over all the archives. It's true that the historian in this case is a woman and concerned to exonerate a woman. Nonetheless, one can make out certain things. For example, that the Roman *infante* is perhaps the son of Lucrezia and Alessandro.

Almost finished the *Portrait d'une tragédienne*. A hard yet gentle canvas which I must not push too far if I am to preserve its quality as a large-scale painting, despite the endless work on cheeks, nose, mouth, and eye. It is the unfinished quality of the red curtain and the linen around the head which makes the rest stand out and gives it a certain relief.

It was yesterday, at six o'clock, that the British troops on the [Suez] Canal were to be regarded as enemy troups. No news yet. I'm worrying about the circumstances of our British friends in Cairo. The news comes; as anticipated, extremists (in Egypt, synonym for looters) are attacking the British troops. The situation may well turn against Farouk. The British are sending in reinforcements. Egypt's action is incomprehensible *without powerful support*. If the English want to take advantage of this excuse, Egypt can be occupied in a few days.

I had written as much in *Maalesh*. Egypt is not a nation. It is a place. There are the rich and the looters. The ruling family is

Turkish. The Arabs think only of stealing. *La coca-cola** flows faster than the Nile. The Sphinx looks on. If only it would talk . . .

. . . .

October 18 · 1951

Telephoned Jean-Louis Barrault. He would like to put *Bacchus* on by the holidays. This seems to me too soon.

Finished the book on Lucrezia Borgia. Boring and confused. Some of the fault lies with these intermarrying families, these military cardinals, these countless bastards of popes and dukes. But not even the crimes manage to make this torrent of worldliness seem serious. These people believed they were eternal; they were bored and covered themselves with gold, ermine, ridicule, and shame.

They frequented bad poets. They thought themselves witty, learned, glorious. One divines, in the margin of these rather vile intrigues, the real Italian life, that of the people, of the artists. But the historian never mentions it. What is left of Julius II? Michelangelo. And these pretentious daughters of a pope? A profile on a quattrocento fresco. A bluestocking recounts (in poetical descriptions) the empty years of a wretched woman and of the queen of bluestockings, Isabella d'Este. The early death of Beatrice d'Este. The Villa d'Este. I have never been so tired as after a visit to those hillside gardens. The result of all that leaping, running water is that you die of thirst.

All that overwhelming life of luxury and stupidity is to be found, a few notches lower, in today's café society. (Beistegui Ball.)

Hitler's Jewish star is not new. After the prophecies of the monk Raphael, a (rather brief) crisis of reformation burst over Ferrara.

---

*In the early fifties the gender of "Coca-Cola" was not determined. *Le Trésor de la langue française* gives a feminine example from Cocteau: "*Pauvre Egypte! . . . Son eau rare, sa coca-cola . . .*" *Maalesh* (1950).

The Jews were ordered to wear yellow hats "so they could be recognized at a distance."

Millecam writes from Mostaganem: "Yesterday I went to Oran to do a commentary on *Les Enfants terribles* at the ciné club. Out of four hundred people there, only two didn't like your film. Moreover, there is now a certain public in Oran that understands you better, perhaps, than the public of the capital. Yesterday someone in the theater told me your film is realistic because it is a documentary not of childhood but of the soul and the poet."

Telegram from Kodak: Cox arrives Monday morning at Beaulieu station.

The Egyptian incident. No power behind Egypt. A wet fire-cracker. Doubtless something to do with finance: maybe Farouk wanted to make good his gambling losses on the Riviera.

. . . .

SUNDAY · OCTOBER 21 · 1951

Did the models, set, and costumes for *Bacchus* (after Holbein and Dürer).

Did the first lithographs for the book with Georges Hugnet: *La Nappe du Catalan*.*

This morning Francine gave a little reception in the studio for all the workmen who built it.

Édouard's painting. When a picture should be unbearable and it is admirable, it is because the painter has surmounted the accumu-

---

*Sixty-four poems and sixteen color lithographs by Jean Cocteau and Georges Hugnet, 1952. Prefatory note: "These poems, written simultaneously, were composed on restaurant tablecloths, during several lunches. Each of the poets left blanks among his verses, which the other one filled in. As for the lithographs which illustrate them, the color is by one poet, the line by the other." Le Catalan was a Parisian restaurant, rue des Grands-Augustins, frequented by Picasso, Jean Cocteau, and their friends.

lation of details by a *tour de force* of which he is virtually unconscious. His soul, the beauty of his soul, passes into the scruple and the patience of his work without his even perceiving it. Air circulates. The canvas breathes. The painter has vanquished that fear of ridicule which impels artists to anticipate the mysterious operation by which their personality is expressed. In the presence of an astonishing canvas like this one, which represents the garage of *Santo Sospir*, one understands that Dermit has thought only of its objective quality. The subjective has created itself on its own. Perhaps this is a typical example of work done under a spell, too simple to be seen by eyes accustomed to any sort of analysis.

When Picasso asked me: "What's Dermit's painting like?" I said: "It's painting that's revolutionary in relation to you."

Don't you think Mme F.* is stupid? Yes, very stupid. Like everyone else.

The newspapers say: "The British are entirely satisfied with France's conduct during the Egyptian incident." Yes, the Suez stockholders.

. . . .

Wednesday · October · 1951

Cox arrived Monday. We began work at once. This morning he had an attack of angina. Raining cats and dogs.

Names. Borgia. The name is fat, ceremonial, tragic. The myth of the Borgias owes a great deal to the name.

Cox in bed. Work with François.† Shooting script for the reels.

---

*Mme Favini, a burlesque character invented by Jean Cocteau (like the musician Rufus, creator of the pantodrama *Das Kreutz*, imagined for the amusement of the composer Igor Markevich in 1934, or like General Clapier, invented during the forties): a typical bourgeois snob.

†François Truffaut, filmmaker.

No news from Jean-Louis (in answer to my letter about Édouard and Nicole*).

Deluged by letters. Will answer tonight. Denise Tual† wants me to organize a production of Satie's *Socrate.*‡ Stravinsky to direct a sort of festival at the Théâtre des Champs-Élysées in homage to Diaghilev.

I finished the editing of the film tonight, much to my satisfaction. I instinctively shot all I needed, and the sequences fell into place without jolts. I didn't even consult my notes. The film was edited in my head.

Cox will leave next Tuesday, with us. This morning the doctor filmed the *Portrait d'une tragédienne* and the *Temptation of Christ* which Cox will put into the reel. Francine, who left ahead of us on the five o'clock plane, took the box, since Kodak won't be able to develop and make negatives until Monday. I'll go to Milly without telling anyone. Francine will meet us at Le Bourget and come with us to Milly, where Madeleine Renaud and Jean-Louis Barrault will come for lunch and dinner Wednesday. Then we'll leave directly from Le Bourget for Santo Sospir.

Madeleine§ in tears on the phone. The Siamese cats have typhus. Visit from Marcel Herrand, who is filming *Fanfan la Tulipe* with Gérard.

Nothing is more tiresome than any kind of writing after editing. Editing is a sport. The time passes very quickly. How wonderful to be able to edit a film without stopping. One forgets to eat. Then one looks for the tiniest retouches to be made, any excuse for not being finished. François, the electrician from Beaulieu,

---

*In *Bacchus*, Cocteau wanted to cast Nicole Stéphane as Christine and Édouard Dermit as Lothar.

†A film producer who participated in organization of "*L'Oeuvre du xxe siècle.*" See below, p. 81.

‡This project was not executed.

§Madeleine Bouret, Cocteau's housekeeper at his Paris apartment in the Palais-Royal.

caught the fever. He doesn't eat, doesn't go to bed, knows all the shots by heart. He would be a first-class workman in the studio.

April sunshine.

Just saw the whole film through again. It seems quite natural: our daily existence at Santo Sospir. I was forgetting that our existence must be incomprehensible because of its simplicity. As a result, the film is as peculiar as *Blood of a Poet* in its day. Peculiar by what it reveals and by its colors, as much by its will as by the accidents which proceed from it.

I am much prouder of it than of my other films. Here *I was free*. In the others *I thought I was*.

. . . .

MONDAY · OCTOBER 29 · 1951

Some people have luck enough to meet others of a color which mixes nicely with their own, and this new color is pleasant; some people meet only colors which mix badly. And some people meet only their complementary colors. (Chanel's case.) From which results certain friendships full of hatred. You are inseparable, and you hate each other. At Santo Sospir the colors mix deliciously. I must belong to the first category. My color almost always meets one that produces a splendid mix.

Yesterday re-corrected the details of the film; showed the film to the staff. I've already redone the flower shots (printed in reverse). The results are not so good as the idea. Tonight, with Dr. Ricoux, we'll retake the shots in Francine's room and in the grand-salle.

The quality I wanted: an amateur's film, is achieved. Bad splices, on purpose. Unevenness of the images. Hasty takes. But the rhythm of the editing is of a professional order. Had to be, to make the rest acceptable.

A journal of amateur filmmakers reports that I am making a very long documentary after having recommended making very short ones. This is untrue, as usual. The film is not a documentary, but a document. Besides, it lasts only three-quarters of an hour. I might add that this film is not commercial; it is a private film, a film Francine commissioned for herself.

Today I'll project the film on a big screen to show Cox where the new shots go. Tomorrow morning we fly to Paris.

. . . .

TUESDAY · OCTOBER 30 · 1951 · Milly

Cox tells me that it is impossible to persuade the Kodak workers to wear rubber gloves. The chemicals are very dangerous. The workers agree to wash with counterpoisons. They wear gloves once, twice, and take them off. They feel lost without making direct contact. The whole difference between the work of a craftsman and mass production.

The Orient's terrible mistake was to have believed itself inferior to the West and to have accepted our example. Our missionaries imported disaster. The East will take its revenge for this dominance, and with our weapons. That is justice.

The Japanese are the people who took longest to let foreigners set foot on their islands. They allowed only one Dutch bank (at Nagasaki) and one cargo vessel a year.

America was the first nation to achieve contact by ruse. The ship's captain was given some sort of title—"Master of the Great Mystery"—and remained invisible. He claimed he could deal only with the regent of the empire (the mikado was too young). This ruse intimidated the Japanese, who till then had politely rejected foreigners without engaging in transactions of any kind.

. . . .

WEDNESDAY · OCTOBER 31 · 1951

China is deep. Doubtless impossible to touch bottom. Yet the disease has broken out. The astonishing thing is the total break with a tradition which, had it evolved, would have created marvels, machines a thousand times stranger and more precise than ours.

The old Chinese painters imitate the ancestors. The young Chinese painters imitate Picasso and Max Ernst. Between them is an abyss.

At Istanbul, when I visited the École des Beaux-Arts, imagine my surprise to see that all the students there were imitating . . . André Lhote!

The noble contaminated by the ignoble. That is the history of Western influence on the peoples of the Orient.

Lyautey is the only one who understood what a Western leader was to Orientals. Morocco venerates him. Westerners lost no time in removing him from his post. Lyautey told me he was to be sent home on an old rat-infested hulk. It was the British who, disgusted, made sure he returned to France on one of their warships.

Lyautey was a Freemason. A Catholic Freemason, Scottish rite. It was doubtless his membership in this lodge that spared him any attack on his sexual preferences, of which he made no secret.

I have been asked for a statement against racism by the *Journal officiel*. I answered that in 1936, on my trip around the world, I was very often ashamed of my white skin.

On the deck of the boat carrying us back to Europe (through the Golden Gate), Chaplin turned to me and said: "Back to the savages."

Jolivet's concerto on the radio: unfortunately he comes twenty years too late (after *Le Sacre*).

When we performed *Britannicus* in Cairo* before the royal family, every scene became an allusion and, to put it frankly, a *faux pas*. The young princesses were made to leave before the end. Besides, the acting of Jean Marais and his colleagues rid the work of that patina which comes from the boredom of school. *Britannicus* gleamed, like a gold coin in an age of paper money.

This is what gave me the notion of filming it, of adding to its vitality, its intensity, by close-ups and camera movements. I gave it up because of the untranslatable text and the limited range of the French language, which makes it impossible for an expensive film to pay its own way. Olivier is luckier with *Hamlet*, for the English language, even Shakespeare's, opened a much wider distribution to him.

EVENING

Read *Bacchus* to Jean-Louis. We understand each other and proceed to do the casting immediately. Madeleine had an angina attack and could not come. We telephoned her the news. Then Jean-Louis takes her the manuscript and the drawings of the set and costumes.

I have given my play not *to a theater* but *to friends*.

Dreadful weather. My hands suffer badly during the night.

Taking the plane at Le Bourget tomorrow at three. Will be at Santo Sospir by evening. Cox telephones; the shots are good.

---

*In March 1949. Yet in *Maalesh*, Cocteau does not mention this presence of the royal family at one of the performances of *Britannicus*.

. . . .

THURSDAY · NOVEMBER 1 · 1951

Age. My body wakes up after I do. I awaken long before my legs do. When I stand up, I have to be careful not to fall.

Sleep always has an anesthetic effect on me. I used to sleep despite the worst pains. (Neuritis, for example.) In my dreams, I was not sick. Upon waking, for a second or so, I would think I was cured. The pain wakened after I did.

Jean-Louis has reached my stage: he used to be afraid of Paris. Now resistance to everything doesn't matter to him. He's no longer afraid. He stages what he wants and the way he wants to.

The response we invariably get abroad has a lot to do with this abolition of our fears of the family—i.e., of Paris.

Telephoned Jean-Louis from Le Bourget. Madeleine thinks it would be a dreadful mistake to stage the play after the holidays. She and Mme Volterra* would like us to get it on by Christmas.

I am astounded that Madeleine and Jean-Louis are seriously discussing an Egyptian tour. And that Karsenty envisages a French tour now. Ideally, Egypt will refuse the tour, and since Mme Volterra is doing an operetta at the Marigny, some other theater will open its doors to us.

. . . .

FRIDAY · NOVEMBER 2

Santo Sospir. Splendid weather. Corrected the proofs of *Reines de France* [1952]. Did new lithographs for Hugnet.

Theater. A gentleman is pointing out the celebrities in the house to his neighbor. "Look, there's Jean Marais! And there's Danielle

*Simone Volterra, director of the Théâtre Marigny, where the Compagnie Madeleine Renaud–Jean-Louis Barrault gave its performances.

Darrieux! And there's X, and there's Y! And you see that gentleman with the white hair—that's Paul Valéry." "But Paul Valéry's dead!" "Dead? Look . . . he's moving."

. . . .

NOVEMBER 5 · 1951

Letter from the Marigny administration: necessary to draw up the guest list even before the play goes into rehearsal. In other words, cook the sauce in which we will be eaten.

Simone B.*'s husband came to see me. Points against Jean-Louis. Still, no question of a change. Simone had offered me October. Too long to wait. Once written, a play has to be put on.

Lists. One forgets one's closest friends. They jump into your head, all day long, one after the other, both feet together.

Dinner at Beaulieu with André Bernheim, Nadine, the Gabins, the Darrieux.

. . . .

WEDNESDAY · NOVEMBER 7 · 1951

After horrible atom bomb tests, a radioactive snow falls over the factories of New York and paralyzes them.

Declarations of peace replace declarations of war. The word *peace* replaces the word *war*. Peace is being hurled at our heads. President Truman, who must find an answer to the Russian "peace offensive," offers a control of the bombs or their total suppression. If the Russians reject his offer, he can say: "You see, the Russians reject the American peace overtures." [. . .]

Jeanson, slapped in the face in the street, exclaims: "You dare strike a coward!"

---

*Simone Berriau, director of the Théâtre Antoine.

Uneasiness of the week of departure. We are no longer at Santo Sospir. We are not yet in Paris. We are suspended, and we suffer from a void.

Today a sun like summer. Francine and Doudou take sunbaths.

The doctor and I have redone a sequence which I hope will be final: the hibiscus in three shots, so that I don't have to work out the speed necessitated by the spring mechanism: 1. I place the pistil (close-up). 2. I place the petals (middle shot). 3. I readjust the torn petals (close-up).

I have sent the whole thing to Cox.

Édouard Dermit. With the portrait of me he's just done, he shows himself superior to all the painters of his generation. One wonders where he gets this knowledge of painting, through which he shows his nobility and purity of soul. People detest listening to praise. But if I put them in front of one of Dermit's canvases, their faces express amazement. (And even disappointment, for they cannot speak ill of it.)

To the American peace offensives, the Russians reply that these are declarations of "hysterical gentlemen."

Vincent Auriol, who makes the speeches of a king (even of a prime minister!), finds himself attacked by M. Duclos. Auriol proposes a meeting between Stalin and Truman in Paris.

Splendid article by Thierry Maulnier on the United Nations and on the strange buildings run up for them in the gardens of the Trocadéro, whereas our national palaces are falling to ruin.

What can be done, in this great crisis of chaos? Nothing. In a world of disorder, set oneself in order. To choose a single element of this disorder would be to lose one's equilibrium by adopting a factitious equilibrium. In Berlin, I dined at General Carollet's with the German musicians and painters of the regime. I wondered, at the table, why Brasillach had been shot and Abetz sent to jail. Why my poor Desbordes was dead. A man who commits himself to a political party is necessarily a dupe unless by so committing himself he serves his own ideal, admitting all the discouraging consequences of his action.

With Vilar's undertaking [the Théâtre National Populaire] we shall see if snobbery has changed sides and if a "popular" public will accept works which snobbery tolerated lest it not seem to be up-to-date. I wonder what Pichette will offer a public not tamed by that fear.

Gérard has broken another rib while shooting *Fanfan la Tulipe*. The Vilar series begins with *Le Cid* on the seventeenth.

Rain.

What accumulates in a house and even in a room in eight months is incredible. I have three days left to collect, to sort, and to send.

Work. I accept death. But I refuse to live and be dead. After my death, all this work must live in my place. I must create a robust health for it. Solid organs. This is why work devours us. It seeks our disappearance. Filial and even animal ingratitude. Already our work emancipates itself abroad and no longer concerns itself with us. It escapes our control.

One wonders how a nation's intelligence resists the radio. Moreover, it does not resist. The radio is a faucet of foolishness. The only thing I can bear listening to is the sports reporting. The high-speed precision of the speakers. They are forbidden stupidity. Which exists only in the fact that some men are kicking a ball around a field and the whole world is excited by the fact.

Rimbaud appears on the postage stamps.

NOVEMBER 8 · 1951

The American arms-control proposal is exactly the contrary of what it seems. "Let us make war impossible" means "let us make war possible." "Let us limit the danger to those who are fighting. Let us protect ourselves."

If it is the horror of war that is speaking and not certain selfish fears, it would be better to act conversely and make wars impossible by the monstrosity of weapons. Otherwise it is the infantryman who suffers, and who always will.

Offer to suppress atomic weapons. This means "Let us keep only classical weapons. Let us fight classical wars. It is classical to send a whole generation of young men to their death. It is not classical to run the same risks behind the lines." But since the danger remains virtually the same (as the Berlin bombardment proves), we must also suppress classical weapons, which have produced such great progress in classicism. We should not say: "Let us humanize war." We should say: "Man must try to pit his intelligence against a destructive law of nature."

Instead of saying: "Make babies," which comes down to saying: "Make soldiers," we should disencumber the earth and no longer call upon it to shake off its fleas. That is what the UN's task should be.

Men want to be farsighted, yet they have short ideas. They should see myopically and have long ideas.

What is the *Entente cordiale*? An arrangement reached at the Folies-Bergère and Maxim's. England's "divide and conquer" is no longer in fashion.

Storm. Splendid weather in Paris, someone calls to say. Obvious repercussions of the atomic tests.

Coco Chanel has just given me the contemporary French translation of the trial of Charles I. I read it tonight. The language and spelling give these texts a strange and tragic quality. The king knows only one thing: he is the king. It does not occur to him that these privileges can change. He stubbornly refuses to acknowledge the authority of his judges. He has no desire to speak before the sentence. Only after. He is kept from doing so. Then he is disturbed and talks incoherently.

Obvious that Charles I, still believing in the validity of the legal system of his reign, thought he would gain time by demanding that the tribunal give proofs of its powers, which he believed contrary to the fundamental laws of the realm. But it was arranged that he be tried in three sessions, and questioning the court's jurisdiction would serve him no better than kidnapping the executioner in Dumas's novel. As for torture, Dumas, for all his personal inventions, remains very correct and entirely in accordance with the text. The head was cut off with a single stroke, and not by several, as is often said.

Charles I paid the bill for Buckingham's extravagances. The duke's name is not mentioned in the trial, but his harum-scarum shadow dominates it. It is because of Buckingham that the royal power had become purely symbolic in England.

Exhausting sessions sorting out papers. We leave tomorrow by car. Very amusing letter from Aubusson: "We are beginning on Ulysses's head."

Francine wants to commission Aubusson to do a second example of the *Judith* tapestry.*

Just named honorary president of the Playwrights Club. As I already was of the British Poets' Drama Guild. Just named honorary president of the Film Club of Nice.

At the United Nations, [Andrei] Vishinsky, USSR delegate, declares: "President Truman's proposals kept me up all night . . . laughing." The gentlemen did not find this "constructive." (Terminology of the period.)

Watching the mountains of paper go into the wastebasket: twenty letters to ask me for something. Not one to thank me for doing it, for giving it.

The fatigue of sorting and classifying is much more devastating than that of making something. It has a certain funereal aspect about it. Hundreds of letters that crush us under the weight of

*Today this tapestry is in the Musée Jean Cocteau at Menton.

those who wrote them and the events which result from them. The problem of accumulation. Where to put what you keep? If you pile it up, you'll never find anything again. Why keep it at all? Out of a sort of respect for the pains taken by the people who send them to us. And how much energy lost! Bones broken, nerves stretched. No exchange of powers. The body empties itself. Grim. This morning I cleared out two rooms filled with letters and manuscripts.

Abetz's condemnation remains incomprehensible to me. An ambassador is inviolable and responsible only to the country which appoints him to his post. Abetz would have to appear before a tribunal of the new German regime. That would be the only court qualified to condemn or absolve him.

. . . .

NOVEMBER 14 · 1951

Too busy to write. Very swift return in the Citroën. Lucky—floods blocked the roads and caused detours behind us.

Saw Escoffier at Karinska's. Started on the costumes. Saw Jean-Louis and Madeleine at the theater. Already Bertin* wants changes: wants to come on at the end of the second act, and a thousand other nonsensical things. Madeleine and Jean-Louis propose replacing him.

Saw Jeannot and his models for *Britannicus*. He seems happy with his work. At Milly, I am back in a house where each object, each plant has been placed where it is with love.

Just heard, in a letter from the Lubiczes in Luxor, that Varille was killed in an automobile accident on the same road we were just on—in Joigny, I think. An irreparable loss for Egyptology. That

*The actor Pierre Bertin appeared in *The Wedding on the Eiffel Tower* (1921) and in Cocteau's film *Orpheus* (1949).

huge gnome's head was its leader. The Egyptologists' dispute, which I described for the first time in *Maalesh*, was based on his experiments. He had a noble soul. And he was *clear*, which not everyone in his circle always is. Only he could answer Abbé Drioton.†

Glimpsed last night in passing, the UN building: almost beautiful, it's so terrible. *Metropolis* style.

. . . .

NOVEMBER 18 · 1951

Work begun on *Bacchus* and on the film. Read the play to the actors. Started the model for Laverdet, which I will finish Tuesday. Escoffier is researching materials for me at Karinska. Chapelain is working on the wigs. The problem is to find a style without period exactitude, to re-create a living fashion, to avoid "costume."

I cannot understand how the company manages to rehearse four plays in one month without completely wearing itself out. Jean-Louis envisages this inhuman labor with great calm.

Saw Météhen and Rossif for the recording of the film (text and music).

The procession begins all over again at the Palais-Royal. I have had to escape to the country.

Last night, *Le Cid* at Suresnes. Pup tents and union managers. Like it or not, Vilar was right, in relation to the times. He has scored a triumph. True, in this dusty old shed, Gérard Philipe sparkles like a thousand-faceted diamond. Rodrigue could not be better acted than by Philipe last night. He illuminated the work

---

†R. A. and Isha Schwaller de Lubicz, Egyptologists and authors of several works on "Egyptian wisdom"; Alexandre Varille, Egyptologist. Cocteau saw them in Luxor during his Egyptian tour (1949). Canon Drioton, an Egyptologist, encountered at Cairo during the same period. "There are two groups of Egyptologists in Egypt. One which digs in the sand. The other in the mind." Cocteau's words (in *Maalesh*) suggest, though scarcely summarize, the controversies which were to echo in the French press of the period.

and the performance. All the skill and the discoveries he contributes have the grace and the naturalness of a child playing with his toys. Relieved of its rhetoric, the play is seen from a very comical and very magnificent perspective.

Vilar seemed tired. Besides, Don Diègue is a sinister old fool. Chimène a pain in the ass. Only Gérard made them tolerable, communicated something human to them.

The house full, anonymous. A concert had been given in the afternoon: Chevalier had sung. Today—Sunday—Brecht's play *Mother Courage*: Yvonne [de Bray] was to do the part, but she didn't realize she would have to sing. So it's Montero who will act and sing.

Alexandre Alexandre comes this afternoon to decide what we will send to Munich.

. . . .

November 19 · 1951

A reporter from *Samedi-Soir*, after a questionnaire to find out if the paper should keep its scandal-sheet format. They say no—that the public is tired of scandal. We'll see. I doubt it. I gave them some written notes. Usually they correct what I say to please themselves. Which is to be dreaded. The reporter says: "What's wonderful about you is your continuous good luck." I stare at him, like a pauper to whom someone says: "What's wonderful about you is that you've always been rich." This young man knows nothing of my struggles nor how many doors have been closed in my face. He imagines my talent is enough and bubbles up of its own accord. I try to make him understand what work is: a struggle against talent. A struggle against oneself.

Back to Paris this morning for the play and for the film.

Apparently Vilar's second performance—Brecht's *Mother Courage*—was dreadful. He should have been more cautious about a

Théâtre National Populaire. The public loves pomp and elaborate staging. His formula works only if he offers the public the very best. Poverty shocks the poor, who come to the theater to forget their own. In *Le Cid*, the work's pomp replaced that of the spectacle, and besides, Gérard illuminated and enriched everyone by his mere presence. Thanks to his moral "lighting," mediocre actors and actresses seemed to have talent.

Strange times. Tual* telephones to say that I talked for an hour on the radio yesterday (?). I had no idea—I was at Milly; it must have been a replay of an old interview with Parinaud.

Found the way to stage Stravinsky's *Oedipus Rex*.† I did all the drawings. The execution will be very easy and very striking.

Jean-Louis telephones. Bertin has decided to play the bishop. Difficulties with Nicole, who is torn between stage fright and her fits of aerophagia.

. . . .

NOVEMBER 23 · 1951

Work and the procession, Palais-Royal. Jean-Louis wants to work too fast. True, he is willing to postpone the play if it seems to be suffering. Nicole worries us. It is a very heavy role for her shoulders. There are two kinds of crisis. If we replace her, and if she is inadequate. My duty is to encourage her, to rehearse with her more than with the others. Her intelligence will let her make the decision herself. Today blocking for the first act. At five I will go to Karinska for the costumes.

---

*Roland Tual, a friend of Max Jacob and the Surrealists, the husband of Denise Tual, referred to previously.

†The festival *L'Oeuvre du xxe siècle* had included in its program the revival of the opera-oratorio with music by Stravinsky, the text after Sophocles by Cocteau, translated into Latin by Jean Daniélou. This revival, with seven *tableaux vivants* by Cocteau, took place at the Théâtre des Champs-Élysées on May 19 and 20, 1952.

. . . .

NOVEMBER 24 · 1951

Seeing Bernstein opposite me, the other evening, at the Marigny (*Lazare**)—I remembered an old story that made me laugh. There was a dinner at Bernstein's, with theater directors (if I'm not mistaken, the day after the premiere of *Sacre*)—Hertz, director of the Porte-Saint-Martin, who covered his wife with jewels and forbade her to open her mouth. Same business for the Quinsons. After dinner (this is on the eve of the First World War), Klotz, the finance minister, speaks of Wilhelm II. "I know him—I know Wilhelm II," says Hertz (alluding to the Coquelin tour). Then Mme Hertz gets up from her armchair, opens her mouth, and declares, anxiously, "Only slightly, darling."

The first act is blocked. Bertin's comic touch contributes a great deal. His absence would have left a gap.

Received Claude Mauriac's book on Gide. Dedication: "*En souvenir.*" In memory of what? Of the betrayal wrought by his book on me?† Of his excuses in Venice? Of his third article on *Orpheus*, where he retracts what he had said before? And all this because I published an article in *Les Lettres françaises*, whereas Jouvet, Kessel, etc. published there and no one—not even Jeanson—dreams of reproaching them for it.

I have begun cutting patterns for the costumes.

Vivaldi's orchestration for "Autumn" is not to be found in France. Only in America. Météhen has found those for "Winter" and "Summer." I must listen to them again at Milly with the records and choose something to replace the allegro of "Autumn." Recording the text Monday morning at nine.

---

*A play by André Obey, created November 22, 1951 (7 performances).

†*Jean Cocteau ou la Vérité du mensonge*, 1945.

. . . .

NOVEMBER 27 · 1951

Fifteen days ago scholars and journalists gathered in Philadelphia to witness the spectacle of Einstein confounded by a scientist who claimed to have found a mistake in the master's latest calculations. For two hours this scientist covered a blackboard with incomprehensible signs and then said: "There is your mistake." Einstein smoked his pipe. Stepped up on the dais, studied the calculations, took the eraser, and replaced the incriminated sign with another, easily chalked in. Then the other scientist uttered a kind of harsh cry and rushed out of the room like a madman. The account of this "abstract" proceeding is one of the oddest I ever read.

Work on *Bacchus* continues. The first act is turning out quite comical, and the actors have a tendency to push in this direction. Yesterday I "moderated" Bertin. His colleagues could no longer rehearse they were laughing so hard, and he was eating up the lines from other people's mouths. He wanted to act all by himself.

Édouard has left the part. Fearing to cause him even the slightest pain, I risked doing him great harm. His lack of craftsmanship was leaving Nicole up in the air. He is too authentic to excel in this profession. He floats there; he drifts. His profession is painting and occasionally acting in one of my films.

Madeleine and Jean-Louis couldn't get over the nobility with which he yielded his part to someone else and the next day came to applaud that actor's* work. He must have been sorry to give it up, but let no one notice. . . .

---

*Jean-François Calvé.

. . . .

NOVEMBER 28 · 1951

I recorded the text and had the music recorded as well: Vivaldi, Bach. All morning we indulged ourselves *à la* Ludwig of Bavaria: we listened, alone in the hall, to splendid virtuosos lovingly perform music quite different from their usual work.

. . . .

NOVEMBER 29 · 1951

Crisis at the theater last night. After the rehearsal Madeleine takes me aside and says: "Nicole has just told me she's scared to death and afraid to tell you. She doesn't feel strong enough to carry such a role so quickly. Her frankness overwhelmed me. If she gives up the part, we've decided—Jean-Louis and I—to take her on in our company. Jean-Louis will sign her contract tomorrow."

I am compelled to admit that I was worried myself. After dinner Nicole came to see me at home. I told her: "Out of negligence and lack of forethought, you are depriving me of an actress who is ideal for the character. You have the physique for it, the voice, the passion. Only the articulation is too much for you. It's a great pity." I telephoned Simone to see if she would take Nicole on. But she takes no students. Besides, she believes teachers are no use when it is gymnastics and tenacity that count. She will see Nicole and give her exercises.

I'm going to try Simone Valère because I don't have time to look for another actress (whom I won't find). Valère has the craft. What she doesn't have is Nicole's personality. I'll have to set fire to her—to get what I hoped to get from Nicole.

Lunch yesterday with Green and Robert.* My first relaxation in Paris. Green is writing a play.

Saw the set. Solid. Good for acting. Doesn't change the mechanism of our rehearsals in the lounge of the Marigny. All Laverdet has to do is paint it; I have given him samples of the colors.

Did a broadcast this morning for German radio. At two-thirty, another broadcast of the indiscreet-questionnaire variety. And during the recording session, a parade of people trying to break down my door.

Lunch at Véfour with Greta Garbo. Paul-Louis comes with her to the house first. Oddly enough, no one in the restaurant seems to recognize her. Oliver† will tell me the next day that he's been asked if Garbo wasn't Madeleine Sologne! And when Oliver said: "That was Greta Garbo," "Ah, we thought it was something like that." The sense of greatness, of the sacred monsters, the sense of the legendary are lost. There are too many things, and too many confused things, overlapping.

. . . .

SUNDAY · *Milly*

I rehearse *Bacchus* while the company is rehearsing Claudel. Hard on their memories. The further along we get in our work, the more I realize the danger represented by a text without stopgaps, a text which seems simple but which is not, and in which each word risks shocking a stupid mind, whatever its allegiance.

Boisdeffre's book *De Proust à Sartre*. He throws one filthy shovelful after another of that absurd legend under which so many are trying to bury me alive. His insensitivity to poetry is alarming. He believes

---

*Julien Green and Robert de Saint-Jean.

†Raymond Oliver, Cocteau's friend, owner and chef of the restaurant Le Grand Véfour in the Palais-Royal.

only false prophets. He has no notion of my pathos. Nothing odder or more significant than to contrast this essay with Millecam's book, in which he understands me in every sentence.

. . . .

DECEMBER 4

Marigny. We worked yesterday on the third act, which blocks well, except for the very last scene, which was turning into melodrama. At first I thought it was my fault. But after studying the text, I realized that it came from a disorder of the first contact. This scene is written like chamber music. An instrument, or a note forgotten, and order becomes disorder. Today I plan to explain this to the artists and to ask them to do a close reading around a table.

. . . .

DECEMBER 5 · 1951

No-man's-land. The painful phase where the actors are racking their memory, searching for their text, losing it, making mistakes, starting over. Jean-Louis knows his first act and almost his second. I observe that the smaller parts give less difficulty.

I have thought a good deal about the Barraults' offer to put the play on with other actors and in another theater during their tour. This tour (my play is not being done in Egypt) is a ruin for me. There was a certain amount of laziness in my reluctance to accept their offer. I wonder if I shouldn't have agreed after all. If the play is a flop, I shall not discuss it. If the play goes, I shall consider the offer.

Claudel's stamina. He made the actors rehearse all day yesterday. He wears them out. He himself showed no sign of fatigue. When I arrived, he continued discussing the tiniest details of the costumes.

If I had two months more, everything would be done in the last fifteen days. I have fifteen days. After all, it comes to the same thing.

It appears that Claude Mauriac has managed to attack me in *Le Figaro*, along with Jean-Louis Barrault, even before the play gives him an excuse to do so. I realize I shall be attacked from all sides.

I have signed the contract for *Oedipus Rex*. Stravinsky will conduct. I shall be the speaker, and I shall direct and design the spectacle, which will be staged above the orchestra, at the Théâtre des Champs-Élysées in May.

Suppression of the author's rights is on the way. The Council of State can do nothing about it. America proposes an international measure which would *facilitate* exchanges (sic). The creator is identified with the industrialist and would lose the rights to his work almost immediately. The Bern Convention* will be revised and annulled.

. . . .

DECEMBER 8 · 1951

My work is such that I must "guard my rest" and resist the lure of chaos. I have looked at all the materials for the costumes; fittings begin Saturday.

The play is taking shape. There are shadows and halftones. But the text is still inexact. I excuse the artists, my style consisting in tongue twisters of the *Chasseur sachez chasser sans chien* variety, to avoid flabbiness and to compel the mouth to accentuate the words, to separate them from each other.

---

*For the protection of authors' rights, the Bern Convention had established in 1886 the principle that the author benefited, in states belonging to the convention, from the same protection as that granted to their own nationals. Cocteau is here doubtless echoing the anxieties provoked by the project of a universal convention under the aegis of UNESCO. Was literary ownership in Europe to be reduced by establishing a worldwide system of registering works on the model of the American copyright? The convention signed in Geneva in 1952, and ratified by France in 1955, dissipated these anxieties.

Yesterday I discussed the possibility with Madeleine and Lulu Watier (if the play succeeds) of continuing the run, after the Barraults leave, in another theater and with other artists. Work would therefore be doubled.

Lazare is a flop. Jean-Louis is closing it on Monday. We shall rehearse evenings.

Yesterday morning, at the newspaper *Opéra*, a dialogue was taped between young directors—Hermantier, Jean-Pierre Grenier (Grenier-Hussenot), Georges Vitaly—and myself in defense of Jean-Louis Barrault and in opposition to *Opéra*'s headline: "Jean-Louis Barrault Worse Than Usual." This headline had outraged the entire profession by its insolence. On my way out, I ran into Nimier, author of the article. I asked him if the paper was responsible for the headline. He answered, quite courageously, that he alone was responsible. I spoke of the deadly habit France has of slinging mud at its bright lights until they are put out.

. . . .

SUNDAY · *Milly*

[. . .] Yesterday Claudel's *Échange* was rehearsed onstage and in costume. I rehearsed *Bacchus* in the lounge. Shouting on all sides. Only Claudel, who is hard-of-hearing, made out nothing—neither his play nor mine.

Recorded the foreword for *Le Cap de Bonne-Espérance* and other texts to go with it. (*Studio d'essai*.)

Greetings to Japan—a note for *The Three Musketeers*—help to all and sundry devour what minutes of peace I have. On the thirteenth, fourteenth, and fifteenth I edit and mix the sound track for the film. *Bacchus* begins the twenty-first. I've tested the patterns for the costumes and Christine's wigs. But I can't do anything for the artists' memory.

Hoping for some relaxation in the country. A hundred letters to answer. Lipnitzki says he's coming, with his machinery and his assistants.

Letter from Aubusson. The *Ulysses* tapestry will be ready in fifteen days. Selected all the drawings for Munich.

The day before yesterday Jean-Louis thanked me in front of the whole company for obliging them to enunciate a text in which the least mistake changes the meaning. The actors, at first glance, always think my texts are easy.

Bertin, who illuminates the first act with his comical presence, cannot keep from adding to the text. He does not realize that the effects derive from a mathematical precision of the words. The opposite of what people take for style.

Olivier Quéant, director of *Plaisir de France*, was bludgeoned on his way home by some blacks wearing American uniforms. He lost his left eye. The embassy's apologies will not give it back.

Our struggle to achieve something precise in a world which favors the approximate, to find our equilibrium in a world which wants to lose its own. Our insistence on remaining honest in a dishonest world. Our belief in a triumph of truth *in the long run*. Renan: "It may be that the truth is sad."

The only strength of a "human truth" is to be continuous.

I play my part scrupulously, aware though I am that the world is a vile farce. What astounds me is to see so many persons play theirs so badly and without scruple, while taking the world quite seriously.

Wrote the article on trees for *Plaisir de France* [1952].

. . . .

SUNDAY · DECEMBER 16 · 1951

A week too overwhelming to allow taking notes. Set, costumes, text, direction. Seats that I am denied and that friends insist on. Film I am editing, etc.

In the morning at Genevilliers, I help Jacqueline and decide on music and words. Noon, costumes at Karinska. Three o'clock, theater: rehearsal. Journalists. Six o'clock, shoes, hats, wigs. I come home dead with exhaustion and find a pile of telephone messages and letters.

Monday night, December 17, after the performance, I'll repaint the set with Laverdet. At six, I'll have seen some of the costumes. I'll have a vague impression of the whole thing only on Wednesday—the night before the performance.

My only goal is to be right with myself. Whatever I do I shall be judged, accused, insulted. Success or failure does not count. The essential thing is to create an atmosphere more lasting than the dates, to unite and release powers.

. . . .

SUNDAY · DECEMBER 23 · 1951

From one Sunday to the next as in *Bacchus*. A tornado in which it was impossible for me to write.

Dress rehearsal: considerable success. Gala (society night): success. Mauriac leaves his seat in a rage while I greet the audience from the stage, machine-gunned by photographers. One wonders why this action—why he behaves like the society public he condemns in his article on the Claudel performance (*l'Échange*).

The *répétition générale* was a real triumph. Between the gala and the *générale*, I thinned out, cut the scene of the archers which ends the second act. The curtain comes down on the scene in which Lothar lies to his father.

Last night Jean-Louis telephoned me from the theater. Everything is going wonderfully, but I find their rhythm of booking disconcerting. I'm not used to it. Their productions are slow to gain momentum; they never begin as if the play were a sure thing. The public seems afraid of an austerity it no longer fears once it is in the house. Yet it has to get there; its pleasure must spread, rise, and surmount the criticisms. Anouilh's *Rehearsal*, which did best, started slow. Besides, this is the season when the theater suffers from the holidays and the expenses of Christmas and New Year's. Bookings doubled yesterday. Not to worry—just wait.

Sartre called me yesterday. He believes Mauriac is going to pour out his poison in a *Figaro* editorial and that if he does, I shall have to answer. I've prepared an answer in the form of a "*J'accuse*. . . ." I'll have lunch with Sartre Thursday, and we'll see how things go.

All the effects are working. Each scene is applauded. The end is cheered. It would be disastrous if the company did not benefit from this perfect atmosphere and if the press were to present an obstacle.

A strange thing: the public endures long stretches and dead spots in all plays. Since I suffer from these, even the least of them, there is a rhythm in *Bacchus*, for example, which does not allow me four adventitious exchanges. I have had to cut lines right and left.

The triumph of the *générale* must have exasperated the critics. They will slaughter me, if they haven't done so already. It is my fate to be demolished on all sides and to pass for a man of good luck. Nothing will change this curve. I must accept it patiently and never be distressed by it. Sometimes it is hard.

. . . .

MONDAY

Jean-Louis and Francine telephoned at midnight, after the performance. Same enthusiasm for details and for the whole. Applause for exchanges and for whole scenes. If we manage to overcome the critics, we shall win. But it is clear that everything possible will be done to stand in our way.

I attribute the notion of a Catholic scandal to inattention. A Mauriac is incapable of understanding the nobility of the Cardinal, who divines Hans's soul and wants to save him at any cost. The final lie is a pious fraud. The Cardinal assumes responsibility for it in order to avoid the Ulrich business, so that Hans can be buried in holy ground.

A young heretic, a pure young man with an anarchist's soul, cannot express himself in harmony with what Mauriac wants to hear. The play would not exist.

Desailly serves the role by the goodness which his whole person exudes. Jean-Louis is like Raphael's young cardinal. He is Stendhalian, but his heart prevails over his intelligence. I find him marvelous.

Tabooizing and detabooizing. Jean-Louis is the typical example of one of those taboos that the press would one day praise to the skies whatever he did, and then pull down from the pedestal a day later. Obey's play served as an excuse. In mine, he indulged in none of the excesses for which he is reproached. He is simple, supple, hard, without gesticulation. Yet he will be overwhelmed with reproaches nonetheless. Besides, they will make me pay for the page in *Opéra* where I spoke my mind about criticism. They will not even bother to realize that I spoke respectfully.

Nothing stranger than criticism. A gentleman in the house, by some mysterious privilege and as a consequence of some mysterious circumstances, says what he thinks and believes he is the depositary of a right of life or death. Jean-Jacques Gautier, the critic of *Le Figaro*, sent me his book last week with the following dedication: "To Jean Cocteau. The executioner without rancor."

Christmas. I turn on the faucet of the radio. Out flows dirty water.

My crime is to revolve as little as possible in theater circles. I frequent no critic. I never go to the tax remission committee, attended by my colleagues. I never go to a cocktail party and rarely to a performance. Never to the *répétitions générales*. All of which is regarded with disapproval. The world that irritates me supposes

I despise it. If I "went out," I wouldn't have time for my friends. The only thing that counts.

Jeannot had lunch here yesterday. He is rehearsing *Britannicus*. It is the first time in the history of the Comédie Française that an actor has assumed responsibility for the whole performance: set, costumes, direction.

In *Bacchus*, too, it is the first time that the author undertakes direction, costumes, set. Our destinies advance side by side. He will be shot down as I shall be shot down. He must win his victory over *the public*.

Madeleine Renaud telephones that the critics are not against us, except for Jean-Jacques Gautier, who disgusts her. I expected as much. Mauriac in the wings. [. . .] For Madeleine, it is *Le Figaro*'s clientele which the theater risks losing. For me, this is natural enough. I am not disturbed about it. I am used to it. (Either J.-J. Gautier is stupid, or he writes in bad faith. One can dislike *Bacchus*, one cannot say that it is "a battle of Negroes in the dark."*)

People say: "You should read Gautier's article to see how far foolishness can go." But I want to have no contact with foolishness.

. . . .

TUESDAY

Christmas *entre nous*. Francine, Édouard, and the P.'s. We had decorated the tree, and each of us brought out his presents. This morning, mass in an icy, almost empty church. Neither pomp nor intelligence. The style of Mauriac and of his newspaper. I was thinking of the pope's strange and dangerous speech about the relations between science and religion. How far away that seems. There remain the organ's wrong notes, a few old maids, an absurd

*J.-J. Gautier wrote in *Le Figaro*, on December 24, 1951: "Starting with the second act, we founder in dialectic. A battle of black ideas in a Negro's brain in the dark."

sermon in which the curé speaks of the beginning of eternity and the goodness of God who abandons His heifers (sic) in order to envelop each person with His love (sic). Christ could enter into victorious combat with communism. The church doesn't want him to.

Jean-Louis telephones. Same success. Half house (but the best seats are all booked). Is it the vacation period? The newspapers? Too bad. The verdict won't be in until next week. It seems difficult for me to regain my balance. I believe that Americanism is giving more power to the press. And I have no stars with whom to counter it. I feel no sadness. A little disgust and a great deal of curiosity—confronting an experiment.

The *Ulysses* tapestry has arrived. Francine is bringing it. Another Aubusson miracle.

And now, no flagging. Get down to work on the film, and for Munich.

. . . .

LAST SUNDAY OF THE YEAR

Week of brawls and, oddly enough, brawls in which our houses take no part. On the contrary, success seems tripled by a reflex against the attacks. It would be tiresome to recount Mauriac's attitude and that of *Le Figaro*. Mauriac and his circle claim to sit on God's right hand and to judge in His place. Last night, a full house. Father Carré, in civilian clothes, applauding in the first row.

Our presents included books on painting. What genius, down through the ages! But in the final analysis, it is Vermeer, Piero della Francesca, and Renoir who prevail.

Finished the cover for the catalog of the Munich exhibition.

Did the mixing for the film. Kodak can make a first copy for Munich.

Mauriac had to be answered blow for blow. Too bad. There

was still something to be said. For instance: "You have tied a friend to a newspaper column and you have insulted him." "I accuse you of having usurped the privileges of a priest. Who are you, François, to seat yourself on God's right hand and to judge in His place? Angels will urge you to confession, and Figaro—even Don Basilio—will weep bitterly on his confessor's shoulder. I forgive you. He alone can absolve you."

Letter after letter from young people who thank me for having spoken to Mauriac as he deserves and as cowardice keeps people from doing.

Another possible paragraph: "I accuse you of having taken advantage of my reluctance to answer insults. You have known it for a long time. You believed you could with cowardly impunity sit down at your desk and compose, so to speak, your 'purple patch.' "

I accuse you of having composed, in cowardice, a "purple patch." [. . .]

The dogma of papal infallibility dates on from 1870. The bishops are fallible. As is evinced by the example of Bishop Cauchon, who must be biting his thumbs, if he has any left, for having usurped God's role. From the point of view of dogma the worst blasphemy is prejudgment.

Yesterday I went to see the rehearsal of *Britannicus*. Everyone is so entirely—and rightly—sure of himself that the lines have hardened, and the play assumes a density colder than a picture by David. They have realized this, and will add some fire. Regrettable that Jeannot, who has no "timbre," must force certain effects that result from a halftone. His scene with Narcisse was extraordinary in the little Salle Mounet-Sully. It fades out in this oversize house. Yet we must change nothing, merely pull a darker proof.

The tragedians of the old Comédie-Française were usually stupid and had no fear of being ridiculous. This is what gave them a certain sublimity. The company of tragedians-comedians in *Britan-*

nicus is too intelligent, too afraid of ridicule. This dampens their fire.

The only serious article on *Bacchus* came out in *Paris Match*. Mauriac, a dishonest journalist, dares attack this young—and honest—journalist,* who has simply seen my play and reports what he saw.

What is amusing about the *Bacchus* incident is that I had written my answer to Mauriac on the eve of his article. I was sure he would sit down and touch up some anthology-piece buffoonery. All I had to do was correct two or three paragraphs in order to make them into a suitable response. To respond "ahead of time" is an excellent method. It gives a certain elevation. I've already prepared an answer to Pierre Brisson if his newspaper starts in again.

. . . .

JANUARY 1 · 1952

Radiant sun. Phone call from the Barraults tonight. Full house. Ideal audience. It seems to me a mistake to do a matinee on New Year's Day. People are sleeping, visiting, or out walking, especially with this sun. Some theaters are closed.

May this 1952 continue the happy calm of the last ten months. I have no knowledge of the angels Mauriac speaks of, but I know my own, the ones who stand by me at every moment: Édouard and Francine. [. . .]

Jacques de Lacretelle in an article in *Le Figaro*: "Why has Drieu la Rochelle not yet committed suicide? He's too much of a coward." Drieu committed suicide shortly thereafter [March 15, 1945].

---

*Jean Farran, "Cocteau Has Made a Good Play Out of Good Feelings," *Paris Match*, December 29, 1951.

. . . .

JANUARY 2 · 1952

My sense of time. I send a toy to one of my godsons. He had just been made a colonel.

Inexactitude of the press. *Combat* has me saying: "And I had just sent some lead soldiers to Mauriac's grandsons." Those lead soldiers, too, must have become colonels.

. . . .

SUNDAY · JANUARY 6 · 1952 · *Milly*

Difficulty of scribbling even a line in a noisy city. Besides, my bronchitis is wearing me out. Mauriac seems to have tied a tin can to his own tail. Not only am I overwhelmed with letters of congratulations and thanks from all sides—from Leon Bailby* to obscure priests, including any number of students—but even the newspapers are making hay out of what they call "*l'affaire Bacchus.*" In one sense it is admirable that a city can still get excited over a theater dispute. (Though one that transcends the theater.) In another sense, I know nothing more disagreeable than these mountains of dirty laundry. My last article is entitled "No More Words, Once and For All" (a line spoken by the Cardinal in *Bacchus*), but who can keep journalists from talking? Luckily in Paris stories quickly stop being news.

Yesterday we did a kind of visit-sketch for television at Madeleine and Jean-Louis Barrault's house, avenue de Président-Wilson. The street was full of huge vans, the house crowded with machines and floodlights. The furnace had stopped. We had to do the same

---

*Journalist and director of two important prewar dailies, *L'Intransigeant* and *Le Jour*.

little improvised sketch twice over, from the beginning, for two different broadcasts. Francine and Doudou were watching the program on the Peyrauds' set, in the rue Saint-Didier.

When you broadcast live, there can be no cuts, no stops. The image shifts from camera to camera. Since the Musée Grevin had decided not to lend my mannequin (I am seen in an opera box, next to Mauriac—which attracts people) and since I was supposed to speak to this mannequin, I filled in this part with a monologue-dialogue with a little statuette of Harlequin. Theme: "There you are, my old enemy. I know your method; it consists in treating others as harlequins, in disguising works written in solitude with your lozenges, your colors. . . ."

Dinner with Jeannot. The atmosphere at the Comédie Française has become excellent again. He will light his set tomorrow. Saturday night I had taken dinner with the Doctor in order to give Loulou de Vilmorin a hug*—she's having an operation in London. Other guests: Roussin, the Achards, the Nimiers. At one in the morning Nimier was driving me back to the Palais-Royal in his Jaguar when a car crossing the avenue des Champs-Élysées from left to right rammed us. The shock was terrible, and we must have rocked back and forth about five times. Nimier was amazed at my calm. I was amazed at his. We emerged unharmed from this accident, which might have been fatal. He tore his left sleeve. I scraped my left leg. He exclaimed: "The driver must have been a subscriber to *Le Figaro littéraire!*" The driver was a Negro.

We awarded the Prix Apollinaire at the Brasserie Lipp. Yanette† took me to visit Roger Lannes;‡ I didn't know he was in such terrible condition. There seems to be some infection of the spinal

---

*Jean Cocteau had warmly supported the literary debut of Louise de Vilmorin, in articles in the *Nouvelle Revue française* in 1935 and 1937.

†The poetess Yanette Delétang-Tardif.

‡Poet and novelist, Roger Lannes, was the author of the first serious critical study devoted to Jean Cocteau's *oeuvre* ("*Poètes d'aujourd'hui*," Paris: Seghers, 1945).

marrow; he is drifting away, victim of a disease which is destroying him without the doctors being able to do a thing.

We leave for Germany on the eleventh. Hamburg-Düsseldorf, Munich. The show opens on the eighteenth. "Why not in Paris?" the journalists ask. Answer: "In Paris, one doesn't show; one shows oneself—up."

How far Milly is from all these people who have no control over their nerves. Splendid walk in the garden and the woods. Everything is struggling to be reborn. But too soon, too quickly, deceived by the sun. Last year the whole countryside had committed this rash act; one night of frost, and everything was killed. One wants to tell each bush: "Be careful." But the sublime stupidity of the sap would not listen. A blind and deaf mechanism commands. How little our pathetic quarrels about Lucifer and the Lord matter to the slaves of a very simple chaos which seems so complicated to us. It derives from a secret men have questioned from Heraclitus to Einstein—a secret which, were they to solve it, would make them exclaim: "So that's all it was!"

I shall have had that strange privilege of being the most invisible of poets and the most visible of men. As a consequence, the man draws fire and the poet is never hit. Since it is ultimately poets who become visible and men who become invisible, perhaps matters will be settled someday. Most likely I won't be around to observe the phenomenon, if it occurs.

How eagerly critics and journalists seek to blur my contours, making light pass for dark, deceiving the world as to my person and my works—a veritable orchestra of false notes and bad faith. A certain amount of calculation is involved, and a great deal of stupidity.

NOTES*

Landed in Hamburg on January 11. Alexandre was waiting for us at the field with a considerable throng of photographers, journalists, actors, radio people. Newsreels and television. My German is very weak on arrival, improves later on. The procession of cars to the enormous hotels begins. At the Atlantic, I am given Hitler's suite. Hideous and sumptuous. Alexandre is overwhelmed with telegrams, letters, phone calls. We go to the radio station, and I speak. I am asked whether I knew that my *Orpheus* [the 1949 film] corresponds to the latest investigations of German philosophy. I answer that I did not; that the poet must sleep on his feet and correspond unwittingly to what is happening in the world; that I had more to learn from others about myself than to teach them; and that the countless letters from German students had taught me a great deal about my work and my person. I cited as an example the letter from a student in Berlin who points out the maternal role Casarès plays in *Orpheus*; at the end of the film Eurydice's death does not occur because Orpheus turns around, but because he sees her in the rearview mirror of *the mother's car*. This student happens to be a friend of the speaker questioning me and knows his exegesis. Later on, an extremely intimidating press conference: too many tables, too many journalists, who are as intimidated as I am. I spoke half in French, half in German, Alexandre translating my French. I told how Reinhardt had put on *Orpheus*,† one night, with candelabra, how Rilke and Pirandello were present at this performance, and how Rilke was beginning to translate *Orpheus* when he died.

---

*These notes on the German trip, typed in Cocteau's lifetime, were inserted here in the manuscript.

†Tragedy in one act and an interval, by Jean Cocteau (1926).

Questions about the "*affaire Bacchus*." The German papers had widely reprinted my answer to Mauriac, but not his original article. I said that the dispute was an old and unfortunate one, that Mauriac's article had more to do with Freud than with me, and that this quarrel of ours had nothing to do with the play. That the scandal had occurred in the papers, not in the theater.

We take dinner at the radio station, then proceed to the tiny theater *In Zimmer*. On the fourth floor of a house. Stage and seats are set up in a huge room. Rehearsals are going on—surprising. Not the least trace of expressionism. Artists and direction are admirable, the way I dreamed they would be when I wrote the play thirty years ago. I seem to be watching my own youth. Offstage sound effects astonishingly exact.

The uproar begins all over again first thing in the morning. Lunch with the consul, television (where I draw the *Bacchus* costumes). Performance. *Orpheus* is performed twice; we take dinner in a nightclub between the two performances. The critic from Frankfurt-am-Main had driven eight hours to attend. Typical example of the seriousness of intellectual Germany.

This Germany of 1952 is in upheaval. A hole is being filled. Youth is thinking, listening, observing, questioning, but not yet creating. It constitutes an ideal public. It is as if minds were eating to gain strength. Moreover, techniques are being reorganized too rapidly and too richly (*à l'américaine*), and the young are caught between yesterday's life and today's industrial obstacles. It has missed that moment of active disorder analogous to the one after 1914 when *Caligari* and expressionism made their appearance, born of that lack of resources which excites the imagination and compels self-discovery.

A famous dancer insisted on performing for us this morning, in an upstairs studio at the opera. She symbolizes everything with which the new Germany must break. The public, it appears, is tired of this style and dreams of something else, which is long in coming. This is the reason for our success in Germany and for the enthusiasm provoked by a film like *Orpheus*, because it is direct and because the public can gain access to it.

The kindness of our hosts consists in not resenting the fact that spiritual nourishment comes from abroad. On the contrary, the Germans can't be grateful enough; one is almost ashamed of their thousand kindnesses, every moment of the day.

After the performance of *Orpheus*, the radio people take us down one of the narrow streets that end in an iron fence. Hamburg brothels are tiny shops where women are on display like mannequins in shopwindows. They live, four or five together, in a kind of aquarium. They fix their hair, polish their nails, tap on the glass, and, if you turn around, open the transom and stick their head out. I note that there is more merchandise than clientele. Here, too, business is bad. Yet Hamburg gives an impression of luxury. The city is laid out in endless rows of houses and gardens, the houses half English, half Danish. And everywhere water: the harbor, the sea.

Sunday, went to Celle. Received at the castle by the curator, Dr. Bauer, who keeps somewhere in his vast body a French Resistance bullet—of which he is very proud.

Johann Sebastian Bach walked from Hamburg to Celle to hear French music. I find it just as surprising that a famous critic should drive for eight hours to see a French play.

The castle theater is a wonder. It is the oldest in Germany, seats three hundred, and is shaped like an egg with the audience at the narrow end. The chapel is a mixture of Reformation and Italian rococo. This is rich Protestantism. At first glance you think you're walking into a baroque church. When you examine the details, you see that the angels' bodies end in devils' tails.

I promise the curator and the mayor, who speaks a very pure French and makes me a moving speech, to come back in March and organize a celebration at the castle of Celle. Perhaps with my film *The Villa Santo Sospir* and *Orpheus* (the play). The town choirs will sing Bach in the chapel.

From car to car, highway to highway, lunch to lunch, dinner to dinner, radio station to radio station (Radio Bremen interviews me at the French Institute); now we are in the plane to Düsseldorf, where other journalists and other photographers are waiting for us, Alexandre in the lead, his pockets full of telegrams and articles.

Scandinavian plane from Düsseldorf to Munich. At Düsseldorf, there was not one free minute for writing, and at night I slept like a log. From gallery to gallery, club to club, burgomeister to burgomeister: inconceivable that men should go to so much trouble to welcome another man. Germany has preserved the tradition of long expeditions to see a painting or to hear a quartet. Here we are flying over debris and factories and a river dyed red by the textile works. Then the elevated tram suspended from rails for twelve kilometers. We are offered cognac, and the photographers have their work cut out for them. We arrive at Elberfeld. It was the Elberfeld Horses that gave me the idea of the horse that dictates sentences in *Orpheus*. Our guides show us the empty lots where their ancient houses used to stand. One of them found nothing but his mother's hand on the bible (as in *Le chien d'Andalou,* he tells me).

We leave the elevated tram to get back into limousines and climb the Huguenot hill with its ravishing little white houses timbered with black beams and with bright green shutters. Up here it is snowing, the wind blows hard, and we sink into deep mud. The theater is bombed out. When flames were devouring everything, mothers threw their children into the water, where they drowned. Strange performance of *The Human Voice** in a schoolroom. My play is badly translated and cut very strangely. Nothing is left of it but an actress who weeps but fails to make her public

*A one-act play by Cocteau (1930).

shed one tear. Huge lunch with the mayor and the troupe. On the way back, see the Brekers at home.* Düsseldorf shuns them. I tell how they saved Paris and spared us so many catastrophes. Their old house is very lovely, very comfortable. Then I talk to the film club audience.

I told them what I thought of the massive industrialization of the cinema and of the obstacle which syndicalism puts in the way of young people who want to express themselves by this means. This was quite comical, since in France I am president of the unions. I add that there is a shortage of film in Germany and that all these young people mistake ink for the manual labor a film requires. I try to make them understand these things, which does not keep them from overwhelming me with scripts. I admire the fact that France preserves a certain anarchic disorder and leaves a door open to beauty, which is produced only by accident.

It is to be feared that discipline will triumph in Germany and that her walls will leave no door open to those who can contribute something new. That night, gala showing of my film *Orpheus*; I was given a gold crown and scrolls wreathed in flowers. I spoke to the audience, first in German, then in my own language when the things I had to say became too difficult for me. I was made honorary president of the Düsseldorf Film Club.

Lunch with our ambassador and the mayor of the city. Meeting with the Düsseldorf actors. In the evening, performance at the Schauspielhaus: *King of the Mountains*. When I arrive at the theater, the executive secretary hands me a telegram from Gründgens, who is in Zürich, asking me to send him *Bacchus* as soon as possible. This telegram astounds our hosts. Gründgens is not in the habit

---

*During the Occupation, on the occasion of an exhibition of work by the German sculptor Arno Breker at the Orangerie, Jean Cocteau published "*Salut à Breker*" in *Comoedia*, May 23, 1942. In 1963, Arno Breker produced a bronze bust of the poet.

of being agreeable or of putting on French plays. When I take my seat in the theater, the audience stands and applauds for a long while, and I am obliged to greet them.

A very odd play. The first part inspired by Molière. The rest fantastic and brilliant, the source of plays by Brecht and Weill: *Threepenny Opera* and *Mother Courage*, a mixture of song and drama, the comic and the sentimental, solo, duet, and chorus. Recitative scanned against a musical background (later I learn that the play was put on this way because some of the actors couldn't sing and that the resemblance to Brecht and Weill derives not merely from the features I had noted but from the way in which the work is now being presented. In other words, it inspired Brecht and is inspired by him). The actors are first-class. And the audience. A gesture, a glance are applauded. At the end, there are twenty curtain calls, and no one dreams of leaving the theater. I go backstage to thank the actors. In our hotel, the corridors and rooms are covered with drawings by Sem,* which mean nothing at all to our hosts but which recall my youth. Oddly enough, in Francine's room are caricatures of her family, from the Baron and Baroness Alphonse down to Henri de Rothschild and Mathilde, Alec's grandmother.

Dinner at the Jacobi Goethe house, surrounded by Prud'hon wallpapers. In his speech the president remarks: "Goethe is the great unknown of Germany, he is worshiped, which dispenses people from having to read him." Which consoles me somewhat for the impossible translations of my work now available.

Here I again encounter M. Hertz (at the film club lecture); he once came to the Hotel de la Madeleine with Dr. Wiene when the doctor asked me to play Conrad Veidt's part in the talking

*The caricaturist Georges Goursat, known as Sem (1893–1934), greatly influenced Cocteau's early drawings.

version of *Caligari*. I had accepted the offer. Dr. Wiene died, and I did not play the sleepwalker. Herz wants me to do a modern *Caligari*. It's too late.

At the reception for the performers, M. Half, representing our steel-coal program, tells me: "What we're trying to do is no use. We can only trail behind. France has nothing left but the prestige of her mind. Not to realize this is a disaster. Your trip is doing a thousand times more good than our wretched schemes." I answered that unfortunately France refused to understand this and was still trying to be what she is not, what she has never been. France's glory escapes her and seems to be of no importance. My trip, which has nothing to do with propaganda and which is due to a German government initiative, will seem no more than a personal triumph; now in the individualist countries it is only personal triumphs which matter. France's only excuse is that her blindness suppresses the danger of massive and intolerable propaganda. What propaganda exists is produced despite France and without her realizing it. All our ambassadress can think of is to order her gown from Dior.

. . . .

JANUARY 23 · 1952

The Brussels–Paris line. We proceed by ricochets or postal relays. Munich–Düsseldorf: stopover. Brussels–Paris. I left Germany after twelve days during which I did not have a single free moment. Sometimes I would speak in public in the morning, the afternoon, and the evening, as well as answer official speeches at dinners and artists' groups. Not to mention the radio, the television, and the throngs of photographers who preceded us through the streets. A German city is almost an autonomous country, it has its theaters, its religion, its press. To go from one city to another is to go from one country to another. Sometimes, in fact, a different language is spoken, or virtually. My exhaustion far outstripped exhaustion.

Each time Francine and Doudou were afraid I wouldn't manage; when I was in danger of losing the thread, I would let Alexandre translate for me, and then I would catch up with myself during his translation, which was slower than my speech. I repeat, the German cities have their customs, their languages, their press, their radio. You do not speak in one as you do in another. You must figure out their style, and what they expect, from your initial contact, from the look of the buildings, the faces.

Hamburg–Düsseldorf–Munich–Augsburg, and back to Munich, this was our schedule. Alexandre was overwhelmed by government invitations arriving from every city in Germany. Except for Hanover, where I will be exhibiting in March, it was impossible to accept these offers, having only one head, two arms, and two legs. A man would need a phalanx of hands and arms and legs, like Hindu gods.

The central feature of the trip was the show of my canvases, tapestries, and drawings at the Haus der Kunst in Munich. The directors had organized this with so much skill and love that my canvases, instead of being hanged until they were dead, as usually happens, seemed to be floating in space and living the same life they have at Santo Sospir. The trip leaves me a certain atmospheric memory, and what finally struck me most was that Augsburg theater filled with four hundred children who had just seen *Beauty and the Beast* [Cocteau's film of 1945], whom I addressed amid cheers, stamping, and caps thrown in the air. In Augsburg there is a remarkable tradition of chamber music and of people who do not leave home. What we call cinema is unheard-of and impossible. Only exceptionally do people leave home to see films. Montaigne, Mozart, Goethe stayed in the inn now transformed into our hotel.

Snow and cold. Mortal cold in the church and cloister of Saint Anne, where Luther stayed during his first interrogations. It was at Augsburg, when I was giving a speech one evening, that the burgomeister named me president of all the film clubs of Germany. After Augsburg, returned to Munich where demands threatened to become overwhelming. [End of typed notes.]

At Munich, the carnival lasts five weeks. A carnival king and queen are chosen. They visited me the last evening, at the *brasserie.* The king took off his order and put it around my neck, amid applause. A delightful decoration which weighs nothing at all and wonderfully crowns a journey of friendship without heaviness, without pomp.

Forgot to note that I had seen, with Alexandre, the main German publishers, all amazed that our rights are sold so ignorantly and so unfavorably. Kurt Desch [a Munich publisher] wants to do a big monograph on my drawings.

Les Parents terribles, because of ridiculous contracts, is performed in a tiny theater in a hateful translation and adapted by the actors without knowing the original text.

Few young Germans understand that film is a manhunt—the camera a weapon which captures human life—and that we cut a text for our sleeping partners, but that we change everything on the set, since you can never tell which angle will be best for sighting the game.

At the Ws in Düsseldorf, saw the actress who played in *The Eagle Has Two Heads*. Very beautiful. Looks like Daisy Fellowes.*

I am taken to a Hamburg cabaret to see a troupe which is about to go on tour and which stays in town so I can see its performance—very entertaining. Two political scenes (in one of which all the major figures of Germany are shown in jail for fraud) seem to embarrass the public—because of my presence. There is an

---

*Marguerite Decazes de Glucksbierg (1890–1962), wife of Reginald Fellowes. Cocteau admired this friend's beauty and elegance. See his article "*La Présence*," *Vogue*, September 1935.

amazing takeoff of Thomas Mann: the actor made up as Mann is giving a lecture; during the lecture, he pretends to catch sight of me and bows toward my seat. There is also a sketch of an aristocratic Stalinist lady—actress first-class.

I've seen and heard so much that my memory fails me. What is striking about the whole trip is a very swift reconstruction—and a very slow reconstruction of mind.

The young people who come to hear me are between twenty and twenty-five. They have been brought up and formed in one ideology and have fallen into another. The shock is excessive. Naturally, they haven't got their balance. One realizes that Germany lacks Jews, and that they would now be helping this country to revive.

In Hamburg, the episode with the dove: there is a dove in my play *Orpheus*, but now the dove has become a political bird; I decide to cut the dove altogether. I could hardly have suspected, thirty years ago, that this dove would become an eagle.

. . . .

JANUARY · 1952

Milly snowed under. My cats roll in the snow. Everything is decorated, down to the tiniest detail—very festive! When you walk, you produce the sound of a horse chewing sugar. How far this is from that grim city where people no longer like anything—where the haggard young are concerned only with jazz, where [Gian-Carlo] Menotti's *Consul* plays to half-empty houses.

Bacchus earned 600,000 francs last night. Jean-Louis telephoned the news to Doudou. I was asleep. When I woke up, I couldn't get over it. We've got into the habit of hearing bad news.

Tomorrow night we're going to *Britannicus*.*

---

*Jean Marais had first directed, designed and acted (the role of Nero) in Racine's *Britannicus* at the Théâtre des Bouffes-Parisiens in February 1941. He had directed and

FEBRUARY 2 · 1952

Discouragement. Too much work. Too much fakery. A city where you are asked to do everything, and where you are insulted as soon as you do anything. The free man's attitude—increasingly scabrous. Every word, every gesture are interpreted awry, politically, which is intolerable. The greater the work's invisibility, the greater the man's visibility and the more the work is hidden beneath legends.

France: less and less likely to understand what is serious and what avoids assuming that serious expression beneath which is concealed a dreadful frivolity.

Misunderstanding all around. If I were not afraid to leave those I love unprotected, I should prefer to get out of this misguided world, the victim of irreparable errors. An honest man would admit: I know I am unfair, I know I am lying and you're not, but I want to lie—and I want your truth to be a lie. My "commitment" compels me to such an attitude. Thus is forged a horde of individualisms obeying some command to extinguish whatever glows and to beat down whatever rises.

Britannicus, insulted, overwhelmed by unfair commentary according to the usual system, triumphs at the Comédie Française, not without a certain discomfort which constrains the warmest audiences and grounds the electricity exchanged between stage and house. Perhaps this imbalance is France's true strength. But it is difficult to survive and pains the heart. Jeannot has won this round, I can tell—but without joy.

---

performed the play again in Cairo, Alexandria, and Istanbul from March to May 1949. (See Cocteau's *Maalesh* [1949]).

. . . .

February 3

Fame is the consequence of a misunderstanding. It is like the crowd which gathers around an accident. All beauty is merely an accident. A few people stop and wonder what is happening. Others imitate them, question them. Then comes the crowd, which no longer sees anything and is content to swell its ranks. Since everyone invents the accident, no one knows what has happened. Gradually the accident is distorted and becomes the work of this close-packed crowd, which has seen nothing.

Yesterday morning, a showing of Menotti's film *The Medium*. I regard it as a masterpiece as a whole and in detail. Who will enjoy, who will support this film? I wonder. In France, no one, except perhaps the ciné club. Another solitude—and in the realm of cinema, solitudes are rare.

The Barraults are leaving February 29. They are not taking my play; impossible in Egypt, in Italy, in Canada. Never mind. After this uproar, silence is indispensable. The play will be published and be revived on stage as fate decides.

. . . .

February 3 · 1952

Yesterday had to preside at the union sessions. Lumière Prize. From eleven till seven at night, futile chatter. Too many naïve people who think they are cunning.

I am told of visits to ministers and deputies without my informants' realizing that these very ministers and deputies have in their pockets orders that countermand our directives. Of course, the adoption of *author's rights* would be an ideal solution. But the gang of the theaters, comparable to that of the casinos and gambling houses, is, electorally speaking, much stronger than the five hundred signatures which the eighth Arrondissement brings to M. X, who couldn't care less.

Even the press, which attributes the cinema's collapse to the stars and the technicians, is subject to this gang. So? Around seven I propose a public discussion, which would force the press to disregard them. My proposal is adopted. But between four and seven I have to endure all that chatter and the hope of obtaining results by the old, hierarchical methods. Carlo Rim [a filmmaker and writer] discusses the moral side of the matter at great length—after which I force him to acknowledge to our colleagues that America suggests substituting for the Bern Convention that of Washington, i.e., suppressing the author's rights on the excuse that control would be impossible because of a future expansion.* For years now, we have been trying to institute a cinematographic author's rights, and if it were now to succeed, it would do so on the eve of its final suppression.

I am extremely uncomfortable as the president of the unions. I speak one language, and my colleagues speak another. They revel in legislative terminology. *I cite facts.* I told them: "You create concrete works which pass for abstract, and the filmmaker's money is abstract (though not for everyone). No money at the outset, and no money left at the conclusion. Money falls into pockets, but not ours. Everything's wrong at the bottom. Taxes and frauds. To hope for a gradual remedy is madness. You will overcome the gang only by a show of strength, by an aggressive and revolutionary attitude. Never by commissions and visits to cabinet ministers. I won't have anything to do with such tactics. I haven't the time to waste."

Went yesterday to the rehearsal of *Antigone*.† Honegger's work

---

*Some years after these professional discussions, the law of March 11, 1957, established in France, in the realm of the cinema, the principle of an author's rights proportional to the film's receipts: the "ideal solution" Cocteau mentions.

†Cocteau's *Antigone* after Sophocles (1922), transformed into a lyric tragedy by

is very ungrateful. I had left Beckmann free to reorganize the production according to documents and written directions (gesture by gesture). This is the first time I have been assisted, and I approve what Beckmann has done. Of course, a certain vitality is missing, but the whole is not too far from the original performance. Tomorrow I'll go and have a look at the lighting and sharpen two or three points which have become blunted.

I'm still getting huge numbers of letters expressing astonishment about the *Bacchus* episode. I wonder if this business is not all a dream—if Mauriac didn't fall asleep in his seat and dream a play, if this mechanism is not fate working to place dramatically a work which risked, in our frivolous day and age, falling between two stools.

. . . .

TUESDAY · FEBRUARY 12

Submerged by letters, visits, telephone calls. I have to escape or else fall ill. Here it's the Mexican method. They cover you with honey, and the ants eat you alive. We'll be leaving Monday for the Côte d'Azur.

Mauriac runs into Fraigneau. "Do you ever see Jean?" "Yes." "He's not mad at me? . . . I'm not mad at him . . . after all, I did his advertising for him."

That does it. His article was an attempt at murder. Yet that's how Paris takes such things. And it's grim frivolity like that which accuses us of frivolity.

Antigone at the Opéra. The performance remains quite tough, quite noble. Then Claudel's *Jeanne au bûcher* [. . .] The public ecstatic. If Captain Dreyfus were there instead of the maid, and the

---

Arthur Honegger, had been first performed in Brussels in 1928, and revived at the Paris Opéra in a production with sets and costumes by Cocteau in 1943.

general staff were being flouted, what a scandal! But Claudel can flout the church. He forgets that he, Mauriac, and *Le Figaro* would have condemned Joan of Arc. Arthur is very sick. It is painful to see how hard it is for him to walk out onstage and back into the wings. [. . .]

. . . .

FEBRUARY 14 · 1952

Too much to do to write. Union meeting. I said what I think. But it disturbs everyone. They prefer vague generalities and indirect approaches. Then Roger Ferdinand [a filmmaker] comes in, late. He is questioned. He repeats word for word what I had just said. Thieving all around—by the theaters, by the distributors, by the producers, who are robbed in turn. *Abstract money*. None to start with, none at the end. Somewhere on the way, it falls into pockets—not ours. A deal that's shared turns out to be a disaster. Telling the truth becomes dangerous. The state is being asked for billions; if they must vanish into the same pockets, that's the end.

Daquin tells me that L'Herbier [a filmmaker] has resigned.

. . . .

FEBRUARY 15

Stopped in at the theater. Same success. Sad that the troupe's departure will interrupt the run. Mauriac knows the manhunt of which I am the victim. He wanted to be in at the kill. Léonard [unidentified] tells me about the cold feet in our cities; even Lyons, where Gantillon [director of the Théâtre des Célestins] is on my side. Brussels goes along but is afraid of Antwerp, etc. Except for Germany, foreign countries and our provinces don't have the same recovery speed as Paris.

Have piled up what's left to do as if in a bulging suitcase. To break with Ci-Mu-Ra as my exclusive representative. To arrange for the transfer of powers. To deal with the false prints of *Blood of a Poet*. To record a radio talk on *Bacchus* in Sweden. To preside at the ciné clubs' committee. To see Claoué about the cyst in my eye. To embrace Jeannot at *Britannicus* before I leave. A life like this is intolerable. Tomorrow, more of the same. Take Alexandre to Milly and try to settle the German contracts. Monday I'll answer the letters which have accumulated, and then we leave for Santo Sospir. Francine will be there tonight.

A man is smothered on one side by his name, on the other by his work. As if name and work were in complicity to suppress the man and meet over his dead body in a life of their own. The man gets in their way.

Snowing. The Palais-Royal sends what looks like the glow of footlights into my tunnel.

First copy of *Bacchus*. I open to a misprint: *place* instead of *glace*.

Grasset reports *Reines de France** is selling well. He suggests a two-week trip to the Kremlin, after which I would write a *Stalin Intime*. He suggests this quite seriously and without realizing the countless impossibilities such a project contains.

I hear the latest parlor game is "Bacchus": one of the players is told he can do anything he likes, and then he is asked what he plans to do.

The poet's invisibility, covered up by visibility. Noise protects our silence. Lies and legends conceal us. Once we were surrounded by silence. Now we are surrounded by noise. Once, when we emerged from silence, we emerged intact. Now legends and lies must fall one after the next. Not so easy.

---

*Cocteau's text *Reines de France*, first published in a limited edition with illustrations by Christian Bérard in 1949, was republished in a commercial edition without illustrations.

To be covered up means it is possible to be discovered. Meanwhile, you smother. Millecam's book. Dubourg's.* The carapace has holes. They will have a terrible time publishing works that "discover" me. As if a mysterious and unconscious power were opposing these attempts at doing justice. I wonder if this is the result of a kind of watchword or of some higher sort of mechanism that controls me.

Millecam's book is metaphysical; Dubourg's objectively precise and a little academic. A very accurate study of my plays and films. Millecam ranks me very high. His book will exasperate. He adds himself to the evidence in the trial I am undergoing at the hands of the critics. He does not argue. He acknowledges what the rest refuse to see. His invisibility is added to my own. Dubourg's book tries to make me visible by disdaining the false visibility by which I am masked.

A poet's work is not, strictly speaking, a creation. It testifies to an inward ethic. It is this ethic which constitutes his misery and his strength. The public, responsive only to ornamentation, to decorative styles, turns away from works which are an ethic and toward ornamental and decorative works—works which I accuse of immorality. (And which are usually based on conventional morality, and not on an ethic [or line] proper to the man who considers himself only the vehicle of certain deep forces.)

Do the gods live because they are *named* by men or are they *named* because they make use of men for this purpose? Yesterday I was listening to a Sorbonne discussion of this strange problem on the car radio. It must have been a lecture on poets.

People do not understand that our night directs us, that there is no question of orders external to us, but of internal orders, which can come from the depths of time. Primitive man, if he was

*Pierre Dubourg, *Dramaturgie de Jean Cocteau*, foreword by Thierry Maulnier (Grasset, 1954).

afraid, carved a god of fear and sought its protection against fear. His fear did not seek to become a god. But his fear took the form of art. He expressed himself. That is what I call an ethic. (It is the intensity of his fear which provokes the intensity of the object he worships and which he readily believes exterior to himself. He fears the materialization of his fear.)

. . . .

FEBRUARY 20 · 1952 · Santo Sospir, Saint-Jean-Cap-Ferrat

I had to leave Paris as fast as possible. My nervous system was losing its organization. By "bearing up," one loses one's bearings, in the exact sense of the term. We made the trip without a hitch: left Milly at ten in the morning; lunch at Nevers; dinner at Avignon (with Désormière, at the Hôtel de L'Europe). Reached Santo Sospir at 2:00 A.M.

Thirty years of this manhunt of which I am the victim and this 1952 in which Mauriac thinks he can give the finishing stroke with impunity—that's what makes the mechanism go haywire. The soul resists. But what can that fuel, that gasoline do, when the gears and valves weaken?

I reached Santo Sospir an invalid, and I thought that at least here I would be left in peace. The next morning a telephone call and a telegram inform me that Darantière and Guillaume [publishers of the original deluxe edition] have instituted proceedings against the commercial publication of *Reines de France*. The lawyers are weltering in their arguments. Lucienne Watier is in tears. Etc. The city sticks to you like a monstrous wad of chewing gum, and you drag the threads of it behind you. My mind and spirit are viscous with it. Rest and work: equally impossible. No matter how much Francine and Édouard lecture me, indulge me, the glue has set. It takes patience. Wait till this glue disappears of its own accord in the air and the sunshine.

Too many matters have been left unsettled because I was thinking only of works. I was naïve enough to assume the rest would follow naturally. Unfortunately our mind is preoccupied by works, and other people's minds by the advantages to be derived from them. As a result, the work circulates, and others profit from it. Add to this the 80 percent for taxes—8 percent for agents, 8 percent for authors. It adds up to ruin.

Pierre Peyraud's plan is splendid but still undeveloped. Any agency that wants to help me out would find itself face-to-face with an agency that owns all my papers and has all my powers of attorney. Not so easy to break. The day before yesterday Ci-Mu-Ra had agreed to study my accounts with Pierre and the lawyer Abelès. Yesterday (Abelès having written to Chaperon to confirm that he was representing my interest) Chaperon took umbrage and declared that Ci-Mu-Ra would refuse to show accounts and that my papers had to pass through his hands. Now Chaperon is Ci-Mu-Ra's lawyer and not really mine at all. Nothing says I cannot take a lawyer who will represent me and ask for accounts as if I were asking for them myself. Moreover, my exclusive contract with Ci-Mu-Ra concerns only the cinema. Ci-Mu-Ra handles the rest of my affairs only for convenience's sake and by verbal agreement. The business is so complicated that it seems inextricable to me. It leads to nothing but scenes and quarrels which illuminate nothing.

That is the tar pit I'm sinking into, and I see no way out of it. I've written to Ci-Mu-Ra: "You'll be quarreling over my grave."

. . . .

FRIDAY · FEBRUARY 22

Dinner at Monte Carlo last night with Colette and [her husband] Maurice [Goudeket]. Fifteen days ago a letter from Colette* was

*Hôtel de Paris, Monte Carlo, Sunday, "Why aren't you here, Jean, my dear? I

quite legibly written, and she sounded content. Today I find her quite low and far away. I've already seen eyes like hers, so blue they seemed black; they belonged to my green cricket when it was singing its death song. I had called Chaplin into the hotel room to hear it, as I mention in *Mon premier voyage*. We were just leaving Japan.

Maurice rolls Colette's chair into the bar. Then into the amazing velvet and gold dining room filled with draperies, caryatids, huge frescoes of naked women, peacocks, tigers. As soon as we pass through the doors, we are in another age. But except for Maurice de Rothschild, Sem's heads are missing. We "recognize" nobody. And the gypsy violinist playing *Gigi* at Colette's shoulder seems out of another age, forming—with Colette, his violin, and that tune from *Gigi*—a kind of phantom group, invisible to the other tables.

Maurice penetrates the padded cell that encloses Colette as little as possible; only essentials get through. Sometimes she hears me; sometimes she tries to hear me and can't. Francine and Doudou dare not raise their voices and fall silent. Moreover, the stories that entertain her are those of a past of which nothing is left, scenes in which the actors are Arthur Meyer* and Bunau-Varilla.†

Great sadness. Old age: this is how I will be. This is how the end begins.

Maurice seems to handle his wife's affairs admirably. She believes there are a few thousand-franc notes in her bureau drawer. Her bank account has always been that drawer, which she filled by writing articles and which she emptied in order to pay Pauline.

---

had forgotten how treacherous the wind is, and how many white stripes are laid across the sea. Did you know that the strawberries are already ripe in Antibes? Aren't you coming down? With much love, always your Maurice and Colette."

*Director of *Le Gaulois*, a monarchist and anti-Dreyfusard newspaper (1844–1924).

†Philippe Bunau-Varilla (1859–1940), engineer, director of the Panama Canal Company at the time when the canal's route and the form of its future administration were determined (1903).

According to the income tax estimate, Maurice acknowledges, she must have earned very large sums. Colette is a peasant and a child. She goes on living, almost content inside that cloud which protects her against a cruel world no longer coincident with her flowers and her animals.

Colette does not disturb the world, and she is surrounded by respect. I do, and insolence surrounds me. Sometimes I envy her insulation, her wheelchair. I have all the afflictions of youth without its advantages.

Back to see Colette this morning at the Hôtel de Paris. She is transformed, and quite renewed. She hears us. She comes into the bar, wheeled by the bartender. I recognize her fine eyes swimming in the liquor of the best Marennes oysters, her olive-tree hair, her mouth like an arrowhead wound.

On the rock of Monaco where old queens of fashion come to die, facing the Temple of Fortune, luck disguised as Prince Rainier or Pierre de Polignac installs her in this dowager's wheelchair. She tells me stories of her "old comrades," the days when she played Monte Carlo as a mime. Mme de B. once told her: "You're a fool. I'll take you to the casino and teach you how to gamble. Give me one louis d'or." Colette gave it to her. Mme de B. put it on 23. Twenty-three came up. She put it in her bag. She changed tables, asked Colette for another louis d'or, put it on 23. It came up. She put it in her bag. "There," she said, "now I've taught you how to gamble. Go on for yourself."

Money. Modigliani sold me my portrait for five francs in 1916. I couldn't pay for the fiacre to carry it. It stayed at La Rotonde and later crossed the ocean. In 1939, it was sold for seven million francs in England. Where is it now?

Ideal weather. Transparent air. Fragrances. We drag about our shadows—our glue. Wait till it all dissolves and mixes in. Till we take on the colors of the coast, like a lizard. Turning into things is the only safeguard when our singularity, our individualism banish us from them. Play dead. Disappear.

. . . .

SATURDAY · FEBRUARY 23

Crocuses are out. Green grass. The lemons fall from the trees. I am gradually reorganizing myself.

Yesterday, a visit to Matisse, at the Régina. He is receiving acupuncture in bed, a veritable throne of some Negro king, almost in the center of the huge room. He has a high pink color. He wasn't sleeping; now he sleeps. He talks about his fatigue. I tell him that the work of certain painters (Corot, for instance) corresponds to their successive ages, while Picasso's work and his own are of the essence of youth, inventive, at grips with the age of the men who create them. Picasso breaks everything, like a naughty child. Matisse cuts up paper and colors images like a good child in bed with scarlatina. Matisse is old, Picasso old, their works young and demanding (intolerable). There is an imbalance. Picasso escapes it by not stopping for a minute. Matisse is beginning to show impatience at the demands of the work. He has just finished a big panel of cutouts (David playing the harp, with a dancer). The thing has an incredible freshness and youth. He says: "It's my last panel. After this, I'm stopping." I remind him of Goethe's remark: "I've finished my work. If something else happens to me, it will be *over and above*. . . ."

He tells me a funny story. A Russian arrives from Moscow and asks him if our poets in France are starving to death. Why? Éluard has been in Moscow, wearing worn-out shoes and a dirty suit. Matisse is astonished. He asks Aragon, who says: "Of course, on a trip you don't wear your best clothes. I myself . . . et cetera."

I remind him of our old friends the Bs, who have two cars. A little one they drive in town, and a huge one they keep hidden and use only on empty roads.

Matisse talks about Picasso's fits of depression. "At those moments," he says, "you feel that Picasso is trying to get rid of something."

I add: "Or else you pay a lot for it afterward."

Several lovely girls in nurses' uniforms move through the room. They paste, cut out, pin up, and by a peculiar mimicry look just like the drawings on the walls.

Matisse says he noticed some strange spots on the Rubens in Munich. They were left by the copyists trying out their colors on the picture. And in the Louvre he noticed that a Chardin still life was peeling; fragments of paint were actually flaking off. He informed the curator, who saw the damage and exclaimed: "But that's terrible!" Then he added: "But I won't say anything, it would make too many complications."

(Matisse): "Time was when I didn't think of painting 'thorough'; I learned to paint that way so the picture couldn't be spoiled, being photographed in colors, poorly reproduced, et cetera, so it would express a certain strength no matter what. Michelangelo used to say that a statue should be able to fall off a roof or down a mountain and still be strong, even if it broke into pieces."

Picasso's pigeon that turned into a dove (by Aragon's mediation) once belonged to Matisse. He used to own those fluffy pigeons, and since he couldn't feed them anymore, he brought them to Picasso. That's the origin of the Communist peace slogan.

Matisse says: "I no longer have any faith, but I built a chapel. I'm a bourgeois. I made my first communion. Sometimes I pray in order to fall asleep. It makes me feel peaceful.

"It's about thirty years since they stopped making fun of me—stopped insulting me. I'm sorry about that. Be glad when they still insult you."

At the Musée Grimaldi in Antibes, before he was sick, Matisse installed himself in front of the Picasso with the amphora in it and began copying it. A lady and gentleman were watching this serious old man, with his white beard and his gold-rimmed spectacles. The gentleman approached. "Can you tell me what this picture represents?" And Matisse: "You see, I'm trying to find out for myself."

. . . .

FEBRUARY 27 · 1952

Last night, since the weather was so mild, I paid a visit to Somerset Maugham at the Villa Mauresque, at Cap-Ferrat. He was rereading *Madame Bovary* in the grand salon.

He had just bought (for an arm and a leg, he said) two canvases by Picasso. A huge monochrome of a standing woman, probably painted in the rue La Boétie, and the dead Harlequin, which is more of a sketch. The woman is in the hall; the Harlequin is in his bedroom. He stammers worse and worse. He talks about Taormina, which he sees through its legend. Taormina is trying to live on a bad reputation, which is more difficult than to live on a good one. I tell him the story of a forty-year-old fisherman, furious because one of the shops in the main street was exhibiting Von Gloeden's photographs of his grandfather completely naked with a crown of roses. The Tahitian Taormina no longer exists. It disgusts the new generation, which regards the tourists askance, imagining that each visitor is planning to make advances. . . .

Began writing the first chapter of a book on the visible and the invisible, responsibility and irresponsibility.*

I find it harder and harder to write, having only a rather small vocabulary which I am compelled to twist every which way in

Journal d'un inconnu.

order to make comprehensible what is extremely difficult to express. A struggle between work, letters to answer, and the sun which lures me out of my room. My jangled nerves are gradually reorganizing themselves.

A letter from Jean Marais. Some adolescent idiots, led on by someone, are trying to bring down *Britannicus*. There are calm nights, and nights of riot. Apparently Marais is being upset by this, though he gives every indication of extraordinary courage; his good nature forgives almost any injustice. I advise him to imitate Sarah Bernhardt: when the city resisted her, she left, circled the globe, harvesting glory and profits.

An actor is doomed to success. He cannot be misunderstood. All he has is immediacy. He must have victory at all costs; if his country rejects him, he must seek it elsewhere, wherever he can find it, wherever the little Parisian intrigues gain no purchase.

Jean Marais has too many strings to his bow. He directs, designs, and acts—and this in a theater of intrigue. He draws full houses. Easy to imagine the nastiness such a fortune provokes.

. . . .

FEBRUARY 28 · 1952

Points of view. During the run of *The Eagle Has Two Heads* at the Théâtre Hébertot, the prompter once said to me, in tears, after the performance: "Ah, Mme Feuillère is simply overwhelming! She has such lovely feet." This is what she saw from her hole in the floor.

When I used to live in the rue Vignon, the cook told me: "The duke of Westminster called . . . he must be a rich man." "Very." "I'm not surprised, with all those chimes!"

When a film is shown to those who have worked on it, each specialist sees only his own realm. He is not concerned with *the film*. The cameraman concentrates on his lighting. The mechanic on his traveling shots. The script girl on where the furniture is. The actor on himself. Etc.

Maurice G. has dinner with Maurice de Rothschild in the amazing Monte Carlo dining room. The maharani, invited by Maurice de Rothschild, says to Maurice G.: "He's an elephant. Look at him! He eats with a trunk, and what he doesn't want he shoves to each side." Maurice the elephant carries a howdah in which there is room for Mme d'Arenberg, the blood-giving secretary, and her husband, a police informer.

. . . .

MARCH 5 · 1952

The day before yesterday the Nice–Paris plane crashed at nine-ten in the morning. Thirty-six bodies burned to a crisp, torn to pieces, flung against the trees.

Meanwhile, the millionaires' yacht anchors at Villefranche. Ten million francs per passenger. These ladies and gentlemen disembark only when the red carpet is unrolled for them. They come back from Nice dead drunk, carrying their shoes, shirts hanging out. Lorent* had sent them welcome carnations, distributed by girls in local costume. Supposing that they had to buy the flowers, they pushed them away. But once it was explained that the flowers were a present, they rushed at the girls, quarreling over who would grab the flowers first.

Thierry Maulnier, in an article in *Nice-Matin*, answers an article in the *Daily Mail*; he ends with this sentence: "France is like a beggar whose mattress, as we all know, is filled with gold." (I'm quoting from memory.)

One phantom government after another. Mediocrity upon mediocrity. The sheet is pulled to one side, and the other is left bare.

*Albert Lorent, tourist representative in Villefranche-sur-Mer.

General uneasiness. Blood is coagulating in the organism. Gold is falling out of the ministers' pockets or remaining in those of the rich. It no longer circulates.

Shall visit Colette in Monte Carlo. Maurice is in Paris, coming back the day after tomorrow.

Back from seeing Colette. She is more "present" than she has been. On the road, what I notice are the telephone poles and lines. They have taken on the charm of fans and fiacres. People will laugh at them the way they will laugh at gas pumps. And those who laugh at the pumps and poles will be laughed at in their turn for their waves and their atoms.

. . . .

MARCH 6

Agrippine:

. . . and put into my hands
Secrets on which the fate of man depends.

Britannicus, act V, scene iii

Did Nero know about the atom bomb? The funny thing about these lines is that we realize (that Racine lets us realize) it meant nothing at all to him.

The bishop of Monaco tells me that he gave up his seat on the plane to do a favor for the little dancer who was the star of the Cuevas troupe. Pure style of the gaming room. (Temple of Chance.)

My little Renoirs. Matisse describes having seen Renoir make these tiny canvases. When he had finished working, he would use up the color left in his brushes on them.

It is true that the tourists collect the earth from his Cagnes garden and that the Americans would pay a lot for his paint rags.

The last canvas that I bought, the day before I left, is a marvelous little profile of Coco.

Finished the chapter "On the Birth of a Poem." Began the chapter which ends with the "*affaire Bacchus*."

Designed new masks for *Oedipus Rex*.* Sent the curtain.

. . . .

MARCH 9 · 1952

At the Padua hotel, a tourist asks the concierge: "Can you tell me where to find the Giottos?" "At the end of the hall, on the right."

A lady behind Chanel at *The Prince of Homburg* (the lady is consulting her program): "Now I understand: the author's a *boche*. Besides, he committed suicide." The other lady: "All the better; that's one less of them."

Finished the chapter "On Our Solitudes." Began the chapter "On Ladies Under the Dryer."

I'm still getting letters congratulating me on having worsted Mauriac. (Many are from priests.)

It's Sunday. We're lunching at La Pausa.†

Received the ballet scenario Marais is preparing on the theme of Dorian Gray, in which he would take the role of the hideous portrait. I wonder why he is drawn to plots which no longer interest the young audience that wants to see him.

. . . .

MARCH 14 · 1952

A young American has found one of my books of poems in the MGM library in Hollywood with this file card: "Unusable."

---

*A revival of Stravinsky's opera-oratorio, produced in Paris in May 1952.

†Gabrielle Chanel's villa at Roquebrune-Cap-Martin.

I've been thinking of the "unsalvageable" in Sartre's *Les Mains sales*. And of that poor French fool mistakenly used in a raid in Budapest. In a shunting station, after five days in a cattle car, they try to make him realize that there is someone who speaks his language and who can explain the mistake to him. He pulls himself together, brushes himself off as best he can, and comes to a hut where he finds, behind a table, a functionary in a goatee.

"What's this all about?"

"I was in Bucharest—"

"I'm not asking you if you were in Bucharest. I'm asking you what this is all about."

"There was a raid—"

"I'm not asking you if there was a raid. Explain yourself."

"But—"

"Be quick about it. I don't have time to waste. Besides, where are the others?"

"What others?"

"The other Frenchmen."

"I'm the only one."

"What? You're the only one and you come in here and bother me in my office? Clear out, and fast!"

The crime is being an individual.

. . . .

MARCH 15

Sketched out the chapter "On Memory." The difficulty is to keep within my domain, not to encroach on the kind of learning I am not entitled to—where I would be lost.

To keep the tone of a sort of Tom Tit of metaphysics. "Metaphysics for Fun"—like Tom Tit's *Physics for Fun*.

Monte Carlo, the elephant graveyard. Old dowagers, old cocottes come here to die.

Maurice de Rothschild has a noisy argument with me in the dining room of the Hôtel de Paris because I didn't treat Mauriac roughly enough. "You should have crushed that Tartuffe." It would be hard for him to understand that I had no such intention.

Last week we paid a visit to the church of Agay. As he left, he handed the curé an envelope. The curé: "One can see that Monsieur is a good Catholic." "Alas, no, I'm only a poor Jew; my name is Rothschild."

I am to write some paragraphs about Gide in the margins of an album of photographs,* to be published by Amiot-Dumont. Very disconcerting. All I can find are nasty remarks (or that will sound nasty).

Letters pile up. Too lazy to answer. Guilt.

In Nice, examined Jeannot's sets and costumes for the Chinese play *The Chalk Circle*. They seem badly executed, but the first act, made out of bamboo, is a real piece of theater.

. . . .

MARCH 22

Too much work to do and still take notes.

Finished the curtain for *Oedipus Rex*. But Stravinsky's letter worries me; they haven't explained things to him properly. He seems to think I'm doing an opera production, whereas my notion is one that follows the oratorio at a considerable distance. I shall write him this—too late for me to take another path.

Finished the chapter "On Memory" and the one "On Translations."

At Daisy's, Lord Pembroke's son and Poulenc tell me that in

**Gide vivant*, text by Jean Cocteau, with pages from the *Journal* of Julien Green and photographs by Dominique Darbois (1952).

1940 a servant of the British embassy in Turkey had sent all the secret documents to Germany. This would have had such enormous and terrible consequences that the Germans did not believe it was possible. They used none of the documents. The servant, having fled to South America, found himself in possession of the counterfeit money which Germany had given him as payment.

Farewell dinner at the Hôtel de Paris, given by the pasha. Lady Michelham, the pasha, the maharani, Orson Welles, Maurice de Rothschild. Big tables covered with flowers at which no general conversation is possible. On my right, the Princess d'Arenberg. I remind her that when we were young, I had nicknamed her *La Source Cachat* because of the color of her eyes. She is one of those dummies who have stuck by their Bernsteins and their Batailles. She thinks I'm "funny" (is he still as funny as he was?). And finds Colette "entertaining." Etc. The pasha (who married Fouad's wife) tells me that in Egypt they narrowly escaped catastrophe (as far as they are concerned). Taha Hussein, who derived his strength from his exile and who had returned to favor, has already lost his place. The maharani is wearing pink veils and fifty million francs' worth of pearls around her neck. This is just the audience that wants nothing to do with us, that knows nothing about us, and that the cost of seats imposes on us. It is for this ridiculous public that I am preparing the production of *Oedipus Rex*. Has Stravinsky forgotten the faces this public made at the first performance of *Oedipus Rex* at the Théâtre Sarah Bernhardt? [In Diaghilev's season of Ballets Russes, 1927.] The audience was expecting ballet. We gave them a Greek oratorio in Latin.

This afternoon I dictated to Colin-Simard a mass of rather odd notes for the Gide book. He asked me questions, and I answered them; this method makes it possible to retain the freshness of a conversation.

Alexandre writes me: "Hurry up and deal with Desch before

he gets discouraged by articles like Sieburg's." Which I find hilarious. For forty years the Sieburgs* and the Mauriacs have been shooting at me, shooting wide. I haven't read Sieburg's article, but I can guess it is like all the others that cover me with a thick layer of stupidity and inaccuracy. After the wave of German praise, one must expect a wave of insults. The usual mechanism by which my invisibility protects itself.

A farmer here on the Côte d'Azur is in despair because the storms have washed out his fields. His son shows him a clearing in the sky. The farmer explodes: "Now we're in for it," he says, "that means the beginning of the drought."

. . . .

MARCH 23 · 1952

Sense of irresponsibility. I haven't the slightest judgment concerning my work. The book is getting written, and I wonder what it's worth. I find it harder and harder to write.

Francine is leaving at seven-twenty for Paris.

Letters from Alexandre show him in a light I never suspected. He understands nothing about my life. He imagines me protected by friendships, advice, guardians who are countering his every move. As soon as we no longer accept his vagueness in business matters, attitudes change. The odd thing is that this change in attitude always occurs in those who have advised us to take charge of our own affairs and to pay attention to what we are doing. Which means: "Watch out for everyone except me."

A letter from Vilar seems to correspond to my projects for *The*

---

*Friedrich Sieburg (1895–1964), German Catholic writer, connoisseur of French literary matters, author of *Is God French?* (1929).

Golden Fleece—a play yet not a play about the Argonauts (the ship *Argo*).

Doudou is finishing a splendid painting of fruit in a basket set on a chair. Who will ever see it? Few people. A splendid painting must suffer the fate of all splendid paintings. They manage to be invisible. What is invisible in 1952—is this: the fruit one could eat. I admire how readily Doudou *finishes off*. It's because, like the despised painters of the past, he seeks no fame whatever.

Poulenc says he ran into Picasso in the Luxembourg—that he looked very bad, that he has been very sick.

. . . .

MARCH 30 · 1952

I have already written 100 pages. With the "tale" Francine is bringing back from Paris, I shall have 150—equivalent to 250 in a book. I have rid myself of a huge weight of shadow. Just now I woke up from a deep animal sleep. I was shaken by snores that woke me, caught in my throat.

A message from Aragon for the homage to Chaplin. And from Georges Simenon, who comes to Monte Carlo Tuesday, staying with Pagnol.

Yesterday it was snowing in Paris. Here the weather is murky. I am having difficulty figuring out what to do with *Oedipus Rex*. I see the date approaching with fear and trembling. I wonder what good it is, presenting such a work to such audiences—the kind of rich people who see nothing, hear nothing. Moreover, it's a work which has to be accompanied by harsh scenic effects.

Finished the work on Gide with Colin-Simard. I have dictated another three pages to him, and a kind of brief preface.

Received the contracts from my agency, which I am to sign.

. . . .

APRIL 1

Visited the *Coronia*, the so-called Billionaires' Yacht. Another fable. There are no billionaires. The cruise costs one to two million—not ten. The *Coronia* is like any luxury liner. Style: boredom. You can bet that for these travelers, boredom isn't part of the reckoning. They exchange the boredom of their residence for the boredom of a trip. They never disembark for over twenty-four hours. The world of pilgrims to Rome. Legend. We know nothing of what we haven't seen.

I have to keep writing and rewriting this first, difficult chapter. I have incorporated into the book the story of the little girl with the cabbages, entitled "Of Criminal Innocence." This book is intended for the few—but they are the only ones who count in my eyes. (The murmur of secrets in one's ear.)

Made new designs for *Oedipus Rex*. What worries me most is not having time to execute the actual pasteboard masks. Judging from Escoffier's letter, Denise Tual doesn't realize the work involved.

Increasingly I find it difficult to assimilate the notion of the atom (bomb) and to live on this terrifying earth.

. . . .

APRIL 2

Lunch with the Pagnols and the Simenons. Inconceivable, three men more different than the three of us, with regard to work, preoccupations, habits. But we have a common aptitude: never to concern ourselves with other people's business, never to envy anyone else. This is the basis of our understanding, invariably complete and steeped in a friendly fluid very superior to mere interests.

Simenon says: "Odd that the three of us here are the only ones to whom America would offer what they ask. Try as I might, I can't think of any others."

To which I answered that it wasn't much use to me and that my finances are going very badly. Pagnol informs me that the Society of Authors has owed me, for the last three years, a retirement pension of 600,000 francs a year. News to me.

. . . .

APRIL 3

Lunch at Grasse with Charles de Noailles. A little house on the edge of the Saint-Cézaire road. Charles has arranged things splendidly, as he always does in all the houses he lives in. After lunch, Marie-Laure, Ned Rorem, and I pay a visit to Marie-Thérèse de Croisset* in the Villa Croisset, where I once lived.†

Since I have no sense of time, I have the impression of returning to the house after taking a stroll. Rorem plays me his music for *Dorian Gray*.

Charles de Noailles says that Rome, which he has just left, is all in an uproar because the pope is making "Communist" speeches and has just dissolved the Order of the Knights of Malta.

Simenon has confirmed what I already knew: that Chaplin is regaining a huge popularity with television, which is buying up his old short films. American young people who knew nothing of Chaplin's work are beginning to know him. So television is a new enterprise which resuscitates the old stars.

Forgotten to note that the Rosen menage was living in the Hôtel Welcome at Villefranche and overseeing my work for the ballet

---

*Daughter of Countess Adhéaume de Chevigné (the model for Proust's Duchesse de Guermantes), and the mother of Marie-Laure de Noailles. She was widow of the banker Bischoffsheim (Marie-Laura de Noailles's father), and her second husband was the writer Francis de Croisset.

†Cocteau's first stay at the Villa Croisset was during the winter of 1917–1918.

La Dame à la licorne. I have invented the details of the plot and dictated them to Rosen.* Now I'm going to paint the model for the set. What have I got myself into! But I accepted the advance, and I must take as much trouble for the left hand as for any work done with the right.

The Opéra and Paul-Louis Weiller offer pennies for my ballet [*Phèdre*] with Georges (the ballet for Toumanova). I refuse. I've had enough of working for glory all my life.

In the car to Grasse, I sketched out a chapter on fables and the power of myth. It will come after the chapter on translations. (If I manage to get it written.)

The Nice papers announce Jeannot in *Britannicus* for the ninth.

No news from Hanover, where my canvases, tapestries, and drawings are . . . The Germans write a lot of letters but never answer when you ask them something. I wrote asking the charming Dr. Reuthel to oversee the sending of the crates. Clarke—the present director of Covent Garden, former keeper of museums in London—told me that he had lost over a hundred canvases in foreign exhibitions.

Naturally Grasset writes that my first title, *Spirit Are You There?*, is better than *Conspiracy of Silence*. The usual method of publishers. He asks me if he can announce the book with the first title. I couldn't care less. Most likely the book† will come out with a third title I don't even know yet.

The list of the *tableaux vivants* for *Oedipus Rex* as I conceive them.

1. The Plague in Thebes
2. Sadness of Athena
3. The Oracles (Tiresias)
4. The Sphinx
5. The Oedipus Complex
6. The Divine Head of Jocasta
7. Oedipus and His Daughters

In No. 1, the scroll *Oedipus Rex*

*Heinz Rosen, choreographer of the ballet *La Dame à la licorne*.

†*Journal d'un inconnu*.

If I were to give speeches and appear in all the cities to which I am invited, I should never leave off traveling. And now all I care about is Milly and Santo Sospir. The rest means extreme exhaustion. Yesterday, on my way to see *Fanfan la Tulipe* in Nice, I noticed that Maurois is lecturing at the municipal Casino. He never misses a trick.

Pagnol says it's ridiculous that I'm not in the Académie Française. Which is also the opinion of Pierre Benoît, though Pagnol claims that Benoît leads you on and then never votes for you. I told Pagnol that I would never ask anyone to do anything for me in this regard and that I would enter the Académie Française only if I were offered a chair.

I'm told that Mauriac wrote his open letter to me to prevent my becoming a member of the Académie—to make sure the doors were shut against me.

. . . .

APRIL 6 · 1952 · (Palm Sunday)

A mother here in the provinces: "My daughter plays the radio very well."

Letter from Loulou [Louise de Vilmorin], discussing Jean Hugo's* trip to Russia: "When I listen to Jean, it was as if I were reading the *Guide Bleu* or the Children's *Tour de France*; the same descriptions of sentimental tourists. They've received a lot of stupid criticism because they went, but I'm glad they made the trip. I promise you, if it were *my* great-grandfather who was being celebrated in Moscow, I would certainly join in, and everything they've told me about it would encourage me to do so all the more."

*The painter Jean Hugo (born 1894), an old friend of Cocteau's, collaborated with him on several theatrical works—sets for *The Wedding on the Eiffel Tower* (1921), *Roméo et Juliette* (1924), *Orpheus* (1926).

. . . .

APRIL 15 · 1952

Several days since I've taken notes. I was ill and in a sort of cloud. And though I'm never bored, I was bored. And it was impossible for me to do anything to exorcize my boredom. I was like that dog in Jules Renard: I kept looking in the other rooms to see if I was there. I wonder if it's because of the shots I'm taking—or if it's the Côte d'Azur and its climate. Michel Simon, whom I've just seen at Pagnol's, says these are days when you register destructive currents. Maybe. I never like it when a general takes power. Which is happening in America. New talk about flying saucers, possibly the vehicle of another world more highly developed than ours. In short, uneasiness. Despite the flowers, despite the friends I care for and who care for me. One tries to get well, or at least one imitates the sick by reading Alexandre Dumas. We come back from Monte Carlo with three or four more novels, besides the ones in the house. Jeannot has spent three days at the cape after *Britannicus* at Monte Carlo. He didn't take his nose out of his book. Francine in one corner. Doudou in another. And me trying to read but realizing even while I was reading that I should be working and that I couldn't do a thing.

The film technicians having asked me for a few lines to head the amnesty petition for Greek antifascists, I was foolish enough to reply. My letter appeared (in facsimile) on the first page of *Les Lettres françaises*. I'm very much afraid I will be denied a visa for our trip to Greece. My Quixotry is incorrigible, a real intoxication with self-compromising situations.

Alexandre behaves worse and worse. He acts right and left in my name. I ran into him at the Nice airport; he was with Mme de Saint-Exupéry, so I couldn't open my mouth. After that, he managed to avoid me. God knows what he's plotting in Germany;

I'm still getting no answer to my letters there. Except for a message from Petersen, who informs me that my show which was supposed to take place in Hanover will be in Hamburg. I have no idea why this change has been made. . . . No doubt some skulduggery of Alexandre's.

Finished the set for *La Dame à la licorne*. Letter from Rosen. Hartmann wants to put on the ballet in Munich in April '53. We're leaving Saturday. Will be in Milly Sunday. Monday at three-thirty at the Théâtre des Champs-Élysées, where Denise Tual is getting the troupe together. I am still worried about this work for a luxury audience and a theater booked in advance. Since Stravinsky doesn't seem to want my *tableaux* to be used during the oratorio, I will make them coincide with my texts. All I want is to finish this disagreeable work and get away. Messages come in from Belgium, Switzerland, Italy, Germany, Austria. I turn down everything. Enormous idleness—a sense of the utter futility of everything active and brilliant. A need for my den and depression at being in a den. Contacts alarm me, and the absence of contacts demoralizes me. No idea where I am in all this.

Marcel Sablon, director of the theater in Nice (Palais de la Méditerranée), has given Jeannot a letter he received from Roger Martin du Gard after *Britannicus*. A long and admirable encomium of Marais as Nero. Jeannot was made happier by this than he was made wretched by the unfair criticisms in Paris.

. . . .

APRIL 29 · 1952

It has not been possible to write. Paris is overwhelming. Books to sign. Letters to answer. Countless problems raised by Alexandre's recent attitude. Contradictory messages from Austria, company forming, journalists, etc., whereas I need all my time for the production of *Oedipus Rex*. Some relief while the painters and carpenters begin their work. Laverdet is painting the curtain. The carpenters are making the pasteboard masks. All I want is to be through with it, to get rid of Vienna, and to leave for Greece, where I can board the *Orphée II* for an island cruise.

Every morning brings a pile of letters in every language. I am always being asked to do something impossible or else to read manuscripts which pile up here and risk getting lost. I sent in my resignation as president of the unions. Whereupon five-page letters in which it appears I am being "influenced." By whom? I wonder. Unfortunately I am quite alone in the midst of this labyrinth. Impossible to break out of it. They'll only insist the more. As I write these lines, the telephone never stops ringing. If I were not to make my escape, I would be stuck here, *immobilized in the movements of chaos*. I still don't understand how others manage, the ones who go out, eat lunch, dinner, write—without seeming the least bit hampered. Someone tells me I need a secretary. What would a secretary do? My work would be doubled if I had to tell a secretary what it was, and then had to dictate . . . (Enough of this, enough.) Just now the theater called: be at Orly at three to meet Stravinsky. But at three I'm supposed to be out at the Parc Montsouris, supervising the work I'm doing for him!

Luckily the weather is fine. Yesterday I took a walk in the Bois de Boulogne. I couldn't take the city anymore. All those chestnut trees, those lakes, those bicyclists lying on the grass, those empty racetracks, all that pale green did me good. And now the telephone starts again. And the articles. And the visits. And the problems mount up. And the friends I'd like to see whom it is impossible to see. And the contracts that are never what they should be—and someone revises them for me, and life grows even more complicated. And memory—my poor memory, which blurs and makes mistakes. And the discipline of work that I struggle to preserve in all this monstrous racket. I'll never make concessions on the work schedule. My book at Santo Sospir. The production of *Oedipus Rex*—that is the center; the rest revolves around it at top speed. One step outside, and I would be swept into the dizzying whirl.

I was forgetting the series of shots after the first set I took on the cape. And the dentist and the barber, and time *which does not exist* and which makes demands *as if it did*—which devours us.

. . . .

MAY FIRST · *Milly*

No sunshine. Stormy weather. The Achards for lunch. We listened to records by Mauriac and Claudel. If Mauriac's article was a prayer on the grave of a friend, his record is his own funeral oration. Yesterday the Académie du Disc convened at the Grand Véfour. I voted for Pascal read by [Pierre] Fresnay, without having heard it. The rest is mediocre, and neither Colette nor I can give *ourselves* a prize. With Pascal on one side and Fresnay on the other, there's no danger of absurdity. My colleagues take such meetings quite seriously. Kemp tells me after the voting that there are three empty seats: "After all, we can't have someone like Vuillermoz here."* I answer him: "Oh, Kemp, you know, critics are all more or less the same."

Yesterday morning examined the work on the masks at Vallat's, at the end of the rue de l'Estrapade. Marvelous workmanship. The newspapers say that when Stravinsky stepped out of the plane at Orly, he asked: "Where is Jean?" And I was working for him! Everything was explained. Now the work has to be done by some

*Robert Kemp (1879–1959), theater critic for *Le Monde*, hardly a partisan of the moderns. Émile Vuillermoz (1878–1960), who wrote chiefly in *Opéra*, defended the modern composers of his day, from Fauré to Stravinsky.

miracle while we devote ourselves to everything that *surrounds* the work. I have ten days left, and nothing is ready. The prospect of nights of work. Have agreed to a television contract with Herbier for *Orpheus* and one with Rossif to show almost all my films.

We were talking with Achard about our delight when friends succeeded in their enterprises. Juliette said: "You're abnormal—you're monsters!"

The little room behind the Panthéon where Vallat is executing my masks. No perspective. He looks at his work through the big end of the field glasses, so as to see it at a distance.

. . . .

MAY 3 · Milly

Went to see the work on the masks for *Oedipus* before I left. I will collect everything at Laverdet's for the finishing touches.

Pichette's *Nucléa*. The Théâtre National Populaire was suggesting that this is the work of the age. Schoolboy work—classroom verses, childish symbols. The names—*Gladior-Tellur*, etc.—had warned me right at the start: a marriage of Claudel and Prévert. Calder's mobiles confined themselves to a few rather agreeable patches. Jarre's prerecorded music of some interest: but in its determination to create "poetry," unreality, it falls back on a kind of realism (actual noises, piped in from all sides), and soon returns to the easy old lies of the theater.

A disconcerting evening. The journalists flung themselves upon me to find out what I thought. I answered: "I am not a judge. I belong to the race of the accused rather than to the race of judges. I don't judge."

Stravinsky arrived yesterday. Telephoned him this morning. We will take dinner together tomorrow night.

Apropos of Pichette's play, I quoted to Thierry Maulnier Anna de Noailles's remark to a poetess she had just read: "Madame, I have just read your book. I was scared out of my wits."

The Lettrists released a few paper flyers in the theater. Supposedly a protest. Real scandals no longer occur.

Very little time left to finish the very difficult work on *Oedipus Rex*. Paris is still insisting on work at excessive speed, one of those "miracles" which never occur in the theater. In the theater there is only very slow focusing and hard work.

Berg's opera and Büchner [*Wozzek*, presented for the first time in France] scored a triumph. I told Nicholas Nabokov: "The French want to be *forgiven* for the Occupation."

After twenty-five years, Paris is discovering Berg. Frau Berg was in a box—we were photographed together.

Invitation from Moscow, from the minister of film. Work to be done in Paris and Vienna keeps me from even considering such a thing.

Another extraordinary thing. I haven't seen Picasso for a year. Stravinsky for fourteen. Chance (if I dare use such a word) would have it that tomorrow I'm dining with Stravinsky and that the next night I'm dining at André Dubois's with Picasso. The two men who have had the greatest influence on me. These two men of genius separated by politics—about which they couldn't care less.

Took extreme pleasure in rereading Charles d'Orléans in Paul Éluard's anthology. What a crutch the orthography of that period was to a poet, in his exquisite lameness.

Corrected the Apollinaire proofs for the Mazenod edition.

Pichette's pretentious play reminds me of one by Arnyvelde [performed 1906, published the same year], *La Courtisane*, which was put on just once by the Comédie Française and which the entire press heralded as a masterpiece.

Moreover, Gérard Philipe declaims in the manner of the worst

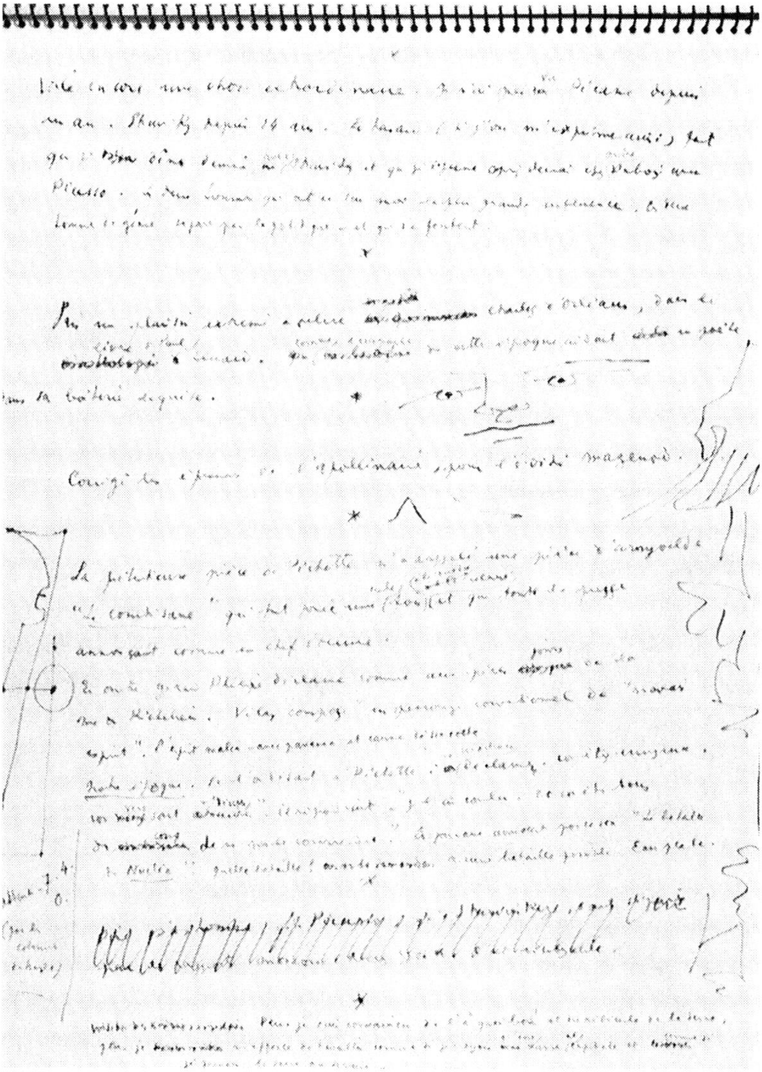

Voilà encore une chose extraordinaire. Je n'ai pas vu Picasso depuis un an. Stravinsky depuis 14 ans. [illegible] Stravinsky et que je [illegible] chez Dubois avec Picasso. [illegible] grande influence. [illegible]

*

[illegible] Charles d'Orléans, dans [illegible] poésie [illegible] dans la [illegible] déguisée.

*

Corrigé les épreuves de l'Apollinaire pour [illegible] Mazenod.

*

La [illegible] pièce de Colette [illegible] "La Courtisane" [illegible] annonçant comme un chef-d'œuvre. [illegible] esprit". [illegible] Colette [illegible] [illegible] Nuits" [illegible]

*

[illegible] Picasso [illegible]

[illegible]

*

[illegible]

days of the house, and Vilar confects a conventional "bad" character—the cunning villain with a Panama hat and a cane!

Our times. If someone said to Pichette: "Your actors declaim. You're boring. Your verses are mediocre," he would answer: "That's the way I wanted it. And you're all idiots for not realizing it." For tonight's performance the papers are already printing their headvlines: "The battle of *Nucléa*." What battle? No battle possible. Smooth sailing.

The more convinced I am of the absurdity and the futility of the world, the more I try to work as if I believed that what one creates is of crucial importance and as if I took the world seriously.

Vilar has a success to the degree that he unites a broad public with an elite, that the state supports him, that he puts on his productions in the theaters he chooses, in the city and in the suburbs. What does he put on? Pichette's play. Never so much as last night have I realized what a division there is between the people who used to know something and the people who no longer know anything. Anyone can put on a production imagined a thousand times over by us, by Gordon Craig, by Reinhardt, by Piscator, by Tairoff, by the Germans and the Russians, and at once young people suppose it is new. If a new production were put on, i.e., one that breaks with these old formulas, our unaware youth would regard such a production as behind the times. There is a huge misunderstanding here, and besides, there is no critic writing who knows what's what and can disabuse these poor fellows. What we have here must be the last spasms before the total extinction of any experimentation, any boldness. The Parisian intelligentsia admires a Japanese film [*Rashomon*], unaware that many very interesting films are made in Japan, and that this one, with its prize from the Venice Festival, is incredibly weak in relation to the Japanese tradition. American-style images—camera angles imitating those of *Beauty and the Beast*, a confused and childish story.

Never have countries been farther from each other. One wonders why Japanese animated cartoons are never shown over here, for instance. Some that I saw in Tokyo were extraordinary.

If it had occurred to me, last night, to say that this absurd play was sublime, I should have had no difficulty convincing a lot of people of the fact.

. . . .

MAY 7 · 1952

Emotional meeting with Stravinsky. He is unchanged. Dinner at Véfour. As soon as you begin talking to this man, everything is numbers, and disorder ceases. I suspected that the little *mise-en-scène* for *Oedipus Rex*, based on numbers, would suit his needs. I explained it to him at great length and drew diagrams on the tablecloth. We drank a lot of red wine. He told me that in America, wanting to see *Orpheus* again, he had a terrible time getting seats a month into the run. The house was never empty. Same story from one of Francine's friends back from New York. "Never has a French film," she said, "provoked such interest." America regards

me as the most deluded—and the most ripped-off—man in France.

When dinner is over, Vera [Stravinsky] and two young Americans join us. We could not bring ourselves to separate.

The next day, lunch at André Dubois's, with Picasso and Françoise [Gilot]. Picasso has regained his healthy appearance, his glance that murders and creates. He was wearing an odd cap with fur earflaps knotted on top of his head. I embraced him for Igor. With Stravinsky, with Picasso, I feel at ease. I feel at home. Nothing vague. Numbers rule. (The invisible—as solid as houses.)

Stravinsky quoted Shaw's description of his visit to Sam Goldwyn: "We had no trouble understanding each other. He talked art and I talked money."

Explained the whole program to the three dancers. Saw Stravinsky again at the theater after my rehearsal. He's thinking about a film opera on *The Odyssey* and wants to get me involved. (To be shot in Spain.) I didn't say yes or no. He took three years to write *The Rake's Progress*. I don't suppose you could plan such an undertaking without two or three years of preliminary work.

I told Picasso: "You're the first Communist king there ever was."

Stravinsky says I look younger than thirteen years ago. "Your photographs don't look like you. It's true that the photographers who shoot us shoot themselves."

While I was talking with Stravinsky in the French Radio box, we were watching the rehearsal of Auric's ballet *Coup de feu* through the glass. Cassandre's set: a set. Dances: dances. No experimentation, no shock.

Wretched article by Jean-Jacques Gautier on *The Medium* in Cannes. Stupidity is always amazing, no matter how used to it you become.

This afternoon, I tried the pasteboard heads on the dancers.

. . . .

SUNDAY · MAY 11 · 1952 · *Milly*

Spent my day with Laverdet. The masks are done. Their splendid monstrosity suggests the masks of African ceremonies. I try to give them a power which will overcome even great distances. The workmen show no surprise at this unaccustomed enterprise; they are dedicated to this work as to certain problems to be solved, and even if the faces scarcely resemble faces, they sense their humanity. They never make the kind of mistake that has anything to do with aesthetics. They look for the arbitrary places for the eyes, the ears, the hair—and they find them. I rarely need to correct them.

Critics and public alike will despise this production. I'm used to that. Yesterday *Le Figaro* printed an adorable piece of writing by a ten-year-old student, disowned by his teacher, who regarded the text as an absurd response to her assignment and a proof of the lowering of academic standards. The child had been told to describe a cat. Among other wonders, he wrote: "The cat has two front paws. Two hind paws. Two paws on the left side, and two paws on the right. His tail follows his body and stops after a while. Sometimes the cat wants to have kittens, so he has them. This is when he becomes a pussycat."

Unfortunately our works encounter schoolteachers very often.

Why not walk out onstage the night of *Oedipus Rex* and say: "Poor fools, enjoy your filth. I'm clearing out, and you won't ever hear from me again." It would be so easy. Picasso said, yesterday: "We've always worked with the understanding that what we were working on would be enjoyed." Is it our fault if these fools believe we're making fun of them? And in a way it's true—we *are* making fun of them. But not the way they think.

I didn't sleep all last night. I kept seeing a production. Correcting it. Changing it. Making it right. And for whom? For spectators who still don't see what is new and who no longer see what is old. Who never see anything. Except themselves—and even then! If they saw themselves, they'd run away.

There are two spirits in the realm of business. The spirit of *fortune* and the spirit of *pocket money*. Nothing is more difficult than to make them understand each other. I am richer with fifty thousand francs in my pocket than with fifty million "working" in the abstract zone of the Bourse. Money makes deductions. "Suppose something happened to you?" The money I inherited from my mother is in London. I'll never see any of it. It's "put aside, in case something happens to me." Something will happen to me. I will die, and never have seen any of it.

Annam is installed at Milly. Annam is a rust-colored chow puppy. At first he growled and tried to bite. By this morning he never leaves my heels and licks my hands. I'd like to take him to the cape, but I promised him to Louis. Incredible how casually we treat animals. We take them away from their father and mother, from their friends. They grow attached to us. We leave them. And then they have to become attached to new masters.

Back to Paris. Work with Laverdet.

Television tonight. L'Herbier. Leave for Vienna from Nice on the twenty-fourth, after the performance.

Annam watches the suitcases being closed. He whines, and wrinkles appear all over his face.

. . . .

MAY 22 · 1952

What if I had to describe our work on *Oedipus Rex* every day! Impossible. Never one moment's peace. There were three performances. A *générale* and two public performances. Triumph. The papers couldn't help acknowledging it, despite the stupidity of the articles. Except for the paper *Combat*, the whole press is absurd, ignorant. Deaf and blind. Nothing has changed.

There occurred—for the ensemble of the orchestra, the chorus, because of our presence and because of the staged pantomimes—something monumental, something liturgical. I saw, from where I stood as the speaker, all the tense faces. My fatigue was such that I couldn't turn around and follow the *tableaux*. I had to follow them in the audience's eyes. The house cheered so much that I was told they had to turn down the microphones—they would have burst.

Last night a few people tried to produce a scandal—when Jocasta remains alone onstage. I said: "Stravinsky and I have always worked with great respect for the public. We ask for the same respect in return." I spoke in a different voice from the one I used for the texts. I thought that the scandal would start up again when blind Oedipus comes onstage. But we finished in calm, and at the last note a thunderous applause covered all the rest. We took bow after bow.

The production requires so much tension, such an emanation of waves, that I was unable to do it a third time. Stravinsky conducted the first day. Rosbaud the second. It was difficult for the press not to record the work's triumph, on account of the two radio broadcasts. They did so reluctantly and insultingly. Stravinsky and I are quite used to this procedure.

Sent flowers and a note to Mme Auriol, since I am leaving for Vienna, and a luncheon at the Élysée is impossible.

Milly. Iris. Peonies.

Wrote the text on Radiguet for *Les Nouvelles littéraires*. Wrote the text for Air France. Wrote the text for the directors' gala.

. . . .

MAY 26 · 1952

We are in Vienna after a flight which I spent most of in the cockpit with the pilots.

On arrival, the radio interviewers asked me what caused the "terrible scandal" of *Oedipus Rex*. These are the lies spread by the press agencies. The more the means of communication multiply, the less information we receive as to what happens anywhere but at home.

Raining, freezing. The director of Air France lends us coats. The Hotel Sacher (the one in *Mayerling*) is the only one in Vienna which has been modernized in the right way, without altering the carved beds embellished with angels playing harps, the red damask, the chandeliers with pendants.

Everywhere in Vienna, the look of an aristocratic province, a spiritual elegance. Yesterday, Sunday, we visited Schönbrunn in a mortal cold which was like the dreadful wedding night of Empress Elisabeth. How could the duke of Reichstadt, galloping back and forth in this cold, help becoming tubercular? But everything here is simple, light, good-humored: dinners, rehearsals, broadcasts, press conferences, photographers. In spite of this rain, under which the processions file by heroically. Lunch with Hindemith. He wants me to do an oratorio with him.

Today, Monday, I rehearse *Oedipus* at five. Apparently a name spreads faster than a work, but the invisible work haloes it with a phosphorescence. Apparently the work becomes futile; it is sniffed out around the name, around the person who represents it. I regret not having been able to bring the production of *Oedipus Rex*. It is true that Paris is a city of the eye and Vienna a city of the ear. In Paris, without a staged production, the music might have seemed long. Here people listen, pay attention (with less "obedience" than in Germany)—with respect.

The voices are magnificent. Boehm conducts with precise passion. Sitting on my chair, I am surrounded by many more sonorous vibrations than on the stage of the Théâtre des Champs-Élysées.

This week, all my films are being revived in Vienna.

. . . .

MAY 27 · 1952

Splendid rehearsal. Magnificent ensemble work and then Bach's *Magnificat* with the astonishing passage for flutes, harpsichord, and cellos.

Evening, after dinner at the Three Hussars, at the Art Club. A nightclub in the manner of Saint-Germain-des-Prés. Except that here there are very poor, very innocent customers, not yet playing a part. The young artists meet with no response and huddle together to feel less alone. They draw, paint, write, sew with whatever comes to hand. The cellar is lined with what in our Midi we call *canisses*. We are cheered, surrounded by affectionate concern, photographed, filmed, received with that grace so characteristic of Vienna. We drink cognac and *vin nouveau*.

In the bars (except at the Art Club, where a classic jazz trumpet is played) the pianists play only French songs and Strauss waltzes (as in New York).

Vienna is poor. The most expensive restaurant seems very cheap to us. You could live here for almost nothing, and the Viennese cannot live. But they are so dignified that they never complain, and all of them give the impression of being rich. Many beautiful and elegant women. No one ever stares. One is free. One circulates effortlessly.

Schubert's house—very moving and quite lovely on its little square of vines, bushes, and songs. It is in this little square that children are confirmed. They are brought here in cars covered with white flowers.

From the hilltop you can see all Vienna and the broad Danube, which is not blue.

The Donau Verlag has published my *Théâtre de poche*. I am asked to sign many copies. But I have managed not to do a public signing. I've spoken on the radio about the theater in general and about the little book. The radio people work in an impeccable building which was finished the day before the Anschluss. The next morning the place woke up as Radio Germany.

After the concert tonight, we were invited to a reception at the house of the president of the Wiener Konzerthaus, Dr. Manfred Martner Markhof. He wears old-style Austrian sideburns. His wife is delightful.

May 28 · 1952

I have never seen a hall so crowded; there was such cheering when I came out onstage that I couldn't open my mouth. No matter how I gestured that I was about to speak, the audience wouldn't stop. Finally there was silence, and I said (in German, first): "I speak German badly and when I am alone. But if I am being listened to by a lot of people, I can't manage a word. So I shall speak in French." (In French): "In France we are accustomed to make a wish when we do something for the first time. This is my first trip to Vienna." (I repeat this in German.) "I shall make a wish for the happiness of Vienna, for its profound elegance of spirit, for its sacred liberty." (Here the audience burst into cheers, and many wept.)

"Stravinsky's opera-oratorio is a severe work, a mythological liturgy—which accounts for its being in Latin. In Paris, we have just put it on as a stage work, and I was looking forward to bringing that production to Vienna. Unfortunately this proved impossible at the Konzerthaus. I take comfort in the fact that Paris is a city for the eyes (*Augenstadt*) and that Vienna is a city for the ears (*und Wien eine Orenstadt*); music circulates in your streets like air. And now I must thank you for Vienna's unforgettable welcome. *Herzliche Grüsse*."

Here there was endless applause from the audience and the orchestra. Total silence during the oratorio, and the faint noise of the program pages turning as the audience followed the text. Difficult to describe what occurred when it was over: endless calls, bowing to a standing ovation, the audience screaming and stamping.

Supper in the Markhofs' fine house. Afterward the minister took us to a tiny club to hear a violinist, who played until three in the morning; I realized I had never heard a violin before. It was so fine, so noble, so insane that despite my tendency to suppose that the whole world is a wicked farce, I regained my confidence in human creations. Accompanied by an accordion and a piano, another violin, and a bass, the violinist was sublime. I was listening to the end of a world—at the extreme tip of that Austria-Hungary, of that Central Europe which once ruled Europe by its grace, by its heart.

I plan on proposing to Hindemith that we do an *Apocalypse*. The themes Mme Hindemith suggested are exhausted by masterpieces: Don Quixote, Don Juan, etc. *The Apocalypse* is not a masterpiece. It is better still, and it is inexhaustible.

After Greece, I shall go to Spain. I want to see the end of that world—before the total and definitive denial of everything I love, or everything that seems to be the only reason for living. Before man the imbecile spoils everything.

In the Air France plane. Leaving Vienna, we rode in the car that belongs to the director of Air France. Doudou followed with Susini.* At the airport, the second car (the one belonging to the

---

*Eugène Susini, French academic, a specialist in German romanticism, director of the Institut Français in Vienna in the 1950s.

Institut Français) was delayed. It had been stopped on the road by the Russians. Doudou did not have his passport, which was in Francine's bag. Mme Susini stammered out a little Russian. They got through, after a cold sweat. The next car couldn't get through in time for the plane. I suppose the Russians were looking for someone, who just happened to be in the last car.

Traffic around Vienna increasingly difficult.

The filming began at the Art Club continues; we are shot with the crew. Quick trip to Zürich. Photographers and reporters waiting for us there.

In Zürich the first thing you notice is the change from poverty to wealth. The wife of the director of Air France tells us about this gold armor that protects Zürich, keeps the city from being alive. Poor Vienna—how rich it seems to me.

A sumptuous car crosses sumptuous landscapes, a sumptuous city, and lets us off at the door of a sumptuous hotel, the Dolder, with a view over all Zürich and the lake.

We go into town, change our money: ten Swiss francs, worth ten thousand French francs. Dinner at the Baur au Lac grillroom: I rediscover the wonderful Bock-Habana cigarettes in their white packages stamped with gold medals.

We have invited the directress of the Cinéma-Nord-Sud, Mme Hindemauer, who laments the stupidities of the distributors and the clumsiness of the agents with regard to French films. It was here that I first presented *Orpheus* (the gentleman who said: "When you speak to the audience, it's the Code Napoléon").

Lots of young people applaud us on the *brasserie* terraces: a warm and loving atmosphere in Zürich as well.

I cannot complain about the audience for *Oedipus Rex* in Paris, but my city always regards me askance.

Le Figaro, the only French paper with world circulation, covers me with mud and ridicule. A few minutes of presence are enough to dissipate this bad smell. Only I can't be everywhere.

To get into the Albertina, you pass through a stage set just like the ruins in *Orpheus*. The director has treasures by Dürer, by Rembrandt, by Bosch taken out of their cases and shown to us: drawings on very thin blue or white paper, even parchment, in charcoal, ink, gouache. It is clear that Van Gogh ardently studied Dürer's landscapes—the cross-hatching, the spare, vigorous line, the blank space for light, etc.

The Albertina wants to put on an exhibition of my drawings and of my big tapestry. The Tyrol, for the *Orpheus* cycle, wants the *Orpheus* drawings. I suggest that they write to Dr. Petersen in Hamburg, to have the whole set sent to them from there and to make their choice on the spot.

Driving rain. We take lunch with Susini at the Institut Français in the Lobkowitz Palace, where Beethoven conducted the first performance of the *Eroica* in the great hall.

Saw the film sent by Millecam. Very odd mixture of Gide, Genet, Buñuel. Mysterious stranger (cape)—crimes—suicides—young boys. The Tlemcen ciné clubs must be astounded.

. . . .

MAY 30 · 1952

I am writing in the garden and in the sun.

This is the weather I thought I would find in Vienna, where everyone—fashionable and otherwise—lives out of doors, drinking and singing all night long. All this had shriveled, frozen, ill protected against winter temperatures.

Yet this journey leaves me with the memory of a city deserving its legend, despite the drama it is living through. French, American, British flags and the red star follow each other over the roofs of all the official palaces. But the musical atmosphere that circulates in the streets and squares doesn't change. We even had a little sunshine in the rose-filled square where I wanted to salute the monument to the empress Elisabeth. That grace, that courage, that thunderous applause, that standing ovation touched my heart. We had the same kind of welcome in Germany, but less subtle, less delicate in its strength.

In Vienna, there were never speeches at the dinner table. It was enough to exchange glances. Fatigue was avoided by a discreet friendliness that sustains you. Just before leaving, we took lunch at the hotel with the Hindemiths. I plan to work on the theme of the *Apocalypse* on the *Orphée II*. To devour my work at Patmos, to digest it and take it up again after returning to Santo Sospir.

Duclos arrested. A brawl. Antagonisms. Disorder. Depression.*

It was only in Vienna, the evening of the rehearsal, that I conceived the right way to speak the text of *Oedipus*, to give it a power equivalent to that of the soloists and the chorus. It lacked the *abnormal* rhythm. I regret having recorded for Columbia before devising this method, which occurred to me because of the extraordinary voices of the Konzerthaus singers. Behind me, the timbre of Oedipus and Jocasta was ringing in my head, forcing me to keep on the same level.

I am not yet dictating my book. I may have to finish it in the Greek islands. Maybe add a chapter on *Oedipus Rex* and the meaning of the masks, on the almost Chinese style of the pantomimes. Performances turn to dust. Only what one tells will survive.

The insoluble problem is to live on an earth still young in eternity, amid dawning and dying galaxies. To exist within an organism whose immortality is assured by the death of our dwelling places.

We imagine we are living the life of the earth, whereas we are

*When General Matthew Ridgway arrived in Paris as NATO commander-in-chief, the Communist party organized demonstrations which proved insufficient; after a few days, the Pinay government arrested many Communists, including the deputy Jacques Duclos.

living a brief period of the earth's life between destroyed epochs and epochs which will follow the final cataclysm of our own (which we call the end of the world).

Before our epoch the Côte d'Azur was glacial; the Côte d'Azur was in northern Siberia. Milly underwater.

A bellboy of the Pátmos-Palace Hotel went crazy. He screamed: "I am John," and devoured the hotel's guest register.

The slaves who worked on the pyramids were buried in them; they were found mummified on the spot. A French scholar constructed a tiny pyramid according to the exact orientation and measurement of those in Egypt. He enclosed some raw meat inside it. Ten days afterward the meat was not rotten but mummified.

Why bother? Any day we can be caught in the tail of a comet. The earth will tilt on its axis, amid a rain of naphtha and bitumen. And our epoch will end and another begin. Let us live out our epoch in humility.

What is found in caves and on mountaintops is still part of our epoch. Of the epoch preceding our own, nothing is ever found.

. . . .

JUNE 1 · 1952

For the Hindemith oratorio. Study of texts relative to the comet and its tail sweeping the earth—taken by the prophets for signs from heaven.

I write Hindemith that I will write chorus verses in mediocre French which when translated are likely to give a certain rhythm to the German prose. The singing will be in German (which is more easily articulated than French). My French texts are for my own use; they will be in German when someone else serves as the speaker. I plan to construct and complete the oratorio at sea. (We leave for Athens on the tenth.)

. . . .

JUNE 2

The right method (which I have adopted) consists, after an enormous effort (like *Oedipus Rex*), in leaving town and not reading the newspapers, which always minimize a success or ridicule it. Best to abide by what one has done, seen, and heard.

Fools admire a pale ruin of Greece; the true Greece is motley. In *Oedipus Rex* I have never been closer to Greece (on the level of the myth's monstrosity).

. . . .

JUNE 4 · 1952

Yesterday we turned on the radio, and there was *Le Sacre du printemps*. I had hoped to hear a rebroadcast of the *Sacre* conducted by Markevich. In a second, this *Sacre* became a nightmare piece—something that was and yet wasn't the *Sacre* at all: a *Sacre* without genius, etc., and I realized that the work was by one of those young American composers who are plagiarists without even realizing it—who naïvely and shamelessly *delight*. . . . The strange racket stopped. We were told that we had just heard, indeed, the work of a young American composer.

Yesterday, a procession of memories, of places, persons, walks, long adventures in hotels, in squares, on roads in the mountain and at the seashore. Hubert's grandmother's estate, where I had a cottage on the grounds, and a house in a huge orchard on the hillside where I lived so long, and restaurants I liked coming back to, and a kind of Montmartre with sinister alleyways I crossed to visit friends on the seventh floor of an apartment building which was surrounded by embassies and from which you could see the scaffolding of a steeple where we got lost and which we could get out of only across bare boards and a garage whose owners are still friends and this villa not far from a little old inn built of planks and logs, where the children of Mme Dourthe* and those of our old gardeners at Maisons-Laffitte were living.

And I began looking up the dates and details which allowed me to see all this even more clearly, until I finally realized that these were places and people in my dreams, dreams I didn't remember when I awoke, and which were accumulating in my memory. Then I realized that my dream life was as full of memories as my real life, that it *was* a real life, denser, richer in episodes and in details of all kinds, more precise, in fact, and that it was difficult for me to locate my memories in one world or the other, that they were superimposed, combined, and creating a double life for me, twice as huge and twice as long as my own.

If one seeks light on the cataclysms of the Apocalypse and those related in certain texts from China, India and Egypt, on the "miracles" which were meteorites, and on how the earth changed its very axis, it is indispensable to read Immanuel Velikovsky's *Worlds in Collision*, published now in a French translation.

In the work for Hindemith, do not attempt a "scientific" oratorio. Preserve the style of the Apocalypse, angels with swords in their mouths, lion-headed horses, locusts and human faces and crowned with gold, the great whore of Babylon, etc.

Plane reservations made for the tenth. I wonder if everything doesn't coincide (and long before my meeting with Hindemith) to take me to Pátmos so that I can complete the oratorio.

Terrifying to think of the number of letters, telegrams, and messages piling up in Paris (Madeleine away, in Milly with Siam and family) and those that will pile up during the trip to Greece. . . . How to deal with them, how to get any work done? How can I ever get through it all? That is the question of a man

---

*Manager of the Hôtel Chantecler du Piquey (Arcachon) when Cocteau spent his vacations there with Raymond Radiguet (1920, 1921, 1923).

convinced of a cataclysm destroying the earth and of the cruel riot of the galaxies themselves. This mixture of metaphysical clairvoyance and obedience to the trivial duties of our rank and station sometimes gives me an uneasiness bordering on disgust (and dreams).

No doubt it is this mixture which makes me incomprehensible to my contemporaries.

. . . .

JUNE 5 · 1952

Tickets bought for the Tuesday flight from Nice to Rome and for the Thursday flight from Rome to Athens.

Strange that Velikovsky speaks of the vastness of our system and the tininess of the atom, whereas such dimensions exist only in relation to ourselves. Our solar system is an atom. The atom is a solar system analogous to ours, and so on, in every direction, to infinity.

This week, strikes have broken out all over France. *Orphée II* is at Piraeus. Telegram from the crew.

In Germany, someone explained how Vermeer painted. He *relayed* his subject by mirrors or *camera obscura*, and copied not the model but the relayed image. We experimented with candles tonight and saw Vermeers: everything took on that astrological look of his canvases—with very distinct shadows and simpler, lovelier relief.

. . . .

JUNE 7 · 1952

Discovery of the perspective of time. Sketched chapter. Supposed I understood—but understood nothing. Very difficult to explain in nonscientific form. (Defense of the unknown—hence apotheosis of the theme of my book.)

Back to our human scale. Commissioned Lorenzi, the decorator at Beaulieu-sur-Mer, to make the ceilings at Santo Sospir. Drew diagrams for him with a wand to which I had attached a piece of charcoal. This is how Matisse works in his bed; he draws on the plaster of the ceiling.

In Greece I shall write the chapter on *Oedipus Rex* with Thebes for a dateline. The chapter title: "On an Oratorio."

On Patmos, I shall finish the text of *The Apocalypse*.

Finish the book before the last letter to René Bertrand,* with the chapter on the perspectives of time.

Apropos of *Oedipus Rex*, the *Nice-Matin* critic speaks of my "furious intelligence." Which means that I am just a little less stupid than he is.

Let us begin work in the new studio, where I am writing these lines.

Uselessness of important things, the human code being based on things of no importance which humans regard as the most important of all. We talk into the void; luckily there is no void. Which is why we must talk all the same.

I realize very clearly that I failed to bring off the film of *Santo Sospir* because I thought those who were helping me were more experienced than I in the realm of 16 mm film and of Kodachrome. The film is odd. It could be much more so. Besides, even though the Kodachrome is off, it captures more than if it were shot in black-and-white. True, if I had shot it in black-and-white, I wouldn't have relied on the interest presented by color, and I would have based the interest on something else. The mistake is to have believed in other people's experience, whereas the important thing is to confront techniques, to invent them as you go along, and to inflect them to your own purposes.

Riddle of time. Acropolis. The Parthenon is there. It is always

---

*Author of *La Tradition secrète* (1943); *La Sagesse perdue* (1946); *L'Univers, cette unité* (1950).

there. It has never been there. It will never be there again, and it will always be there, while never having been there. And even when it is no longer there, it will be there.

Eternity lamented: "How tiny I am!" and earth lamented: "How huge I am." They were neither tiny nor huge, but their lamentation was called "Bible." And has made a fortune for the publishers.

There is neither tiny nor huge nor slow nor fast nor low nor high nor long nor short nor eternal nor fugitive. There is nothing, and it is this nothing which does everything. And this nothing is no one. And this nothing exceeds us because we believe we are something. And everything is the cancer of something that is dying.

Imbecility of intelligence. Genius misgauges . . . a bit. It is sick. Hence it can participate in the sickness of the world—of the worlds.

What people call my intelligence is the fact that I admit my monstrous foolishness and struggle in it the way a drowning man invents swimming in order to reach land.

We have the strange luck of living between cataclysms (until further notice).

. . . .

JUNE 8 · 1952

Last night I poured out to Francine and Doudou the memories of my youth in society. I could write a chapter on the tango analogous to Michelet's on the café. Everyone had gone crazy—this was 1913: Soto and his cousin Manolo Martínez had brought the tango from Argentina, in a gramophone case. They were living in a little private house, in Montmorency. You saw old ladies there who had never before left their own rooms, aristocratic young women slumming: old ones or young would dance glued to Soto or else to Martínez. The tango madness was almost incredible, when you think of it. It marked the downfall of the Faubourg Saint-Germain. It heralded the war. The whole city was dancing the tango, whose steps were very complicated in those days. Huge gentlemen would step gravely in time to the beat, stopping on one leg, lifting the other like a dog taking a piss, exposing the soles of their patent-leather slippers. They plastered down their hair with Argentine lotions. No one paid any attention to age anymore; they just tangoed. Then came the "*Très moutarde.*" People would dance this to heroic marches like the "*Sambre et Meuse.*" Couples pasted together at the belly leaped and galloped. The ladies, heads and shoulders simulating a faint, clung with one hand to their partner's shoulder and with the other held fast to their rope of pearls. I remember one nightmare: at the princess de Polignac's,* old Princess Amédée de Broglie and Boni de Castellane were cavorting from one end to the other of the huge salon in the rue Cortambert (the one decorated by Sert with black and gold frescoes that looked like Singer sewing machines). The hostess looked like Dante. Her American accent pulverized her words, but she was kind and very funny. How good she was to artists! It was in her house that we first performed *Oedipus Rex*. Pierre Brasseur was the speaker. Instead of saying "Creon," he said "Crayon." He was in full stage makeup and wore a white tie like an airplane. He mentioned it to me just the other night at Simone Berriau's, when Lazareff was giving her the Legion of Honor. To thank the minister, Simone got up on a chair. She was gasping, crying. She unhooked her dress. "If you unhook your dress," exclaimed the minister, "I'll stick your rosette where you're not expecting it." But let's not mix up centuries: the madness of that particular decoration isn't at all like the tango madness before the war. And I hope it doesn't herald any such catastrophe. I always live in fear of such madness.

---

*Winnaretta Singer, Princess Edmond de Polignac (New York, 1865–London, 1943). She was a great patroness of the musical movements of her time. Several works by Stravinsky, Satie, Falla, Ravel, Poulenc, etc., which she commissioned, were first performed in her mansion on the avenue Henri-Martin.

. . . .

MONDAY

Deaf and dumb—that is what the French have become. What pleasure can there be in opposing this stupidity, this weakness, finding happiness despite their eagerness to destroy it, escaping when they believe they have surrounded you, falling in their midst when they've forgotten all about you, splattering them with waves.

A frivolous and academic race of idiots. Everything I detest. Remarkable minds, noble hearts float on this swamp like wrecks of the charming fleet that once was France and the city of Paris.

I shall be—all my life and after my death—misrepresented, insulted, calumniated, dragged through the mire. Doubtless I'm paying for the happiness I find in the calm and confidence of those I love. You never stop paying, and you can never pay dearly enough. An example: my mistake was to have turned, for *Bacchus*, to Jean-Louis and Madeleine. I thought we belonged to the same family. I was wrong. They are *prudent*.

The saddest spectacle is a mind between two stools.

A visit from Jean H. He has neither the sense of reality nor the sense of unreality. He cannot manage to get inside himself; he topples over with every breaker. A handsome wreck. I try to tell him something, but the words I use change their meaning when he hears them. And his weakness is stronger than any strength. He demoralizes . . . Beware of the weak who write and ask advice. Terrible demoralizers.

Finished and sent off his preface to René Bertrand.*

This morning, I tossed my cigarette butt into the water, close

---

*René Bertrand, *Sagesse et chimères*, preface by Jean Cocteau (Grasset, 1953).

to a sea anemone. The anemone grabbed it and gulped it down in a second.

Perspectives of time. In proportion as a man left our system to approach another, the time of our system would accelerate and that of the system he was approaching would slow down until it took on the rhythm of human time. If we were then to return to our system, centuries and centuries would have passed. But the perspective of time allows us to return to what man thinks is the past, according to the normal time necessitated by our journey.

Eternity exists no more than immediacy. Immediacy, eternity are words that have managed to convince us. All this must be of a dreadful simplicity.

. . . .

JUNE 10 · 1952

We left at four. And were given, just as we set out, a vile example of the human race: in the charming customs office in Nice, a Nazi-style woman insisted on searching all our bags, even our wallets and briefcases. I had brought my mail to read it on the plane. She insisted on opening all these letters. Etc.

I had forgotten a few banknotes in my briefcase. This woman dragged us into the police bureau and accused us of trying to pass foreign currency. In other circumstances, this woman would be administering torture in a camp.

THE BUREAU CHIEF: "I'm sorry, you see we can't read your names on your faces."

ME: "Then why did all the people in the airport ask for our autographs?"

THE BUREAU CHIEF: "It's a nasty job we have to do."

ME: "I don't blame you for your job. I accuse that woman of

treating travelers like criminals. Those are Gestapo tactics which don't fit in at all with yours."

This Dutch plane will be in Rome in fifteen minutes.

Rome. We are met at the plane. Immediately everything works like a charm. Hotel Excelsior. We take an old fiacre. This is the only promenade possible in a city where everyone seems to be out on promenade. It is because people were not thinking about the things I think about that they chose to build this splendor. Nor do they think, today, of what I am thinking about, and they are building no splendor.

Dinner at a restaurant on the Pincio. Unattractive crowd. Pilgrims, mostly. Among them, at one table, a woman of a beauty, a grace, an elegance which seem lost to our age: something like Garbo as a young woman. At first she seemed to me to be wearing some sort of uniform; she had tied a white scarf over her head; a gray sweater knotted over her shoulders hung down over her black dress. I supposed she was a Roman, though she was speaking French to the man opposite her. You couldn't hear the words, but you saw the shape of the words on her mouth.

I couldn't take my eyes off her, and this was made easier because she glanced at no one and nothing around her. Splendid hands, with a gold ring on the left one. I would have given a lot to know who this woman was, whose mere presence inspired an attitude of respect and discouraged any inquiry among the staff.

She was drinking a lemonade, left the table, and crossed the terrace with that same astonishing gait that Garbo had, crossing the lobby of *Grand Hotel* at the film's end.

. . . .

JUNE 11 · 1952

This morning, photographers. We plan to lunch at The Apuleius (Ostia). Stormy weather.

. . . .

JUNE 12 · 1952 · 6:00 A.M.

The chic thing in Rome is to speak French. At the restaurant last night, what seemed to be all of Roman high society was gathered and speaking French. Rather carelessly. Except for one or two very discreet types, no one recognized our table. This restaurant looked like the one at La Fenice in Venice: you eat out in the street—inconceivable in Paris, where a crowd would gather to watch, judge, deride, and quickly turn aggressive. In Rome people pass, do not watch *other people*, and if they do, it is impossible to notice it.

Fiacre. Hotel. (Yesterday, ran into Cesare Pavani and Ruspoli at the hotel. When he does his film with Pabst,* Jeannot will stay with Cesare.)

Paperwork madness. Absurdity of all the pages you have to fill out on a plane (besides the fact that anyone can write anything) and of the fact that people who are not "regulation" are always perfectly in order. Endless and incomprehensible questionnaires.

In the Rome–Athens plane (English). We fly over the Gulf of Taranto, the Ionian Sea. A confused departure because of the time it took to settle the bill at the Hotel Excelsior. The Marquise† is like a child afraid of missing the Acropolis.

The fly inside the airplane does not share our sense of time. Wrote several notes for the chapter on perspectives of time. Received in Rome a telegram from René Bertrand in answer to my preface. I wrote him from Rome that if some famous scholar would undertake the preface, he should drop mine, which I wrote in case some famous mathematician hesitated to support a philosopher, or a philosopher hesitated to support a historian, and so on. These

---

*G. W. Pabst's film with Jean Marais, Aldo Fabrizzi, and Daniel Gélin was called *La Maison du silence*.

†"The Marquise" and later "The Marquis" are Cocteau's playful designations for Francine Weisweiller and Édouard Dermit.

men of science set great store by labels and fear to lose their standing because of the interest they might show in a work outside their field. In this case, there remains the poet, who is a philosopher and a mathematician and who is not regarded as such. For example, the scientists concerned with the atom bomb never think of the atom as a solar system analogous to ours. They believe in the infinitely small and the infinitely large and never deal with the problem of the perspectives which lead us to believe in different dimensions, whereas there is only one.

My right hand is in deplorable condition. "Desquamation," the Marquise says, and adds: "We're flying over the Ionian Sea." "The Marquise is increasingly lucid," says the Marquis—"it's the cold."

As a matter of fact, the Marquise was shivering—as in the house in London. The Marquis declares: "We have three more hours of shiver, but in three hours you will be even more learned. You'll know everything."

The nice thing about the boat is that when we reach Greece, we'll get back to a regular domicile and our habits. I was careful not to inform the embassy of our arrival; they might make things easier with customs but would complicate our stay. My program is to take Francine right up to the Acropolis, to the Theater of Dionysus—to the little agora. If the cold in this plane doesn't oblige us to be taken to a hospital first.

The Marquise, being frozen, no longer professes. She terrorizes the stewardess, who turns on the heat as we enter the Isthmus of Corinth. Here begins that pastel blue you never see anywhere else and islands the color of suntanned skin.

We are twenty minutes from Athens. The Marquise regains her spirits. Snow on the mountains. Mauve clouds. The plane is warm.

We were wrong not to tell Paul [a sailor on the *Orphée II*] to meet us at the airport. He would have taken the bags to Piraeus, and we would have been free of luggage.

My poor right hand reminds me of Canon Mugnier's, which

were always so amazing when you touched them—tiny lizard hands. A lizard with bright eyes, a crest, a muzzle, and that astonishing swiftness in its movements, so that it flicked from one person to the next: wherever you went, he was there. And yet you could always find him in his rooms in the rue Méchain, his door and his heart wide open to visitors. He was "*ubiquique*," as Misia Sert used to say. I remember asking an old and very famous headwaiter which guests he encountered most frequently around a table, and his answer: "Mrs. Edith Wharton and the abbé Mugnier."

The approach to Greece always gives me the same pleasure—a kind of cheerfulness. I seem to be coming home again. In France, alas, I can no longer go home.

. . . .

JUNE 13 · 1952

Arrival at the Athens airport.* The Marquise upset at not being met by Colonel Fuller. Friendly inspection. Very difficult to make it understood that we are meeting a yacht. The Colonel appears and makes everything easy. He is one of those American warriors who are as little American as can be imagined. Francine met him in Pau, where he was parachuted in during the German retreat. He takes us in his jeep to the little yacht basin, where his sailboat is not far from ours. Here we find Paul, the other sailors, and the impeccable *Orphée II*, after a very rough journey (Nice–Athens) which becomes the Odyssey when Paul tells it. A little more and the fables would begin. What strikes me is how impossible it is,

---

*Though ancient Greece and its mythology were important sources of inspiration for Cocteau (Antigone, Oedipus, Orpheus), he did not visit Greece until March 31, 1936, when he passed through Athens on his trip "Around the World in 80 Days." He returned in 1949, on his theatrical tour (*Maalesh*), and this latter stay, from May 16 to 23, inspired the poem "*Le Rhythme grec.*"

in 1952, to explain that a trip has no other purpose than traveling for its own sake. Espionage rules. Paul and the others have had to endure countless and interminable questionings.

"Why are you traveling?"

"What are you carrying? What are you hiding?"

"Our captain is a young woman who wants to visit the islands."

"That is a meaningless answer."

Moreover, in southern Italy and in Greece, more fishermen refuse to take French money. They want pounds or dollars. They are not even willing to sell a liter of oil.

"The ship behaved very well." That was the leitmotif of the crew. Here, black bread and privation. Athens is the most expensive city in Europe. Not only the first shock of millions of drachmas. The merest thing is priceless. Not much water. It was only four years ago that you got water only twice a week. Now you get it only mornings. This is why ancient Greece regarded springs as divine. Besides, they must have had irrigation systems that were much more ingenious than in our day, when we depend on the faucet.

In Ostia, they had just discovered a huge region of the old Roman roads with splendid plumbing that brought the water from Rome, whereas nowadays there is no water from Rome to be had.

We go at once to the Acropolis, to the theaters, to the Tower of the Winds. The same desire to weep, the same strange anguish. The reason for this overwhelming feeling is that we are visiting the graves of intelligence and of beauty. Everything here will be done away with eventually because *it isn't in line*. And it isn't in line because *it is the line*. That is the drama. The line is lost. At the Theater of Dionysus, to the left of the entrance, we find the gigantic phallus lying in the grass.

At the tavern opposite the Theater of Herod Atticus, I experience that poignant abolition of time—I seem never to have left this place where we saw the spotlights illuminate the tiny marble cage of the Wingless Victory. We heard the choruses. We stayed under the pepper trees, invisible throughout the entire performance.

Sun this morning and the sky a brighter blue than any other sky in the world. Colonel Fuller is going ahead of us to the islands. We'll be joining him this afternoon. Paul has gone to the consulate for the passports. Francine to the bank for dollars.

The elegant tavern of Piraeus is called: Chez Lapin.

The abolition of time is more apparent on a boat than anywhere else. Here you rediscover your carapace. You climb the ladder. You are amazed to be in Greece. You thought this cockpit belonged to Saint-Jean or to Port-Cros.

(For the chapter on the perspective of time.)*

Seems—the word that comes most readily to the point of my pen. It seems to me. It seems, if you look closely . . . For an observer, it would seem . . . It seems to mean . . . If you step back, it seems—it seems, if you come closer. Seems long, seems short, seems small, seems huge, seems far, seems near, etc. Now what seems to be is not or is something else. And it seems to me that this something else is what seems to most people to be the nothingness that seems to me to be a substance singularly stuffed with what seems movement and life.

Paul has spent over four million drachmas since he dropped anchor in the harbor. Everything costs money. The merest stamp on the merest paper costs twenty to thirty thousand francs. To repatriate the additional sailor of the Nice–Athens trip cost Paul fifty thousand francs; he managed to argue them down to thirty-five thousand.

On an island, Paul went to find bread; they brought him a loaf of black bread; he tried to pay. "You can't," he was told. "It costs too much. We'll give it to you."

One of the reasons that makes the *Orphée II* suspect is that little

*This chapter was finally to be called "Of Distances" in *Journal d'un inconnu*.

yachts never come so far in Greece. An ostentatious luxury would be *an explanation*. Francine's invisible luxury — that imperceptible fortune—does not provide a *justifying spectacle*, does not inspire that abject respect for gold.

Many Athenians have never walked up to the Acropolis. And it annoys them to hear it talked about. *Is the past all we have?* Alas, yes.

Invulnerable solidity of myth. It is the lie that becomes truth—whereas history is truth that becomes a lie.

The king and queen are in Ankara.* Marika Kotopouli is on tour in Istanbul. She is to perform in the new open-air theater.

My one pride is to realize that the performance of *Oedipus Rex* would be perfectly appropriate in the Theater of Dionysus. In scale and in style. Of that I am sure. But alas, the Greeks put on very mediocre productions, in which the great tragic ceremony is lost. The scene of Athena and the men with horses' heads would be sublime on the Acropolis.† Today's audiences would think I was making fun of them and of the Greek myths.

I live on a desert island in the middle of our times and of France. Doudou and Francine are my *Fridays*.

Four million drachmas to get out of the harbor. Greece is a powerful organization against tourism. Tourism would be its one and only (and magnificent) gilt-edged security. Apart from tourism, which it frustrates, Greece has no resources. Sand and myths. The tourists enrich Italy and the Côte d'Azur. Greece protects itself against tourism and is ruining itself. A mother of a family tells me: "We can't afford to live in Athens—too great a luxury." And the food is so poor. And the water comes between nine and eleven in the morning.

A Greek in New York. He asks when the water is turned on. Astonishment. And the electricity? Astonishment. Hot water? He

---

*First official visit of the Greek sovereigns Paul I and Frederika to Turkey.

†Second *tableau vivant* of *Oedipus Rex*: "Sadness of Athena."

is told that water, hot water and electricity are on all the time. The Greek: "But that's prewar. You're terribly out of date." Etc.

A Russian to an American: *"You're free to do what you like? That's chaos!"*

Just had an *excellent* lunch on board. We are all set. Leaving in an hour for the islands, where we are to join Colonel Fuller.

In antiquity, Greece was rich on account of her silver mines. The mines exhausted—nothing was left. Olive oil.

Three o'clock. Sailing. Friday the thirteenth.

At Piraeus people have fish to eat—but don't know how to fry it. They burn it.

In mirrors and especially in photographs, I notice that I have grown old. But it is what is young in me that notices it. It is a young man who sees an old one. He is amazed—without bitterness and with respect, the way youth regards old age among noble peoples. (In China, for instance.) My youth respects my old age. My old age protects my youth. That is why I am at peace.

We are sailing for the islands. Sun and a fresh breeze. We drop anchor around six o'clock in Poros—which looks a great deal like Port-Cros. We spend the night in a tiny creek. In the morning we will set sail for other islands (June 14, 1952).

. . . .

JUNE 14 · 1952

The Sleeping Woman. Huge profile constituted by the mountains—extraordinary resemblance to my painting of a sleeping woman, at Santo Sospir.

We sail past the village, or the village past us. Perfect style of the houses—very simple and without the shadow of an architectural affectation. The tile roofs seem to be hollowed out, draped like an awning. Vines decorate the walls.

As we leave the coast, the sleeping woman appears before us, facing the opposite way from the one at Santo Sospir. She occupies the whole background, and several peaks sculpt her: the long black shape of our arrival. The mountains silhouetted in a bright pink sky.

The *Orphée II* navigates through the deep waters of the archipelago. Poros is one of the only green islands. The islands which surround us would have, from a bird's-eye view, the color of human bodies. The Fullers' purple sail accompanies us on the right. Two and a half to three hours to our second port of call (Port Molos, Hydra), (maybe to Spetsai). Navy blue sea. Veering wind. Our sails hang limp. I understand why the Greeks wore out their pockets and their hearts in sacrifices to gain favorable winds. There is always a dead calm, as soon as the wind drops, toward evening. They managed with their galley slaves. The galley slaves were their only motor force—the whip and the oars.

We coast down Hydra, an island without water [sic]. Mrs. Fuller tells me about what happened to Piaf in Greece. She arrived in Athens; everyone was expecting a Parisian beauty. She sang out of doors, with the racket of the streetcars turning at the corner of the stage. Astonishment at her appearance. She sang and was hissed. Pennies thrown. The second night, more pennies and hisses. The third night she triumphed. Those who had hissed applauded. By the end of the week she was worshiped; she had conquered Athens.

One always imagines that films go everywhere. No one has ever seen my films in Athens. (Except for *The Eternal Return* and *Beauty and the Beast*.)

I have the impression that *Orpheus* would astonish—would scandalize. The keepers of the myths would not understand that myths die if they are not adapted to the times.

Bare, bald, myth-scoured islands.

A centaur would not be the least bit surprising in these mountains.

The English are loathed everywhere. Very few remain in Greece. Greece tolerates Americans, who help the country. For them, America represents the war. The advantage of Frenchmen on tour is that they no longer represent anything. Nothing matters but individuals. Personalities.

There are islands one does not approach. Either because of mines or because of DPs. Paul has had to fall back to the entrance to the Isthmus of Corinth; American submarines were on night maneuvers.

High sea. All the bottles in the medicine cabinet were falling out. To our left, the Fullers' purple sail. Its reflections on the waves reached the *Orphée II*: like blood on the water.

We approach the coast. It is six-thirty at night.

The legend of Psyche is *word for word* that of Beauty and the Beast.

Why the Athenians had tiny buttocks: because Theseus dined with Hades in the underworld, but Hades fastened him to his chair. Theseus managed to wrench himself free by leaving half his posterior behind. (Mythologists.)

I have Doudou read me long passages of mythology on deck. It is splendid that the mythologists preserve the seriousness of historians and treat fables as the reality they become by the sturdiness of their texture. I had forgotten certain details of the myth of Actaeon.* For instance, when his dogs go howling after him, trying to find him, and enter the cavern of the centaur Chiron, who to console them carves them a statue of their master.

And Aius Locutius, the god who spoke only once, who manifested himself only once, and to whom Camillus, conqueror of the Gauls, raised a statue on the Palatine.

---

*At the Villa Santo Sospir, Jean Cocteau represented the metamorphosis of Actaeon on one of the walls of Francine Weisweiller's bedroom.

Spetsai

Ruins make me sad. They are the grave of the beautiful. But Spetsai is alive. Is it possible that such an island exists? It is almost incredible. On this island, ugliness has never set foot. It is so beautiful that ugliness detests it and keeps away. So elegant that vulgarity perishes on contact.

Everywhere at sea the soft whistle of the buoys. Under a sky where the stars form a block, a hard rock into which our own world is integrated. The bushel of bees Max Jacob wrote about.

You would like to live in each house, sit in each square, go into every shop open to the soul's depths.

If France were to become unendurable, I know that Spetsai exists and that you could grow old here in one of these little white houses, and no longer see ridiculous shapes around you.

P.S. I was wrong. In the morning, I discovered that ugliness had set foot on the island (in the form of a hotel—Istanbul-style).

June 15 · 1952

Sailed around the island. Enchanting lunch with a family of peasants. Perfect education of the peasants and their children in these islands. Once *everyone* was well brought up, I suppose. What we have learned is not a good education but a bad one. In palaces, alas, all children are badly brought up. They are taught to be so.

Have brought the father, the little boy, and the little girl on board the *Orphée II*. The father, when he drank some framboise, said in Greek: "After this glass I'll go to Salamis. After the next I'll go to Paris."

The children eat some chocolate, for the first time. The creek is surrounded by the noise of cicadas. It looks like the harbor of

Les Porquerolles. But it is Greece. Gods with nothing terrible, nothing vague about them. Gods who are concerned with human affairs, who marry the wives of men and give them children. Births of imaginary heroes who walk on earth and marry one another in the underworld.

Here one suffers less from the anguish of being nothing, and from the lie of perspectives. These seas and these mountains can make you forget the cataclysms from which they resulted. A charm conceals from us the tragedy of their origins.

The gods are the living paintings of a *ceiling*.

One-thirty. Motor working. We leave the gulf. The family waves farewell with bed sheets and tablecloths.

Swam all morning in water that is air, only a little denser.

Five o'clock. We arrive at Nauplia. We anchor in the middle of the harbor, disembark. Uniformed sailors are waiting for us—and we don't understand a word of what they are saying. They seem to be trying to pick a quarrel. Francine, in a rage, goes with Paul to their captain, who speaks French and explains our misunderstanding: the sailors wanted to be friendly, to show us to a hotel, and to offer us freedom of the port—they were trying to tell us, apparently, that the yacht could tie up alongside the quay. It all sounded as if they were working us over.

Nauplia lacks charm. Too many forts and memories of the Turks, the Venetians, the dukes of Athens. Tomorrow we go to Epidaurus (morning), to Mycenae in the afternoon. Huge fish leap out of the gold and purple sea. In the distance, opposite, the mountains of Argos and Lerna.

Tonight a phenomenon I have never observed before: the sea so calm that all the stars in the sky are reflected in it, even those of the Milky Way. Thus the sea becomes a sky, even deeper. If you lean over the side, you get dizzy—the impression of leaning over the side of an ocean liner from a dizzying height. Yet if you throw your cigarette over the side, the water is right there. Such illusions lead to reflections on the illusions of our optic.

. . . .

JUNE 16 · 1952

This morning the water is so transparent that the yacht seems suspended in midair. We are leaving at two for Epidaurus and Mycenae—five hours' sailing.

Dosia Fuller tells me about the death of Beloyannis. All the details in the newspapers. The mistake of making martyrs. If you set this argument against that of punishment, you are accused of being a leftist. Before dying, Beloyannis said: "I am dying the way the first Christians died, with this difference, that I am dying not for heavenly glory, but for the earthly glory of my comrades." My signature has been noted on the petition, but it was not known that the French Communist journals attributed the initiative of that petition to me.

The Fullers are leaving us—going back to Athens.

Last night I picked up some splendid stones on the beach and enlivened them with ink. I was surrounded by the five or six people on the island and their children. Dosia Fuller translated their observations for me. Our own dear critics could learn something. In these islands, the instinct for shapes and lines is admirable. Nothing distorts it.

In order to pay for our meal, we had to make some sort of trade: a little present of gowns and suits for the children. They give us eggs and ouzo.

The huge phallus lying in the grass at the Theater of Dionysus is the proof of general inattention. It seems to have escaped the priests and the archaeologists. Wonderful image of the intellectual freedom of a people without complexes, glorifying the powers which Catholicism teaches its followers to hold in shame. Perhaps we could steal it—camouflage it on the yacht some night. But either because the area to the left of the theater is not inspected or because no one knows where to put such a thing if it is taken from where it is lying, it will remain there in the grass, and other travelers as curious about the real Greece as we are will have to come back and discover the anatomical precision of the glans from which drips a heavy drop of sperm.

It is likely that four or seven of these phalloi supported the stage between curly-haired satyrs. The extraordinary expression of the far-left satyr, fallen back and apparently swooning.

All the radios are on full blast until midnight. French and Greek tunes—or else those Greek songs so tragically weighted with the oriental rhythm of sobs.

. . . .

JUNE 17 · 1952

This morning at nine we disembark and find the taxi reserved for Epidaurus. The father, the brother, and the little boy in front, the rest of us in back. A fine-looking car, but unfortunately the batteries are low and the motor is that of a very old Ford. Endless breakdowns. No water. We turn back. Search for salt water at the bottom of a well among the olive trees, in sultry heat.

Mycenae. Bath. Lunch. Nap. We set out for Epidaurus at four-thirty in another car.

Nauplia. The Lernean Hydra. Lerna has several springs whose water turns to marshes. If you block one, the water pours out of another. These are the heads of the Hydra. It lived under a plane tree. The Lernean marshes and fertilizer plants befoul the harbor of Nauplia. We all feel sick. And Hercules has not cut off all the heads.

Yesterday we performed a retrochronological tour, visiting Epidaurus from four to six and Mycenae from six to nine. This was the equivalent of leaving the century of Louis XIV for the Middle Ages.

Epidaurus. Nothing is left of this sumptuous resort but some rich foliage, some scattered stones, the skeleton of the theater shaped like a megaphone (it holds fourteen thousand spectators), and the museum where you can examine certain luxury details. For instance, the ceiling of the rotunda of the Temple of Asclepius where carefully carved, realistic lilies fill each cella.

On the square of the hotel and the baths, we find a tiny labyrinth in the form of a snail. Here the doctors would shut up their patient; he would be lost, half-dead with fear; fear cured him by shock effect. Votive inscriptions testify to these miraculous cures. It was Lourdes, but of an incredible luxury and wealth.

I was greatly intrigued by the hole at the bottom of the corollas of the lilies in the rotunda ceiling. Most likely a pistil stuck out of them, with a tiny night-light, as in the mosques. Unfortunately there is no one to tell us anything about the thousand enigmas we can only guess at. Dull absurdity of the *Guide Bleu*. It blurs the mind and dries up the imagination. Especially at Mycenae, where we go next.

Mycenae. We happened to get there (because of the breakdown this morning) after sunset, at that hour when solitaries loathe their solitude. The sky was crystalline. Against it were silhouetted mauve, violet, and bluish mountains. Everywhere the plains were striped with yellow lines. The eyrie of the Atridal overlooked a vast amphitheater of empty fields. It was flanked by a cone-shaped rocky mountain. This was the typical site of the tragedies. Her blood flowed from its source. The great names of the Atridae seem to designate giant persons of long life. In reality they killed each other off and perished very young. But they grow huge with distance according to the laws of the perspectives of time, which occur inversely to those of space.

Schliemann must have seen something terrible. That king in a gold mask, buried, hidden, to the right of the lion gate, in a tiny cave, with all his followers sacrificed to accompany him.

The first thing that strikes you is that it wouldn't have been difficult to push the king into the pool and, if he were wearing his armor, to see him drown at the bottom. The water was brought in by an aqueduct, drawn from the depths of sinister cellars. The ground is smooth, varnished, polished by bare feet. I take off my shoes, and my soles slip as though on ice. Agisthus and Clytemnestra had no trouble hiding that splendid service of gold vessels. Mycenae is a scene of crimes of boredom, of neuroses, of furious outcries. Even at Nauplia we imagined that the soldiers were berating us. What must have been the style of that harsh, barked Greek of the period!

Of the sublime palaces of Argos, not even a shadow survives. A tiny, extremely ugly little town replaces the proud architecture of Achaios.

On the other hand, Mycenae is an eagle's nest. Nothing abides, and everything remains. Clambering like goats over these huge blocks, we have no difficulty imagining what it was; the Carpathians and Arabia teach us the mores of these sumptuous creatures of prey.

Which does not keep Barrès from being right: "The hog has rooted out the truffle." One would like to see the arms of the king of kings and his gold mask on the spot. It must have looked like a terrifying bee in a hive, one of those hives that form tiny villages on every rocky slope, villages among which the beekeeper circulates in his black mask, proportionally gigantic, like death.

I was forgetting to say that the road to Mycenae is lined on either side, all the way, with flowering laurel, red and white. It is a Royal Way.

The famous things are the ones that very few persons know. The rest, those that everyone thinks he knows. More and more I realize that no one knows anything.

A girl drowns. The father says: "My luck—the river god has taken my daughter." That was the Greek spirit. A logical and mythological mind.

We left Nauplia at two in the afternoon. Victims of the Hydra. Pestilential vapors. Terrible coughing fits during the night. Convalescence this morning, as though I had been sick for a long time. Slow motion. Fresh air up on deck. Down below, the motor warms the cabins. We head for Spetsai, where we will anchor, reprovision, and from which we will make for the southern islands.

. . . .

JUNE 18 · 1952

Agamemnon. He supposed himself the king of the world. He was the king of a few hills and a few little islands, on our poor little earth. He would give his kingdom for the motor of our yacht. And I would give the yacht for a flying saucer. Etc. What do I not possess? said Alexander. A cigarette lighter. A wristwatch. A jeep.

Took presents to the nice family living at the creek mouth. All the children on deck. Immediate departure for Spetsai, from which we will sail by night for Crete. I would like to see Candia [Iráklion], Knossos and return to the Isthmus of Corinth, stopping off at Santorin. To pay homage to the island of the *gymnopaedias*.*

---

*Dance of naked boys in honor of the Dorian Apollo, which took place on the festival dancing floor of Thera (Santorin). For Jean Cocteau, this erotic memory is evidently combined with that of Satie's *Trois gymnopédies* (1888), one of his favorite works by this composer.

After having dived into the sea, Francine and Doudou dive into *Joseph Balsamo* and *The Black Tulip*. I'd like to see Spetsai again—although by day it was not so beautiful as by night, when it seemed to me a little derelict of beauty.

Since we got away from the breath of the Lernean Hydra, my chest has stopped hurting.

In the distance, our islands and our Cap-Ferrat are as fine as all the islands and capes in the world. All they lack are a few temples. The Greeks had built them there, but the stones have been taken away for the construction of the harbor of Monaco, a principality which possesses the last temple where the worship of the god Chance and the goddess Fortune is practiced—turning on a roulette wheel.

. . . .

JUNE 19 · 1952

Ascot. Alec's horse, Mât de Cocagne, is running today. How far we are from Ascot and from races. In blue water, making for Crete.

When I speak of a frivolous Greece, with accommodating gods of an extreme indulgence, I speak of the Greece of Athens and the Parthenon. A royal and Voltairean age. The other Greece, the one I am visiting, resembles it no more than Catherine de Médicis resembles Mme de Pompadour. Murders, poisonings, consulting the oracle, carrying out its orders. The Greeks must have believed very deeply in their gods to sacrifice their daughter. To them such a sacrifice seemed essential in order to win the favor of the winds. One realizes what this leads to on a sea navigable only one month in the year (June), without a single breeze, and the rest of the year a prey to storms between the islands or to cruel heat.

Noon. Paul has turned off the motor, which was heating up. The sails droop. The water is a methylene blue jelly. We will sail for a day and a night and arrive in Crete tomorrow evening. We shall rediscover oriental Greece. Maurras's old scholars admire only decadent Greece, such decadence being the high point of a civilization, the acme which precedes the decline whose depths we are now sinking to.

Yesterday evening, in the Spetsai harbor, I was looking at the yacht that belonged to a young woman of Athens. (She owns one of the very few yachts in Piraeus.) She herself had an American quality; trousers like ours; a boy's voice and gait. On the yacht, someone had cranked up an old phonograph and was playing Greek records at top volume. Old scratched records. So here was a girl who had escaped the tradition and yet was loyal to the tradition, but without a touch of grace. And since I suspect her of being incapable of sacrificing herself or of killing a member of the crew to gain the west wind, she remains where she is, fallen between two stools.

Each time our sailors land, they are asked if they are Communists. They answer that they live at sea and that at sea there is no politics. Very suspect in Greece, where around six in the evening the squares are filled with groups of men who talk of nothing but politics. Saint Paul's epistles show us that nothing has changed.

No news from France. Neither papers nor letters nor telegrams can reach us. At sea it is as if a flood had drowned all such things.

While I am writing on deck, a little breeze rises. The sails fill. The *Orphée II* gently advances.

Too bad Apollo doesn't embellish our critics with asses' ears to punish them for their declarations. On the other hand, he does grant certain persons the gift of turning to gold whatever they touch. I know such persons, and it is killing them. On occasion avarice obliges them to die of hunger.

Greece attributes the invention of pederasty either to Orpheus (after the death of Eurydice) or to Thamyris, son of Philammon and the nymph Argiope (for love of Hyacinthus). Or else to Minos, lover of Theseus, to whom he gave his daughter in order not to lose him.

Hubris (the personification of Excess and Insolence) is the reigning goddess in 1952.

The birth of Typhon, son of the earth, a monster whose fingers ended in heads and who can step over mountains, cast them into the sea, etc. . . . proves that the Greeks of the earliest antiquity were aware of one of those cataclysms from which our cycle proceeds. What is incomprehensible is that Greece is reduced to dust, to fragments, whereas many civilizations came after the cataclysms, and their landscapes where ruins are lying have not changed configuration. It is difficult to imagine men giving themselves up to this destructive, ruinous, and gigantic labor. I know that Catholics and Turks are capable of anything and everything, but still, they had to possess the means of destruction. Hatred and stupidity are not enough. It is easy to destroy a work by Sophocles, less so to destroy Eleusis.

Morosini's imprudence explains the ruin of the Parthenon. But Eleusis? But Epidaurus? But Mycenae?

Left Spetsai at eight this morning. It is now six-thirty. The boat is rolling. We had to take in sail and turn on the motor. We pass within sight of Cythera.

I have only just now realized why the Greek dances are performed by men who seem to watch their feet very carefully. These dances came with Theseus to Delos, where he invented a votive dance for the young men rescued from the labyrinth. This dance imitated the windings of the labyrinth, and the dancers watched their feet as though seeking their way. Now and then one snapped his fingers, one clapped his knees or a hand against his heel to signify his delight at being on the right path. Back in Athens after Aegeus's suicide, Theseus imports this dance, adding to it a funereal character which you can still observe today on the dancers' faces.

. . . .

JUNE 20 · 1952

What Theseus saw as he approached Greece we saw this morning around eight, in a sun very dangerous for the wax of Icarus's wings. Engine trouble. At anchor in a high swell. Paul overhauls. We are still fifty miles from Candia. We start up again at ten. Patches of snow on the mountaintops.

One o'clock. We turn off the motor, which is overheating. These necessary and unpleasant stops (because of the swell) keep us from arriving before dark. We wait on deck.

Minos in love with Theseus. Pasiphaë still infatuated with her white bull and furious that her son is imprisoned because he has his father's head. Phaedra, who calls her mother a cow, her father a pederast, and thinks of nothing but escaping from the island. Ariadne in love with Theseus; Icarus in love with Ariadne and tells her the secret of the thread; Ariadne tells it to Theseus in return for a promise of marriage. Theseus conspires with Phaedra to abandon her sister at Naxos, etc. A nice play, impossible to write because of the exhaustion I feel at the thought of my contemporaries' extreme stupidity. The closer the *Orphée* gets to the coast of Crete, the more clearly the play looms in my mind, and the more certain I am to give it up—I have had enough of an imbecile Europe.

Scenario. The journey of the twelve young men and the twelve maidens, taken to Crete to be "devoured by the Minotaur." Endless journey, judging by ours. Atmosphere of a tuberculosis sanatorium. Since the monster is herbivorous, it is easy to see that the twelve maidens and twelve young men are destined to serve other appetites.

. . . .

JUNE 21 · 1952

Ugliness and stupidity are two powerful goddesses, against whom intelligence and beauty possess few weapons. The ugliness of Candia is Turkish. We have anchored in a harbor full of wreckage and construction machinery. This morning we went to Knossos. Knossos is worth a long sea journey. Thanks to the wonderful excavations of Sir Arthur Evans, one strolls about *chez* Minos. The palace must have given rise to the story of the labyrinth. If this exquisite anthill were not laid open to the sky, one would easily get lost. One keeps climbing up, then down, and turning back to where one started; one thinks one is getting out and finds oneself back at the final cul-de-sac of a key pattern or a volute. Here is the example of a decadence which is the fine flower of a civilization. Then comes the decadence of decadence and the modern garbage can. The frescoes are astonishingly elegant and fresh.

Majorelle, Lalique, Maxim's—but at the source. The red and dark blue columns narrowing to their base, the doors, the terraces, the chambers, the lyre-shaped bull's horns—all this inextricable entanglement of floors and corridors, surrounded by a circle of mountains, affords no tragic atmosphere, no notion of dread. Everywhere grow the flowers reinvented by the motifs of the frescoes.

The modern Cretans—cretins—respect these enchanting images only to the degree that they bring in money. Like the Antibes museum and Picasso. Picasso is profitable. Detested, but profitable.

Opposite Crete, here is the green sea and the dark blue strip and a wild island whose shape and color are those of the young princes and the lovely ladies on the walls of Knossos. In Knossos everything was noble. In Candia everything is vile. And proud of being so. Once the indispensable was beautiful. Now the indispensable is miserable. To each his own.

The slaves have become the masters. I discover the consequences.

Majorelle. Lalique – [illegible] l'origine. Les colonnes larges à haut, étroites à bas, les portes, les lucarnes, les chambres, les cornes du taureau en forme de lyre, tout est [illegible] pas d'étages et de corridors, au milieu d'un cirque de montagnes, ne donnent aucune idée tragique, aucune idée d'effroi. Partout formes de fleurs [illegible] des motifs de fougères.

Le crétois moderne ou "crétin" ne respectait ces songes délicieux que dans la mesure où elles rapportent. C'est le musée d'antiques et Picasso. Picasso rapporte. On le déteste, mais il rapporte.

En face de la Crète on a la mer verte et [illegible] marine et une île [illegible] dont les formes et la couleur sont celles des [illegible] dans les musées de Knossos. Tout était mollesse. Tout est ignoble à Candie.

Et fin de l'été. [illegible] était beau. L'[illegible] est infect. À chacun sa chacune.

[illegible] J'[illegible] ce qu'[illegible].

[illegible] à Knossos – [illegible] idiote. [illegible]

[illegible] Je ne m'étonne plus que personne au monde ne vienne visiter les îles.

×

[illegible] musée de Candie. [illegible] comme Thésée, [illegible]. Comme Phèdre [illegible] pas vers Naxos mais vers Santorin – vers le large.

*

Forbidden to film Knossos. Wretched ruling. A thousand explanations to prove where the millions come from to pay for our gasoline. I am no longer surprised that no one comes to visit the islands.

At three-thirty we visit the Candia museum. Tonight we shall escape—like Theseus, like Ariadne, like Phaedra, like Daedalus and Icarus, not to Naxos but to Santorini—to the open sea.

The most amazing fresco of all is that of the acrobats. One of them is tossed by the bull's horns. He performs the *salto mortale* and falls back into the hands of a third.

To the left, one of the ladies in blue.

The photographs mistakenly put "lady in blue" under the image of the acrobats.

Candia museum. Shameful. So much genius, grace, luxury, in the hands of officials who follow us from case to case as if we were thieves, and a director who authorizes us to shoot pictures in Knossos for twenty minutes. We return as soon as possible, before the sun makes using Kodachrome impossible; unfortunately all the light at five o'clock is backward—the huge inextricable palace that basked in the morning sun was, after the afternoon hours, in shadow.

Back to the harbor. Paul has had a terrible time getting gasoline. Here everything is a matter of knowing someone and dollars. Everything to discourage tourism. Filthy stupidity. We shall be sailing in an hour, if customs deigns to give us back our papers.

In Minos's palace, the young men and women were vases of flowers. The vases of flowers were young men and women. The frescoes in relief were human hills, and the hills, reliefs in the shape of human bodies. Everything was related, everything matched, everything blossomed into lilies and coiled into volutes. You leave the ruins of Knossos feeling exalted, light, without fatigue. You leave them by passing between a little café and a fountain from which you drink the water. Water in Greece is a treasure.

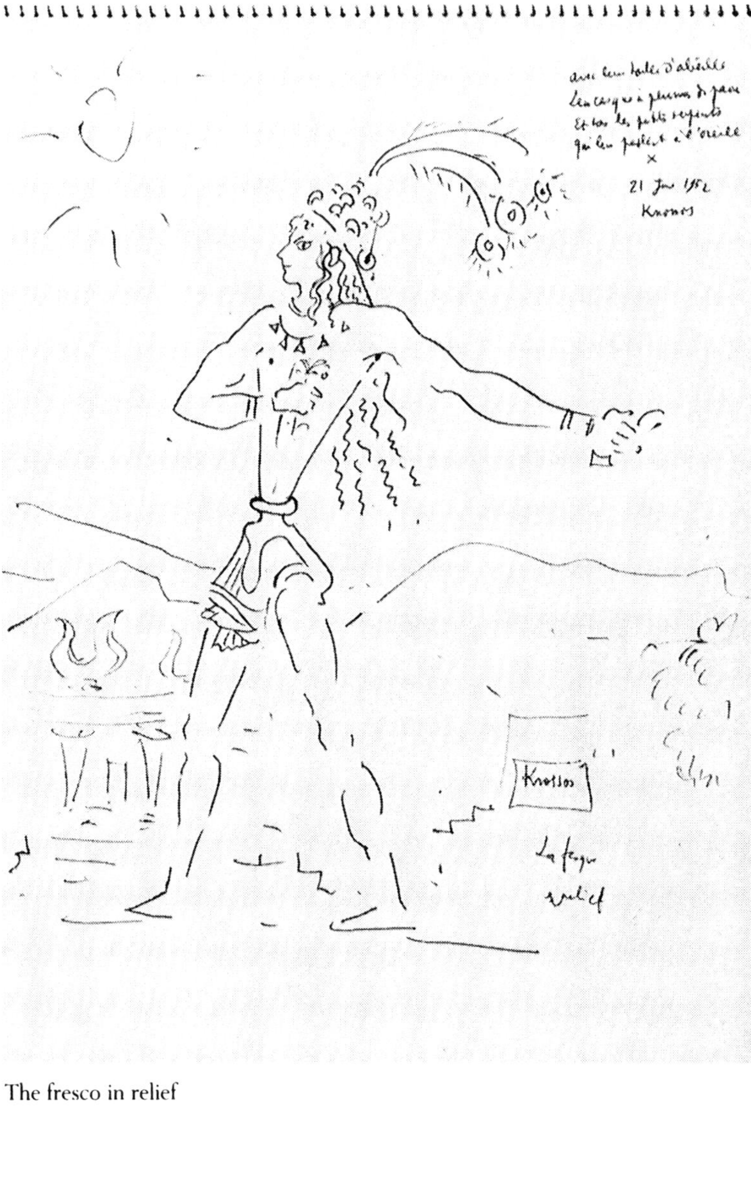

The fresco in relief

At sea. After absurd difficulties. The Cretans have not seen a French yacht since Mme Coty's cruise in 1928. Their rudeness, their ill breeding exceed all bounds. Of course, there are friendly exceptions who try to arrange matters, but they are exceptional. How people so noble and so refined can become so wretched—it is disconcerting! If only the little donkeys that trot along the roads could govern Crete. Everything would be better, as on Gulliver's island of the horses.

A fool is in charge of the Candia museum. I sent Édouard to obtain authorization to film Knossos. The fool asks if it is for commercial purposes. Édouard mentions my name. The fool knows me quite well, for when he authorized our filming for twenty minutes, he spelled my name perfectly. After Knossos, return to the museum. The fool doesn't speak to me. I see him walk off, arm and arm with a plump girl, probably a student. Crete suffers from a murderous inferiority complex. Never has Greek history recorded its resistances and rebellions. Crete takes revenge on anyone who visits: mistakes ill breeding for national pride.

Crete. This is the first time I have been impolitely received in all my travels.

The frescoes I made for Francine are as beautiful as Knossos. But it will take centuries and ruins to make them visible and respectable.

On the excuse of exalting souls, Catholicism has murdered beauty. It is, alas, almost invariably at the scene of the crime.

In Greece, the Catholics and the Turks have ruined everything.

What struck me the most at the Candia museum: the black stone bull's head, white-veined with red crystal eyes; the wooden swimmer; the gold pendant of two bees; the terra-cotta women with movable feet.

One-thirty in the morning. Halfway. Calm sea. Sky seething with what Claudel calls "the great incontestable stars." What is more contestable than these incomprehensible worlds, most of which

The ladies in blue, Knossos

are dead and which prove nothing? Which terrify . . . Lying on my back, I look up at this dreadful silent explosion. *Le Soulier de satin* is stuffed with these empty phrases whose lyricism astounds the actresses who perform it, as the actresses in Voltaire's tragedies were astounded. Mlle Clairon declares she enjoys the roles of Racine and Corneille but so much less than those of Voltaire. Marie Bell imagines herself sanctified by *Le Soulier de satin*. Madeleine and Jean-Louis are close to believing the same thing. Claudel's success in the theater is the success of a gala performance of *Irene*. Voltaire amazed a credulous age; Claudel amazes an unbelieving one. He props himself on the priests the way Voltaire propped himself on the Encyclopedists. Their souls are of about the same value.

. . . .

JUNE 24 · 1952

Saint-Jean—last year we celebrated it in the Calvi harbor, where the winds kept us cooped up. This year, the same thing may happen to us in the Santorin harbor. The *meltem* (Greece's mistral) is blowing, paralyzing us in the harbor, moored to the seawall.

Today we are out at sea, after a night's stopover at Polykandros, a tiny island where political criminals used to be sent into exile.

Today (Sunday) we sailed off Santorin at nine in the morning. It is likely that the island's volcanic collapse dates from the cataclysm which preceded the one described in the Bible by several thousand centuries. All that is left is a crown of rather terrifying mountains, black, greenish, yellowish, dark red, iron gray, around the volcano out of which the tiny lava island belches fire and smoke, blocks of sulfur and gypsum. (Last eruption 1950; before that, 1928.)

Under the crest of this hollow tooth hang white villages which suggest *The Thousand and One Nights*, but when you reach them (by donkeyback), there is nothing there.

Minos 1952, Candia-Palace

Thera, the ancient city, where the gymnopaedias were held, is on the right, two and a half hours by mule on dreadful roads. I decide against it. It is one of the last Greek towns where inscriptions and carved phalluses over doors have resisted the iconoclasts and testify, like Knossos, to the cult of homosexuality (at Knossos, it was obligatory).

The Greek islands are nothing but an idea one creates for oneself. The spirit and the soil are exhausted here, dispelled, drained of their substance. Everything noble that is left lives in the mountains (from which all rebellions start).

The testiness of the islanders results from the fact that we are visiting their ruins. Yet these shadows of the shades of a dead Greece are very much alive when it comes to refusing us gasoline and then selling it for a fortune (they sell it by the kilo) mixed with water and rust from the motors (indispensable on account of the unfavorable winds).

We were to leave at dawn on the twenty-third. But the Greek mistral rises, the sea turns nasty, and Paul decides against it. We remain moored to the seawall. Finally we leave at eleven-thirty. Better risk a nasty sea than be mistreated on the spot and have to give up our place on the seawall to the mail boat, which arrives Tuesday morning.

Painful crossing. Everything shifts position, gets broken. The waves sweep the deck. You feel your stomach turning. We take refuge in a bay of Polykandros, a wretched island where some five hundred people must be dying of hunger and thirst.

We drop anchor at seven. Dinner. Sleep. We set out at seven-thirty in the morning. The wind has dropped, precisely when the fishermen had told Paul it would.

On our way to Piraeus, between islands. Calm sea, fresh wind. Skins and every object on board covered with a salt crust. We must sail day and night, without stopping, if we are to reach Piraeus by tomorrow morning.

Crète. C'est la première fois que je suis dépaysé depuis que je cours le monde. 5

*

Ce que j'ai fait chez Francine est aussi beau que Knossos. Mais il faudra des siècles et des ruines pour le rendre visible et respectable.

*

Chez Minos

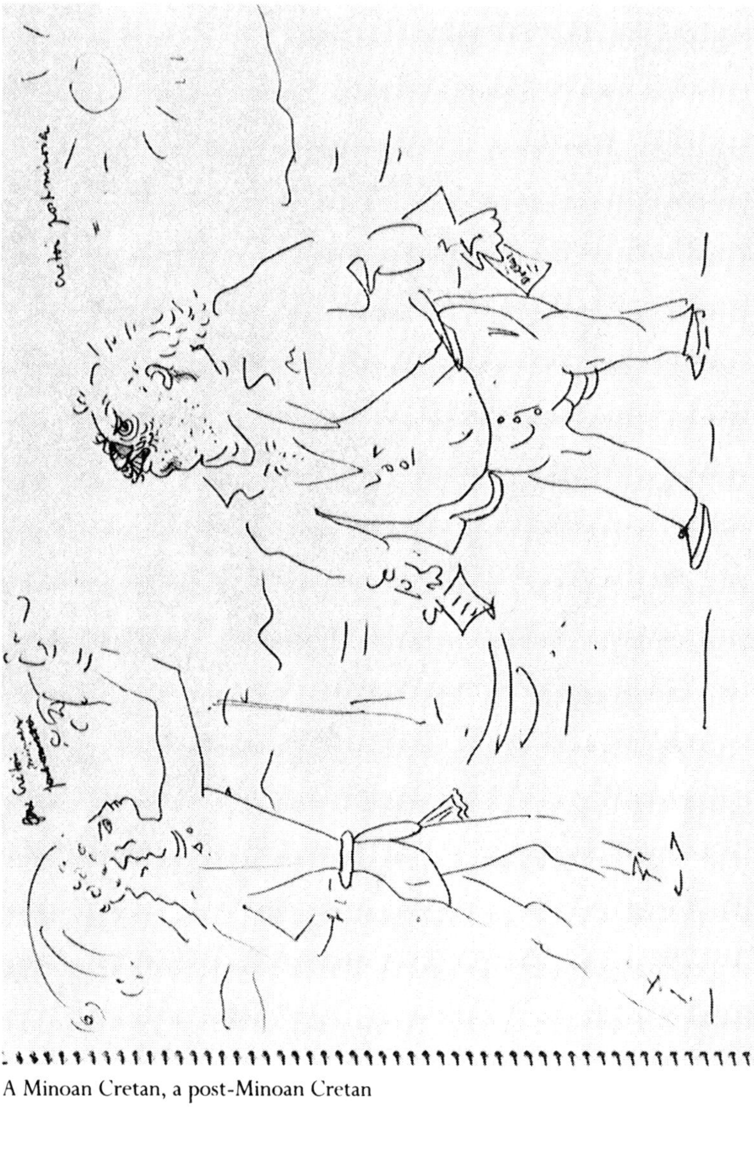

A Minoan Cretan, a post-Minoan Cretan

Let's get out of here!

June 21, 1952. We escape from Crete

Customs Labyrinth and the Clos Ginette

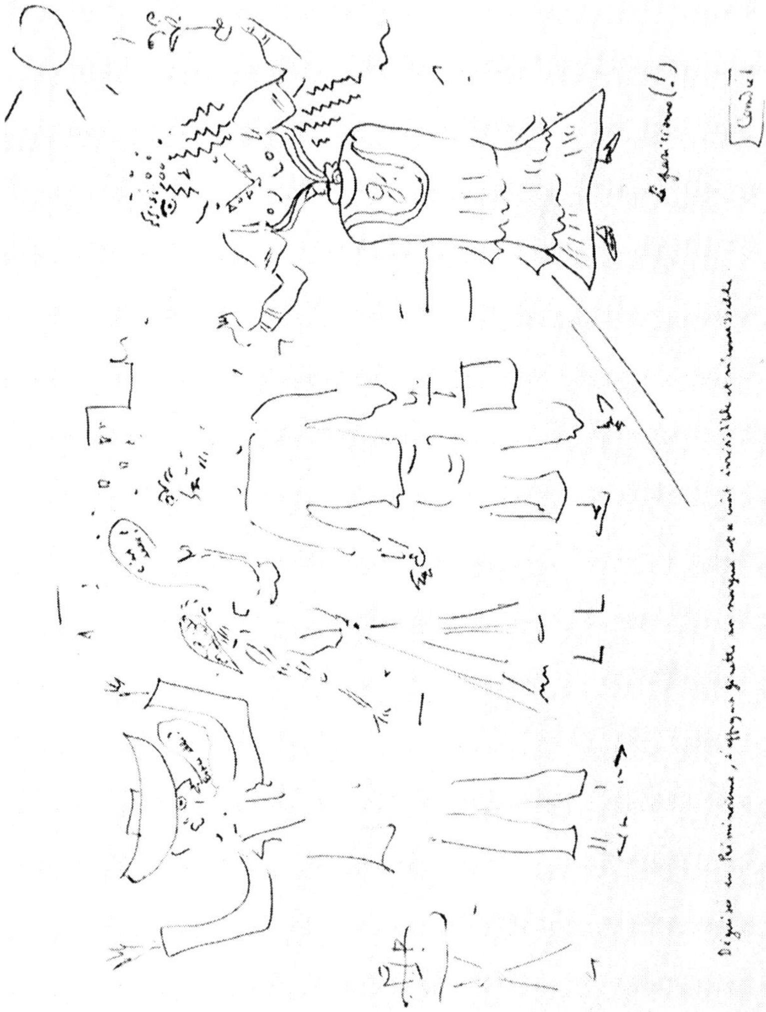

Disguised as a pre-Minoan, the fearful Ginette
challenges us, believing herself irresistible

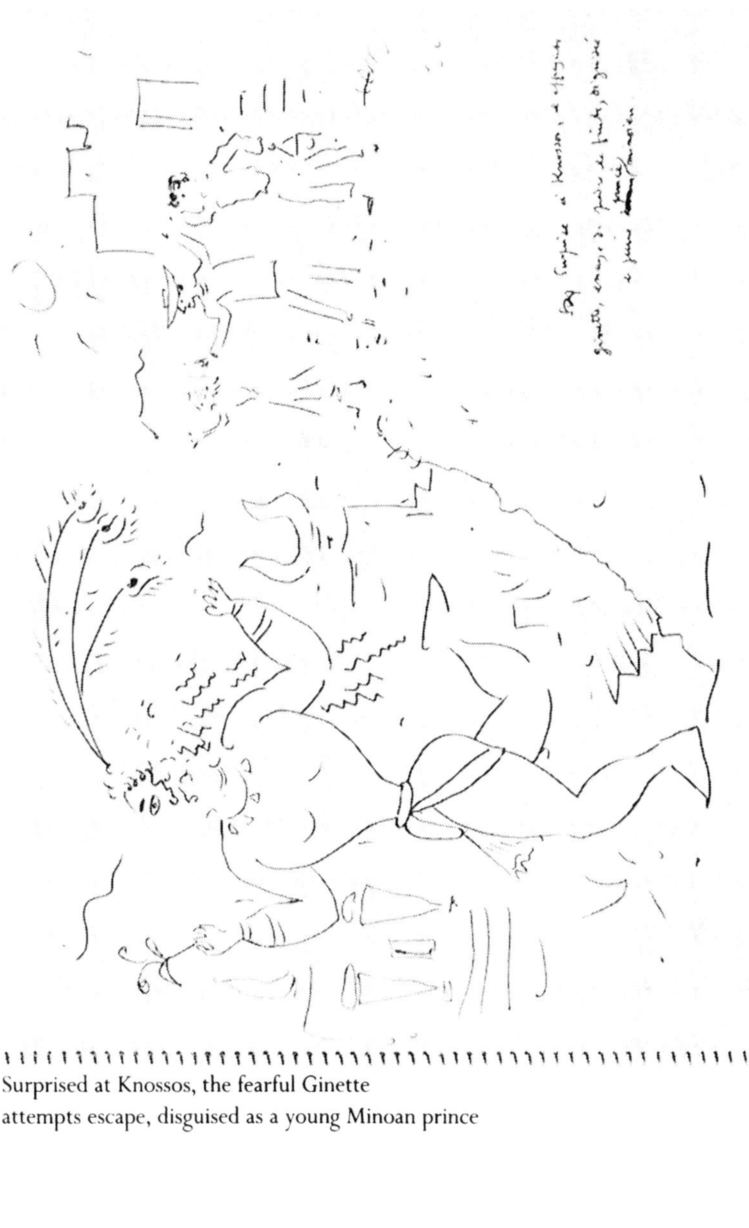

Surprised at Knossos, the fearful Ginette
attempts escape, disguised as a young Minoan prince

At intervals of several thousand centuries, the earth receives a shock, that same shock observed several times a second when we consider the atom's mechanism from that distance which is another, unknown form of distance and which leads us to believe in the infinitely small, which—any more than the infinitely large—does not exist. Each of these things changes the axis of the poles and the configuration of lands and seas. Men perish in them and take them for the end of the world. Their poor effort begins all over again. It is likely that Greece was a continent whose islands are in fragments. What had blossomed on these fragments has been gradually exhausted, like the provisions on a wreck. New means of transport have provided riffraff in their stead. The pirates, now vanished, leave only begging hands and empty heads, a dusty mixture of races and religions. Greece is a corpse devoured by myths. A ghost crowned with legends. Such a journey is enlightening as to our chances of survival in France, and the blindness of the French. (Myself first of all; to me, all these wretched rocks looked like Eden.)

Beautiful Adonis is dead. (Final chorus.)

A single great fortress opposes the dead gods: Mount Athos (forbidden to women, to children, and to eunuchs). This must be more of a beard ritual than a sexual one. The way everything is a hat ritual in Turkey. Mount Athos is forbidden to the beardless. Perhaps a bearded woman would be allowed.

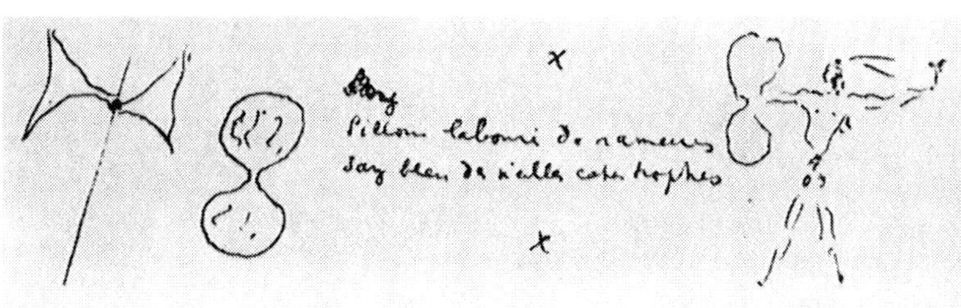

Furrows ploughed by oarsmen
Blue blood of ancient catastrophes

The double (Frankish) battle-axes, the figure-eight buckles (for wasp waists). Everything from the Minoan period is bee-oriented. Daedalus constructed hives. Perhaps the style was inspired by hives and bees—whence their cult of flowers. There are villages of hives on the hillsides. And the gold clouds of the wheat threshed there.

In a case in the Candia museum is a piece of gold jewelry: two bees face-to-face. The motif of bees is seen as frequently as that of lilies and double axes.

Perhaps, as in Egypt, the long curls of the Minoans were wigs. Quite likely. Not everyone would have the same hairstyle and the same hair. Peoples who lived naked wore wigs to protect their heads from the sun. Their version of hats.

Five-thirty. Motor trouble. Bad oil and gasoline. The plugs are filthy. Calm sea. We pass those islands so delightful from a bird's-eye view and so wretched close up. Nothing grows on them. They seem made out of the material used for forts in boxes of lead soldiers. Here it would be better to be born a sea gull than a mule. Only the gulls seem elegant, rich, happy. Besides, on most of the islands we can make out neither men nor animals.

The Athenians know what I have just found out. They go to the nearby and delightful islands. Spetsai, for example, or exquisite Poros. The other islands are our Corsica. The harbors resemble Ajaccio. But Corsica has a green fur; it hasn't contracted alopecia. On the islands we have been visiting, a road like the one from Calvi to Ajaccio is inconceivable. The donkeys' hide and that of the soil are about the same. Corsica is poor, but rich in creeks and splendid trees. And few Corsicans stay at home. They travel; they emigrate and everywhere form colonies where the Corsican spirit does not disintegrate. In the Greek islands, the type is anything but pure. It was pure in Rome, where the Greeks prevailed over their conquerors by their intelligence (of which the power of Trajan's Column is the symbol).

What can be cultivated on these waterless rocks? A few vines. A little honey. Mind would wither here and lose its charm. You end by forgiving these officials. Cheating is their only distraction. They live far away from life, and they know it. They despise what testifies to a lost beauty. You have to have seen the Candia Palace [hotel] to understand what they regard as an ideal and what is happening under the eyes of the old islanders, who still wear the native costume.

The Isthmus of Corinth is one-way. If a ship enters from the wrong direction, you have to wait. You risk waiting several hours. Better to reach Delphi by road. Then Athens, from which Francine will fly to Paris for her daughter's birthday and from which we will fly to join Jeannot in Rome. (I am heartsick thinking of the unanswered letters and messages waiting for me at Santo Sospir. I've been dragging some around in my bag that I haven't had the courage to answer.) Don't forget to pick up the black cup the owner of The Apuleius gave me; he had just found it, part of a whole set. And so many amphorae that they had left them on the banks of the Tiber.

I can't see the customs office of the Athens airport without thinking of Yvonne de Bray, clutching her roses wrapped in cellophane. This was the disguise of a splendid vase from Crete (now at Milly, on the mantelpiece of my workroom).

I wonder if the Charioteer has been returned to Delphi; four years ago, I saw him in the Athens museum. He was the finest thing there, along with the Poseidon fished up out of the sea, the little bronze rider, and the two young colossi from Knossos lying side by side. Everything (except the Charioteer) was still in the statue hospital. (The little rider in the lecture amphitheater.)

The Charioteer's horses lie disemboweled on the ground, like the picador's horses. I suppose that the whole thing is now back in place. After the civil war, they were supposed to return the Charioteer to Delphi.

Il ne se pouvait pas que, comme en Égypte, les longues boucles mesurant fussent des perruques. C'est même probable. Tout le monde n'avait pas les mêmes coiffures et les mêmes cheveux. Les peuples qui vivaient sans porter de perruques afin de protéger gracieusement la tête du soleil.
C'était [illegible].

×

Candie habitant de ruches
Jeunes qui aux tailles d'abeilles
Maintenant les maisons sont mortes
Et la jeune gens s'est perdue.

~~[illegible]~~
~~[illegible]~~
~~[illegible]~~
Fête à Candie, le dimanche
Demoiselles à colliers d'or
(avec seins nus et jupes blanches)
Les promenades restaient dehors.

Corinthe n'est heureusement plus le genre du port.

We pass the intersection of the roads to Daulis and Delphi, where Oedipus killed Laius. I have spoken so much of this place that the craving to see it has a lot to do with my decision to return to Delphi by road.

Ten-thirty. Since seven-thirty, we have been moving under sail (ten knots). We are thirty miles off Athens. In a car, we would be there in half an hour. The *Orphée* will take four or five. Everything that hangs from something seems to be suspended by miracle in the air; you can realize our speed only by the creaking of the wood and the ropes, the delicious murmur of the water against the hull.

. . . .

JUNE 25 · 1952

Arrived this morning at Piraeus. Noon at Athens, Air France. No more seats for Rome tomorrow. So we will leave the day after, another airline. Quick lunch at the hotel bar, in Constitution Square. Air France hires us a car for Delphi.

Nothing is so endless as the road to Delphi. Five hundred kilometers' round-trip. The good road leaves off quickly, and you bump along the ricochets, on steep slopes flanked by uninhabited mountains. Except for goats and their shepherd with the ancient crook, except for donkeys and women whose faces are wrapped in black cloths, we meet no one, no car, no cart, no farm.

A few famous springs, a few pale stones, some empty red boxes, the tiny theater in the huge hemicycle where Alexander's hunt and the chariot races were held, the odd scent of immortelles, a few gray columns under the soft, dripping rain—does all this make up for 800,000 drachmas and the exhaustion of endless roads creeping around rocky turns? No. There are so many lovely things that lie within our reach and which we don't even bother to see, out of mere laziness. And after all, Delphi was Lourdes, less revolting and filled with treasures, according to Pausanias. But the place trafficked in souls, and the pilgrim left with empty pockets. The museum is absurd. The poor little Charioteer with his onyx eyes and bronze lashes is back in Delphi. How many journeys he's made without his horses, which lie gutted on the floor in the hallways of the Athens museum. Here he is, back again, standing on a wooden crate in the center of a waiting room.

I was "dressed" for Athens but had kept on my Italian sandals—*which caused a scandal.* They allow the guard to discover that the Charioteer seems to have feet that are an exact cast of mine, and me to discover that my hands have aged and my feet remained young. As we leave, I dip them in the cool water of the Castalian Spring.

We wonder why bare toes should scandalize a people who used to live in sandals. Except that this people has lost what gave it wings, what rendered it apt to understand the freedom of elegance.

It is raining gently, and the smell of the sun-warmed plants is heady. One would like to know how the crowds climbed up to this eagle's nest, how they brought and carried away the statues. With "progress," Delphi seems inaccessible. I think that this "progress" of ours would amuse the men who argued over the holy city, pillaged or embellished it, rebuilt the temples destroyed by earthquakes and rockslides.

Besides, the notion of cataclysm had nothing to do with their conception of the place. They considered it differently from the way we do. This sinister chaos was nothing but breasts, haunches, shoulders of goddesses, high citadels of the gods. And down below, in her hole, the Pythia, an ignorant old woman, writhed, frothed, stammered out confused sayings which the priests translated, swindling the clientele.

Poor little Charioteer, poor little human and graceful column, poor blind man who stares at everything the archaeologists are ignorant of. The guard is in love with him, caresses him, makes us touch his nails, the lines of his palm which holds the reins. He shrugs about the amputation of the left arm. I am reminded of Alfred, guard of the Potomak.*

When this Greek speaks of the young monster who sleeps standing, his eyes fill with tears. We turn away, for modesty's sake. He remains beside the pedestal, mouth open, in ecstasy. In the neighboring rooms, a young idiot from the archaeological school prowls around in shorts, a stone in his hand, looking for somewhere to put it in the Theseus reliefs. Sad sights which have nothing to do with the problems that occur to us. A little love, a little boldness, a little life would manage to solve them. But life, boldness, love are not on hand. I would excruciate the scandal of my sandals by declaring at the top of my lungs that the performance of *Oedipus Rex* has more to do with the matter than the programs of the school, which derive from the boneyard and the catalog.

I have a headache. I dip my retreating charioteer's feet into the Castalian Spring. We get into our car, not our chariot. And we imagine the group of Oedipus, Laius, the wheeling horses, the terror-stricken servants at the intersection of the roads from Daulis and Delphi. And the Delphi–Athens road goes on and on, winding like the serpent Python to the boat in which Paul rows us out to the yacht, dead with fatigue.

. . . .

JUNE 26 · 10:00 A.M.

The sky is washed clean, balanced at last. It recovers its incomparable transparency. Around us, on all sides, continues that work which never seems to be work, but a kind of maniacal puttering.

*In *Le Potomak* (1919), Cocteau assigns the monster who bears this name a solicitous guard named Alfred.

Our French neighbor takes lunch with his crew; our English neighbors feed their baby, scrape their yellow and blue hull. Others sleep. The huge French yacht (the only other one which flies the French flag besides the *Orphée II*) looks like a ghost yacht. Boats filled with baskets of silverware pass—sardines. Up on the left, the yacht club where we once had an official dinner organized by Marika Kotopouli, on our return from Istanbul. Up there to the right, the strange nightclub Chez Lapin. We can hear its music at night.

This morning the liquid air and the sun show all these Greeks to be children and all their clumsiness at receiving foreigners as child's play. Last year there was no authorization granted for a Frenchwoman to wear her fur coat. Since she was freezing, she could rent or borrow one. This kind of thievery alternates with the greatest helpfulness, the most delicate attentions.

Only you will never explain in these harbors that our radio is an old battery model which doesn't work. This old radio is an *idée fixe*. It requires a thousand visits, a thousand authorizations, a thousand sheets of paper (whose stamps are very expensive). We cannot even throw it overboard, for we would be accused of having sold it. In museums the visitor is followed step by step by men who supervise his every gesture. We were tempted to make off with the phallic column from the Theater of Dionysus; with a car and a yacht, it would have been easy enough. The ruins of the theater lie about like dirty linen and empty tin cans. I first mentioned this extraordinary object years ago, and it remains here, hidden in the grass. We will show it to Mme Fuller this afternoon; she didn't even suspect its existence. It deserves a secret room in the museum here in Athens, all to itself, for it shows what must have been the decoration of a theater where Sophocles produced the premiere of *Antigone*.

We have lunch at the Fullers'. They live in a building next to the Dutch Embassy. If I had time, I would visit the ambassador and his Russian wife. She is the one to whom Mme Vaux-Saint-Cyr, our ambassadress, said: "I went by your place this morning; I should tell you that your flag was upside down." (Blue, white, red, straight across.) It was with this delightful household and the Lebels that we had visited Corinth.

What a performance I could put on in the Theater of Dionysus if I were given a free hand. Unfortunately everyone here suspects us of bad intentions, of lack of respect toward the myths. I could not try a thing. If I did, it would be in Rome, for a performance in the theater at Ostia. Most likely I shall make a (short) film at the cape, using what I have seen at the excavations and the masks and accessories of *Oedipus Rex*.

What has always saved my life is that what I don't see doesn't exist. This is why I never look at a newspaper or an article—favorable or unfavorable—about me. This is also why my dead friends seem to me just as much alive as friends living far away.

Seven o'clock. Back from Athens. No bank open. No museum. We filmed the phallus of the Theater of Dionysus, which the guard says is a tiger. Then a few shots of the Acropolis. Return, dinner on board with the Fullers. Packing. Plane for Rome tomorrow morning at nine o'clock.

. . . .

JUNE 27 · 1952

In the English plane.

From up above, the sea freezes. The islands seem close together. Everything is sculpted, motionless. As with the whirlwind of the stars, which we imagine fixed.

The cold in these English planes!

Postal strike. Impossible to inform Jeannot by telegram. We'll stay an extra day in Rome.

Incredibly, the Greek customs didn't search our bags. Though

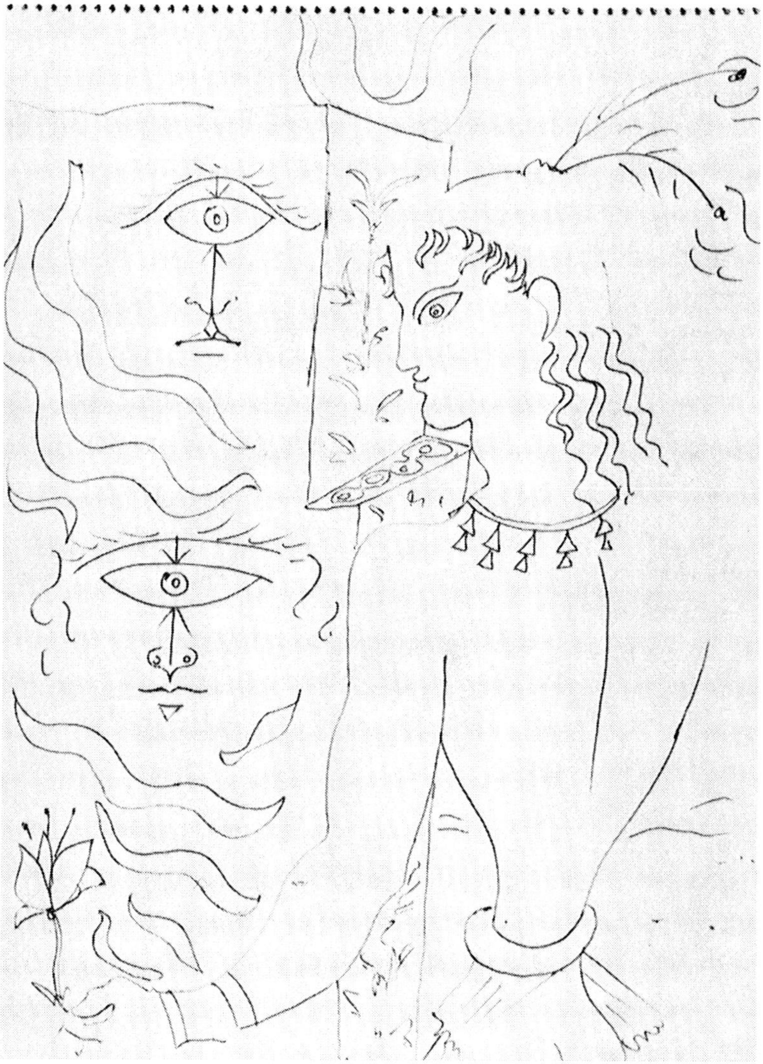

they did search Fuller's, and he travels with a diplomatic passport.

General strike on account of Rhodes, which is demanding autonomy.

Francine leaves Paul millions of drachmas. Paul takes on a Greek sailor for the return trip.

We fly over this sea so difficult to navigate in a boat. From a distance the islands regain their agreeable shape and their pinkish coloring. Impossible to suspect that they are so terrifying. The Athenians know they are, and content themselves with Spetsai or Poros . . .

We have visited the central sites: Mycenae, Epidaurus, Knossos, Delphi. All these treasures, all these religions, all these wars, all these oracles, all these pirates—of which nothing is left.

The Theater of Dionysus. Two Americans early for the performance, in the orchestra seats. They consult the program. The usher should explain that they are sitting in the men's seats with a hole in the marble near the edge so that you can piss sitting down.

JUNE 28–29 · 1952

Rome. The city where you walk under triumphal arches to perform the merest errand. Very pretty women, elegant and carefully groomed. We learn from Cinecittà that Jeannot is filming outdoor shots at the monastery at Subiaco. Dinner at Ostia, The Apuleius. We take our cup and a splendid black vase decorated with ivy which the owner gives Francine. Francine is leaving today at three. At the airport we run into Jeannot, who is taking the same plane for Paris and who had been free last night! Absurd phone call from Cinecittà. The whole company returned every day at two-thirty. We cancel the car that was going to take us out to Subiaco.

Bought a very curious Greco-Roman head. I leave it at The Apuleius and will return to pick it up either with the yacht or with the car. We will take dinner at Ostia and leave Rome tomorrow morning at nine. Jeannot will come to the cape for a few days next week. He wants me to help him rewrite the dialogue for his film which is, he says, detestable.

. . . .

JUNE 29

We leave Peter's city on Saint Peter's day. The result of this brief stay in Rome is that I have changed my mind in that way I have of gladly contradicting myself if my sentiments compel me to do so. In the Athens–Rome contest, it is Rome which wins. Sumptuous Rome with its orange walls wins after this journey. First of all, water flows here and sprinkles everything with its abundance. In Athens, you suffer from drought; and in the islands, from being surrounded by salt water and having no drinkable water—which desiccates a whole population to the very marrow of their souls.

Wherever the eye falls in Rome, it touches life. Even the russet ruins are mingled with life; they live and serve. In Athens, tongues hang around a few scattered bones. If I had to leave Paris and choose some other city, I should choose Rome.

From the plane flying toward Nice, Vatican City resembles a tiny cathedral close. The Colosseum a mole hole. Man has already disappeared.

Flying over Elba, from a height where man no longer has even the size of a flea, I imagine that one of the invisible (from our vantage) creatures has escaped by sea once again to overwhelm this poor world of ours and that from where we are nothing can be seen of such an operation. No need to mount very high above the earth for all man's glory and his wickedness to vanish, for his ambition to be reduced to absurdity. And if we rise a little higher, the very places he dreams of conquering vanish, and higher still, everything freezes, and higher still, everything leaps and rolls, and the centuries become seconds, and this system in which the conqueror imagined himself king becomes a simple atom.

It is a pity that the conqueror is always lacking any metaphysical spirit, any liberal sense of science. It would calm his itch to conquer and to convince the others. As for myself, from this perspective, I have lost the slightest craving for preeminence, and I am quite persuaded of the stupidity of those ambitious fools who end with a rope around their necks. At Rome there is not much distance between the palace window where Mussolini harangued his mobs and the place where those mobs pulled him to pieces and hung up his corpse like a piece of meat.

To write is an entertainment I put on for myself. What happens then is of little consequence. It is not long enough. And I marvel that from a certain height the time in which palaces are built does not exist.

Besides, for anyone who thinks and observes and registers all this, it is ruinous to travel too much and shake up the wine of his bottle; the mind grows confused and no longer finds peace. I brought work along on our trip and have never found a minute to set it in order, having only the possibility of taking these notes. The rest seemed to me like an alien planet to which I am returning and whose language I have lost touch with.

. . . .

July 1

Back to Santo Sospir. Ceilings very well executed with Lorenzi's help. But in Francine's room a crack has formed because our neighbor is blasting through the rock with dynamite.

JULY 2

Francine is back. She found Paris so intolerable that she merely laughs at the dynamite and the drilling. But because of her apprehensions for my frescoes, she calls her lawyer.

The lawyer was comical: a tiny, lively old man who speaks as loud as the explosions. The workmen suspect something and behave very cautiously.

My wine is troubled. I have enormous difficulty answering the piles of letters. In the newspaper, this riddle: who is the most unknown and the most famous? Answer: me.

How could my demanding work correspond to my fame? This paper is right, and the public makes no mistake. To these people, the riddle seems easy to answer.

JULY 4

I've finished my mail. I can't get down to work, though, copying out the notes of my trip. I dawdle, lie on the beach. Reread *The Countess de Charny*. Besides, I adore the book and find Dumas admirable.

In the letters, one from Mme Auriol. She invites me to a private luncheon with the president—I am to name my dates. I'll go if I return to Paris, which I shall doubtless have to do: for the dentist.

The Latin Quarter film club asks me to serve as its president. "We went along with Chaplin. But not with Clair and Renoir. We want you." I accept. On the other hand, my doctor's film club, of which I am the president, is falling apart; everyone is resigning. One pharmacist in Nice blames Dr. Ricoux for indulging me in my follies.

Tomorrow, Saturday, Lorenzi and his men are coming to finish work on the ceilings: those in the pink room and the main room downstairs. Once this villa is found by archaeological excavations, it will be declared remarkable.

The minister asks me for a few lines for the restoration of Versailles. I send them, but Versailles will become something like Delphi. A site and a few ruins. That is the rule.

SATURDAY · JULY 5 · 1:00 A.M.

I am sixty-three years old. 3-3-3. The triad.

For my birthday, a delightful serenade by Lorenzi. The workmen begin work at four in the morning. Francine, furious, cannot sleep and comes down to see me.

Jeannot and Cesare announce their arrival at the Nice airport. Horrified by the racket that will greet them.

JULY 11 · 1952

I have largely conquered that sloth caused in me by the feeling of "what's the use?"—conquered it because of Francine. Her pleasure is the pleasure of others. And to such effort it is natural to respond by an effort of one's own. To get tickets in advance, to organize a trip, to think of birthdays, to order shirts, etc.—all this seemed insurmountable to me. But since she orders, organizes, and makes the reservations, one adds to gratitude the courage which was lacking for packing, for instance, or passports. She leads us along the very roads where I was getting lost in the void or, for fear of getting lost in the void, was paralyzed, drowning in the feeling of "what's the use?"

Francine has seen the lawyer in Nice and the secretary of the prefect (actually this secretary *is* the prefect—who changes often—because she is permanent and remarkable besides).

Lawyer and prefecture have stated that the Villa Santo Sospir is in some sense a national site and that it is their duty to protect it. It is, the lawyer declares, our Knossos, which must be defended against the Turks. This lawyer, Maître Bonello, miraculously happens to be deep in a book on Crete and the Minoan frescoes.

Rereading Proust. His snobbery irritates, even when he is making fun of society people. He only makes fun of them as unworthy of the names they bear. He saves everything by the inspired way in which he tells his story. In the same way, his homosexuality is vexing. At the hotel in Balbec, the grooms seem to occupy him more than the famous and bizarre *jeunes filles en fleurs*. Besides, when he begins studying Charlus, a certain embarrassment compels him to put after the word *vice* and in parenthesis: "(or what is erroneously so-called)."

. . . .

JULY 12 · 1952

The Tour de France no longer interests me the way last year's did. It has lost that epic style caught up by the troubadours in every house by means of the radio.

Nothing but advertising now.

Probably they need an announcer like Koblet. Fausto Coppi is a star but does not charm the householders who listen to the racing exploits. Besides, in this heat the troubadours are exhausted. Briquet, the best of them, gets mixed up. He loses track, as he did on Mont Ventoux, of what he is saying. The mistral and this hot spell knock out even the least indolent. The runners themselves prefer to lose the prize than to pedal in hell for a public insolent enough to shout "Fakers!" at them.

Before we leave Santo Sospir, where the workmen are finishing the ceiling, a letter comes from the prefect saying that measures have been taken and that there will be no further threat to the frescoes.

. . . .

July 12 · 1952 · In the plane to Paris

In this plane, it is uncomfortably cold—air conditioning. If it were this cold in winter, passengers would be demanding heat.

After rereading the first part of *Cities of the Plain*, I have just reread with amazement the first 150 pages of the second part. Was Marcel's illness suddenly worse; was he distracted by his countless letters, his countless "exceptional visits," his nocturnal expeditions? Even the most uninspired novelist could improve on this. Unreadable! And I've reread it word by word. A labyrinth of ill-written sentences, of parentheses after which these sentences remain hanging, vulgar jokes, characters dropped and then reintroduced quite unexpectedly . . .

Marcel's odd insolence—attributing his own sexuality to others, constantly identifying some young woman or other with his own person. Besides, young women of the period did not smoke in trains, nor did they have that boyish freedom of action.

How can the Verdurins maintain the slightest prestige in the world if all the members of the little clan are so grotesque? It would have been so easy for Proust's snobbery to let the Verdurins know just who Charlus is, for Charlus to run on in his usual way, over the heads of the faithful, to the Cambremers, and to put M. Verdurin in his proper place. Especially since Charlus wanted to come off well in Morel's eyes and since his silence could only be attributed to anger and pride, whereas he swallows his affronts in silence and without the shadow of standoffishness. It would have been so easy for Proust to have Charlus say to M. Verdurin:

"I am not the one you have embarrassed, dear monsieur—you have embarrassed Cambremer"—since Charlus, whose attitude would be understandable in a bordello, cannot accept affronts in the presence of Cambremer and Marcel.

Moreover, Proust adds unexpected guests and then abandons them (in order to place a clever remark). Mme de Cambremer-Legrandin, who is a dithering idiot, is less so than the Verdurin clan, who must amaze her by their intelligence and their audacious sallies. But here Proust abandons all verisimilitude because his snobbery forces him to show any other milieu than the faubourg under absurd colors. Except with regard to Céleste Albaret, who is an authentic character and one from his own life.

In short, these 112 pages are a poor sketch of what they might be. They are a smirch on the rest, and I hope I find nothing like them as I continue rereading. You never find this kind of weakness in Stendhal, or in Balzac, or in Gobineau. It is a disaster, giving rise to a terrible revision in one's judgment of the whole.

I have known this society, and all or almost all of Proust's models (except Bertrand de Fénelon). The composites (except with regard to Mme de Chevigné, whose filthy language and cheap cigarettes he has left out, along with her yellow teeth and her parrot nose, keeping only her sapphire blue eyes) are mostly the absence of composites. Mme Greffulhe, Greffulhe himself, and mainly Montesquiou are of great physical and moral exactitude. I remember Greffulhe at a luncheon at Mme de La Béraudière's (his old mistress) at Dieppe. She had invited some young Argentine tango dancers. During lunch and across the table, Greffulhe, raising his Jovian brow and his shoulders, shouted: "Who the hell are they?" as if all the other people at the table were deaf—in short, the duc de Guermantes.

When I knew Montesquiou, he had only the language and the insolence of Charlus, so far. He put on his famous act for me at the Palais-Rose. Later, coming from Le Piquay, at the Gare de Lyon buffet, I saw him, potbellied, made up, dyed, wiggling his behind . . .

Charlus's diatribe about Mme de Saint-Euverte (Mathilde Sée) is, to the letter, a Montesquiou harangue.

The only interpolation is that Proust takes Charlus into houses of ill fame, where Proust himself would go to satisfy his needs. The same is true of the scene with Mlle Vinteuil, in which Proust transposes one of his own sexual complications (the mother profaned).

Marcel's morbid snobbery leads him to make preposterous gestures of politeness, not only to Mme Standish and to the Castellanes, but to Saint-Léger and to Diaghilev.

Proust, better informed than Balzac as to worldly nuances (use of the particle, for instance), never penetrates so deeply into the souls of aristocrats as Balzac, in *Splendeurs et misères*, where the conversation of dukes is a masterpiece of the genre.

One never encounters, in Proust's duchesses, the grace and the marvelous vivacity of Stendhal's Sanseverina. The bicycling girls and Nissim Bernard's grooms tend to become interchangeable. The line that separates them is quite fragile.

Not that Proust's work is diminished in my eyes, but with a certain perspective I discern Proust's connections with that earlier Proust, the Proust of *Pleasures and Regrets*—the Proust of Reynaldo Hahn and Madeleine Lemaire.

He never cites his habitual friends, his intimates: Hahn, Madrazo (something of Ski), Lucien Daudet. He cites those he considers most fashionable and chic in the world of the arts.

As soon as Proust, adopted by the *Nouvelle Revue française*, gained a certain amount of favor, he proliferated his dinners for critics (at the Ritz), his caresses lavished on those he regarded as useful to his reputation.

His rancor toward Mme de Chevigné, who refused to read him,

went so far as to beg me to persuade her. (We live in the same building, 10 rue d'Anjou.)

In short, I admire Marcel. I do not respect him. I feel a certain sadness, for while he was alive, we respected him with all our might.

I have also noted all this for the pleasure of adding that, after page 112 or 115, Proust recovers; his zigzags and tired patches vanish, and he drives straight ahead. There remains only one repetition of the theme "etymologies of regional names" and, putting Proust's pen into Charlus's hand, of the theme of the young Israelites in Racine.

With these exceptions (and it is altogether excusable that Proust should stray a little in the clouds of antiasthmatic powder in that room at 102 boulevard Haussmann), the energy resumes, and if one sometimes loses one's way, it is without awkwardness—even when the intolerable salon theme of worldliness—of being received or not received—dinners in town—overwhelms the story.

Sometimes Marcel's profound malice plays with fire, as when he has Saint-Loup refer to belonging to the Verdurin clan as if it were a question of being homosexual. "My uncle Charlus is one. You're one too. And I'm not. I can't help it."

But from page 115 on, Proust finds himself back in a state of grace, in that aquarium which is his native element, where he moves with the ease of those Hollywood swimmers who dance underwater. But it is the theme of jealousy which he always develops most happily, where he evolves in depth: where the light of day scarcely penetrates and where it is his own body which is the source of light.

After this page 115, Charlus becomes Charlus again, leaves the box to which Proust relegates him and lavishes on Cambremer and Morel explicit phrases which should have reached the Verdurins themselves, through the intermediary of the little clan.

Besides, as I have said, certain remarks of Marcel's would have enlightened the Verdurins but would have spoiled their ignorance of society, which the author wants to emphasize so scornfully.

I even wonder if Mme Muhlfeld wasn't the basis of the character of Mme Verdurin.* When I knew Mme Muhlfeld, she was very up on her *Gotha*, but she had something of Mme Verdurin's, denigrations and clannishness. She regarded as foolish and dangerous for the faithful any society which did not receive her. Moreover, she conducted her flock to the Institute and to the Académie. How many times I heard her use turns of phrase that turned up in Mme Verdurin's mouth! I recognize her more often than Mme Straus, in whose Dreyfusard salon Proust won his first spurs.

For Marcel the architect, the point was to lead Mme Verdurin to where she becomes the princesse de Guermantes. Worldliness obsesses him in the form of progress. What is irritating about the Verdurins is the exaggeration which emphasizes his thesis and their total ignorance of a world whose mechanism the princess Sherbatoff, though not living in it, could have explained to them. The first thing a Mme Verdurin would do, hearing Charlus tell her he is the duc de Guermantes's brother, would be to take Proust aside and interrogate him on the matter. Whereas in the text she simply doesn't believe him.

What inclines me to understand Proust, even when I resist him, is this proof I have of the disappearance of a world one no longer frequents. One has a tendency to believe, as in the case of the planets, that ours is the only one inhabited and habitable. Being

*Wife of the novelist and literary critic Lucien Muhlfeld (1870–1902). Born Jeanne Meyer, she was the sister-in-law of the dramatist and novelist Paul Adam. After 1902 she ran a famous literary salon in Passy, frequented by, among others, her neighbor Paul Valéry, André Gide, Jacques-Émile Blanche, and also younger men, such as André Breton. She died in Grasse in 1953.

young, I "went out," and do so no longer. I therefore imagine "society" to myself as a thing which once existed and which no longer exists, whereas it still exists, though I am too remote from it to see it.

But the Verdurins are in perpetual contact with the newspapers, performances, persons who circulate between one zone and the next. There is no reason why Cottard, a famous professor, should not have aristocrats in his care as well as bourgeois. Now it is possible that all this adds to the fairy-tale aspect of the work. But the Goncourt tone of the Verdurin clan often sinks to Labiche. (A reproach which does not involve Cottard, who speaks his jargon admirably and whose game of cards is perfect.) In short, it is odd that Mme Verdurin, who supposes she is gathering around herself the most brilliant minds of her day and treats all others as bores, should accuse her whole flock of being stupid and boring (Brichot, Saniette, Ski).

The more I think of it, the more I suspect that Proust, who studies society the way Fabre studied insects, is entitled to his mistakes about their extremely and ancestrally complicated behavior. What is funny is the adherence he demands of the insects, as when he begged me to persuade Mme de Chevigné to read his books—which comes down to Fabre's demanding that the insects read his. "Marcel is very sweet"—my neighbor Mme de Chevigné would say to me—"if only he didn't pester us so with his scribbling. I never understand a word of it all—it gives me a headache. He should be satisfied with being amusing. Though his midwife visits at impossible hours are certainly no pleasure." (One recognizes the Guermantes style in that.)

Montesquiou used to say, even more flatly: "Ah! if M. Proust would only write pastiches of Saint-Simon like the one concerning me—" he should have said "flattering me"—"he might well have become a writer."

And Gruffulhe to me: "I'm going off to Bois-Boudran* to write a book. I'm going to answer M. Proust."

Let's be fair. Proust never hesitates to judge society people and accuse them of stupidity. He finds them stupid but superior, which is the real basis of snobbery. It is titles that he likes, and certain prerogatives. He reminds me of Lucien Daudet (his intimate friend) saying: "When I dine in town, I *like* to be at the wrong end of the table—it's the proof that I'm with the right people." He was really surprised that such superior people would admit him to their table. The disease of snobbery is so profound that a famous snob, Georges Rodier, wept on the Nile because that journey to Egypt deprived him of a reception at Mme Moor's, an old American snob who had been taken up by the aristocrats. "I'd have given anything," Lucien Daudet used to say, "if my name were written d'."

The countless letters Proust wrote to members of the aristocracy remained as incomprehensible to them as M. de Charlus's letter to Aimé at the Hôtel de Balbec. Moreover, they were too lazy and too absentminded to decipher those hen tracks. I knew some of these people, who were simply amazed when Proust's correspondence began to be published. "Why, I have heaps of letters from Marcel," the duchesse de G. told me. "I never dreamed they were worth anything. I don't even know where I put them. I'll have to dig them up and reread them. If I can—his handwriting was so terrible, I must tell you I never got through more than half of them." Marcel knew all that, but he submitted to that Saint-Simonian and Sévignesque ceremony. He wanted these ghosts to be what they no longer were and what he wanted them to remain. Which is proved by his letters, in which you might make the mistake of seeing only flattery, whereas, even from this angle, they are no more toadying than Racine's prefaces.

---

*His château near Nangis (Seine-et-Marne).

I was too young and too raw for Marcel's affections to be based on a literary opinion. In me he esteemed the admiring respect with which I surrounded his person at a period when *Swann* was finding no readers. He would read me what he had written the night before, trying out his effects, interrupting them with the hysterical giggles he muffled with his gloved hand, saying: "It's too silly! too silly!" which made it very difficult to follow him.

Sometimes he would leave out a paragraph, saying: "I'm skipping this because this passage won't be explained until the fifth volume."

And then he would write me letters as long and as flattering as the ones to his princes and princesses, which is why I paid no attention to his praise and never cared to publish his letters.*

I cannot approve the recourse that so many of his correspondents have had to this posthumous warranty. They should have realized, reading the letters addressed to others, the value of such praises which they had assumed were meant only for themselves.

At Proust's deathbed, we were heartened to see the pile of school notebooks in which his work was completed. At the time, I wrote in *Les Nouvelles Littéraires* that this work went on living at his left side like the wristwatches of dead soldiers. All the same, Marcel had revised a great deal in proof, and the negligence I find in the first 115 pages of the second volume of *Cities of the Plain* is corrected toward the end. One takes comfort in realizing that Marcel's death might have deprived us of the splendid trajectory which leads—though it falters slightly—from the first line to the last.

This morning, starting with page 203, I was struck by a new feeling: Marcel fell back into a sort of lyrical and psychological stammer, a whole labyrinth of "who" and "whom" and "but" and of parentheses he seemed unable to get out of. Instead of my first amazement, I now felt a certain despair, as if Marcel had been ill

---

*Twelve letters from Proust to Cocteau have been published since Cocteau's death in the *Cahiers Jean Cocteau*, I (Gallimard, 1969).

in my presence, had had his asthma attack, or as if I were blaming myself, confronting this proof, for not having worried about him enough at the time. I make this note after the passage where Mme Verdurin wonders if M. de Charlus and the prince de Guermantes can be invited together, which is a little too much after all, and following the series of suggestive blunders which she throws in his face and where the whole business of "being one" or "not being one" recurs with the indigent insistence of a Montmartre café singer.

". . . while Morel, forgetting that the baron was supporting him in considerable style, with an ironic smile of superior pity, *and said* . . . " instead of *said*, an example out of so many of Proust's confusion; he would doubtless have corrected the errors left in a text where he blames his characters for precisely such errors. We all make such mistakes in our books, and a sort of almost posthumous laziness keeps us from correcting them from one edition to the next. But Proust attached the greatest importance to exactitude of style (he was right), and I suppose that if death had not surprised him, he would not have failed to undertake this labor.

I have not yet finished rereading *Cities of the Plain*. But as of now I discover that the book, by dint of being familiar to me, has lost its essence of surprise and, no longer drawing me on by its plot developments, offers me a very odd temperature chart, where the merest rises and drops, the slightest asthma attacks, Marcel's least exhaustions become as legible to me as the mountainous red line of a temperature graph. This is why, at the risk of letting it seem I am participating in that deadly modern craze for knocking idols off their pedestals, I am making these notes which for me represent a new form of criticism.

The little railway line assumes a charming life, less confused and less clogged with worldly preoccupations: the clan is boring, the gentlemen are boring—but Proust gives these tedious encounters the quality of frivolity, as if he were meeting friends. In reality it is the names of places and people which move him, even when he considers that the route is becoming humanized and that people are taking precedence over the sites blurred by habit. I am thinking of this significant sentence: "They reminded me that my fate was to pursue only phantoms, beings whose reality, for the most part, was in my imagination."

Low level of interest up to where the discovery of Albertine's friendship with Mlle Vinteuil and her friend plunges Marcel back into the depths of that aquarium where I had found him just now and where his developments become magnificent. Albertine remains the type of one of those ghosts whom Marcel's genius manages to make palpable, while leaving them all their ghostly privileges.

. . . .

JULY 13 · 1952

We have arrived at Morfontaine, Anna de Noailles's* little white temple of friendship set here like a magic box in the middle of fields and woods where no fence delimits the grounds. One knows that here the estate ends, that here another estate begins, and that's all. Hence one can imagine that one lives in a marvelous little gatehouse surrounded by vast grounds.

. . . .

JULY 14 · 1952

How ill-natured the French are! We go to Chantilly. Around six in the evening we reach the threshold of the stables where an old keeper rushes up and showers us with abuse. No matter how carefully we tell him that it is no crime to glance at a racetrack, he drives us away, insulting us even more roundly.

---

*Countess Anna de Noailles (1876–1933), a close friend of Cocteau's since 1910. Her poetic works exerted a considerable influence over Cocteau's first poems.

An old keeper with a huge white beard and the rosette of the Legion of Honor appears at the door of a sort of concierge's lodge and, without inquiring what is happening, drills us with a hostile stare. *Douce France!*

. . . .

JULY 15 · 1952

We leave Morfontaine for Paris, where I will stay with Francine. Madeleine is on vacation. Painful dentist's appointment. Cloudy weather.

It is absolutely essential that I break all my ties with the present moment. Work in the dark. Put in no appearances. Fame is absurd when work is increasingly difficult and does not correspond with that rhythm. The invisible takes over its own defense. It possesses other methods than those of muddle. And if this invisibility becomes total, one must resign oneself to it and to hearing it said that one is fading out, that one is finished. That is the moment when truth begins.

The disease of being visible is so powerful in Proust's work that the final sprint of his arrival at glory becomes wonderfully comprehensible. He was *reluctantly invisible.*

Someday we shall have to see what invisibility rejects from his work and keeps.

Saw Pierre and his wife at Morfontaine. Raoul's dissatisfied society, his honesty, his friendliness having blindfolded me to all the rest. He keeps letters in his pockets—says *yes* to everything he is asked to do and does nothing. The disorder in my affairs grows much worse than in the days of Ci-Mu-Ra, where there was not so much disorder as routine. Nothing more difficult in our times than to find real support, the kind you can rely on. Raoul compels me to twice and three times as much work. I am horrified at having caused him to give up his job with Paul *and* the job that replaced it. He must find another job better suited to his indolence and his tastes.

. . . .

JULY 16 · 1952

Back to Paris, dentist, Colette and Maurice. Madeleine and the Siam brood. Went to see [Julien] Duvivier's film (*Don Camillo*). Why distort a book of which each episode gave the film its opportunity? The rage to change everything is overpowering. It is the weakness of this film in which Fernandel proves, as in *Angèle*, that he is a marvelous actor.

I am staying at Francine's, in the place des États-Unis, for a little peace and quiet. No sooner do I come home than a mysterious wave informs the visitors, who question Madeleine.

Maurice tells me about Colette, who suffers night and day and who accepts this suffering because it determines a style of life in which Maurice never leaves her. She prefers such suffering to the health which would separate them, Colette going one way, Maurice the other, whereas the role of male nurse keeps Maurice beside her and forms a sort of household.

. . . .

JULY 17 · 1952

Found waiting for me at my rue de Montpensier address Sartre's huge tome *Saint Genet, comédien et martyr*.*

Newspaper manners. In *Combat*: "Unpublished writings of Cocteau on tragedy." Bits and pieces clumsily pasted together from a chapter of my book on Marais.

In *Vogue* a page of photographs of the masks for *Oedipus Rex*,

*Genet (born in Paris in 1910) first met Cocteau in 1943.

arranged so that they lose all meaning, all style. Photographs taken in my absence.

Art and sport. I have never been interested in *the sprint*. Calculations for the race as a whole have been my sole study.

Genet: never has the word *fairy* used by the English to designate someone like Divine been more accurate than when applied to Our-Lady-of-Flowers.

Paris-on-the-beach. A little boy in the elevator to Cecil Beaton: "Mommy says I can't talk to you. She told my nurse you were a fairy. Are you?"

. . . .

JULY 18 · 1952

The masks and objects from *Oedipus Rex* have just arrived at Francine's in the place des États-Unis. No one realized how big the crates would be. They look like a building. Francine has them put in the old carriage shed.

It is a big mistake to suppose a book is forgotten because it is not being read by the people around us. When literary snobbery withdraws from a book, that book makes its way among its real public, and if the book is a mediocre one, that public is enormous. We know no one who reads *Cyrano de Bergerac* or *Dorian Gray*, yet the circulation of these works has never diminished.

Other worlds. At Samois, on the bridge, I once saw passing under my feet a procession of fine new houseboats; each one had stenciled on its prow the title of one of my books. I never found out who the owner was.

This morning, woke from a disconcerting dream in which I was relieving myself in a bathtub. I had come out of some brown water, and the bathtub and I being outside somewhere near the Champs-Élysées, I was looking for something to liquefy, to flush out the substances inside. Between the Wallace fountain and the pedestal of one of the Marly horses, there was a metal pitchfork with its wooden handle stuck in the ground. I took the pitchfork and walked toward the bathtub, but I was uncomfortable because some farmers were watching me. I turned around to put the pitchfork back. And I said to myself: "Since I'm dreaming, I shall walk around and wait until I wake up." I must have been pretty wide-awake to say this. Wide-awake, I wondered why I hadn't lit a cigarette, as I usually do. "It must be that I never smoke in my dreams," I realized. I had never noticed this before.

Waking, the mind preserves the rhythm of its own confabulation, embroiders on the theme of any subject, the way a vehicle whose motor has stopped rolls a few yards farther on its own momentum. A mirror, a chair, a curtain, a garment thrown on a piece of furniture suffice to construct, then and there, terrifying creatures which a touch of consciousness eliminates altogether.

Note for book. I discover this oddity: as in many theaters, and in all theaters abroad, *there is no smoking in my dreams.* Yet I constantly smoke Gauloises. It is all the odder that I should have done away with smoking in my plays and that I had never noticed, before this morning, this feature of my dreams. It is possible that this suppression of cigarettes, which the waking self attributed to a style (compel the actors not to copy life), came from that dreaming self, without my suspecting it.

For a note to the chapter "on dreams" in my book.

. . . .

JULY 20 · 1952

Proust hides behind *the other*. This is the way to recount oneself with extreme complacency.

Many political intrigues, such as the Regency (conspiracy of the duchesse du Maine), have had their source in boredom. One conspires to overcome it. Councils are quickly transformed into opinions, actions, commitments. Dictators do not tolerate a single minute of relaxation. A governmental Eden would make politicians and journalists despair.

Roger de Vilmorin's valet: "Glad to have a war so you can have something to talk about in the Métro!"

Proust is a snob who is wrong to be one, a pederast who is wrong to be one. He is very harsh in his judgment of snobs and pederasts in order to deflect attention from his own person. This is also a delectation. To write in urinals in order to be read. (Without knowing who has written the obscenity.) To be read and remain invisible. A kind of group exhibitionism.

. . . .

July 21 · 1952

Reading Sartre's book on Genet carefully. He magnifies and idealizes—even the horrors. When Genet meets you, he asks: "How do you find me? I'm fine, don't you think?" Something very frivolous and very pedantic inhabits him in which the great destiny Sartre bestows upon him does not appear. For Genet this book is terrible: he must either abide by it or call it stupid, which is quite in his line but, in this case, hard to do.

The book represents Genet no more than the Statue of Liberty in New York represents American freedom. Like all true works of criticism, it is a monumental portrait of Sartre of which Genet is merely the stone or the bronze.

Sartre acquits Genet, which is to strip him of the glory of failure. He kills him: "a perfect crime"—which could be the subtitle of his study. He turns Genet inside out; hence he puts him right side up. After this book Genet can no longer cheat in any casino in the world.

Jean Genet thinks for those who do not think. He speaks for those who are silent. With Genet the creature known as a *voyou* has found his fabulist.

America is the only legal country which admires the breaking of rules, provided this action is of an exceptional order.

. . . .

JULY 23 · 1952 · Santo Sospir

Finished Sartre's book. The last chapters sink into a disgusting mud. Too bad. Unless the public vomits up the work of which this terrible study is the preface and discovers with astonishment the enchanted aspect of Genet. It is as if Sartre denies this to him. By dint of thrusting filthy rags down his throat, he clogs the plumbing. I put the book down with a dreadful sense of discomfort. Who can swallow such a thing?

We got here last night. Sea like a lake. Heat. I must find a method of work. Alternate work, sleep, bathing. I don't have the right rhythm yet. Slept little; Sartre's book the problem. Unbearable smell. He quotes me a good deal—but except in the phrase *another defendant, Jean Cocteau*, he does not involve me in anything base.

For instance, I should not like either Francine or Édouard to read this book.

It is true that I managed to get Genet out of the law's clutches. I said in court: "Be careful. This is a great writer." The judge sentenced everyone. He was afraid. Afraid of seeming stupid—the stupidity of the French bourgeoisie.

The judge: "What would you say if someone stole your books?"

Genet: "I should be proud."

The judge: "Do you know the price of this book?"

Genet: "I don't know its price, but I know its value."

The lawyers turn their heads as though watching a fine tennis match.

Later we interceded with the president of the republic—Sartre and I—to spare him transportation for life. What is funny is that Sartre had asked me to draw up an appeal for clemency. Still hearing Genet say "transport," I wrote "transport." This appeal for clemency was illegal since it was pending trial. We obtained it against all expectations and all regulations.

Ultimately, I was disgusted. It was all disgusting. Aside from the fact that Genet accepts (and demands) that one militate on his behalf, even though such actions contradict his myth and his goal.

. . . .

JULY 24 · 1952

A magnifying position is adopted instantly: I decided that you had to have the journalists against you because I have them against me. If I had had them for me, no doubt I would have arrived at a different attitude.

I write to Sartre: your greatness is to be the victim of no superstition. You walk under every ladder.

Difficulty getting back to work—even answering my mail. Sweat flows more readily than ink.

(Rereading Proust.) I once said to Mme de Chevigné: "People are always quoting to me the same four witticisms of Edmond de Polignac. Were those gentlemen all so clever?" And she replied: "Not a bit of it. In those days there were five glasses at every place—a great deal was drunk, and everyone was half-seas over. Some people thought they were saying clever things, and the rest thought they were hearing them. Everyone was drunk."

After many years Étienne de Beaumont shed some light for me on a certain absurdity of the bright young things of 1952. "You're forgetting that they all drink!" he said. "You're forgetting that they're all drunk."

. . . .

JULY 25 · 1952

Superficial critics have often taken for a deliberate imitation my faculty of mimetism which derives from a sort of self-annihilation in the presence of what interests me. In a sense, I become it. And to the point of playing the role of anesthetic in pain. Afterward the shape and the moral nuances I have assumed do not immediately leave me. Something of them abides, and it is possible that this is perceptible in certain poems where I have not been careful to wait for a total return to myself. But it is rare that I fail to take precautions on the threshold of an authentic work.

Fashion is important for art. It immediately discredits itself and compels one to change weapons.

Louis XVI is the first capitalist bourgeois at grips with the prodromes of Communism.

. . . .

JULY 26

After the assault of the hibiscus by the rose geraniums—an assault halted by a few swipes of the sickle—the hibiscus takes its revenge: it tries to smother the geraniums by a surreptitious and implacable invasion.

. . . .

JULY 27 · 1952

Fat King Farouk used to say: "Soon there will be only the king of hearts, the king of spades, the king of clubs, the king of diamonds, and the king of England." There is a queen of England, and Farouk, after abdicating this morning, left Egypt on his yacht. Things have gone faster than I expected—but as I expected.

It is impossible for me to work from notes. I lose my way. I have to take notes in my head. I have all the trouble in the world finding my way in the chapter "Of Perspectives."* You have to have the courage to burn everything, to rethink everything, and to write.

For a week now, a strange thing has been happening to the hallway fresco: the saint riding on the centaur. I notice a sort of dimple appearing in the centaur's chin. I get up on a chair and scratch it out with a razor blade. The next day the dimple reappears in the saint's chin. I scratch it out. This morning it turns up in the centaur's chin.

In Proust's last volume, I rediscover the stories about Mme de Galbois, a lady-in-waiting of Princess Mathilde—stories that Reynaldo Hahn used to tell us in the apartment on the boulevard Haussmann. "The princess has a cow so splendid that she is always being asked to put it out to stud."

The duc de Montmorency, of dubious sexual tastes, had invited the young prince imperial for a stroll. They failed to return, and a certain anxiety was expressed. Then they arrived. "We've been," said the duke, "on foot as far as the Jardin des Plantes." "And everyone knows," Mme de Galbois then observed, "that Monsieur le Duc is a famous pederast."

One night, it was snowing, and on the doorstep the duc de Luynes, who was leaving the house, opened his umbrella. "There's no need for that, Monsieur le Duc," said Mme de Galbois, "it won't snow anymore." "How the devil do you know that?" "They've put salt on the ground."

Doudou quotes me the blunders of his Bouligny comrades. "I

*Ultimately entitled "Of Distances," in *Journal d'un inconnu*.

don't want you to pay. I'm your guest." A young lady to a voice coach: "I'd like to take dictation lessons." A young man: "That was in the days of Starist Russia."

. . . .

JULY 28 · 1952

I have just reread several works on the Revolution and on the reign of Louis XIV. It is clear that Louis XIV's pride ruined France. Condé obeyed ludicrous commands. (Hatred of Holland.) This whole period in Condé's life was nothing but failures. He managed to survive by sheer nobility of soul.

Louis XVI was a capitalist bourgeois. He was the victim of an incipient communism. Absurdity of the queen who couldn't say thank you and who might have convinced him to invent the monarchic system of modern England. The queen and the king, in the Temple, set the example of a perfect family. But it is easy to behave well in disaster. That is when a good education shows. (Wilde in jail.) The hard thing is to behave well in good fortune. That is the proof of real spirit. Nothing is more absurd than the stoicism of the aristocrats confronting the guillotine. One scream from a woman of the people (Mme du Barry), and the scales fall from our eyes and ears. Moreover, other kingdoms had so reluctantly come to the aid of the French king and queen that they had nothing to lose in agreeing to serve as examples. The people adored Louis XVI, and it was only her blunders that made them detest the queen. She wanted to "take revenge": she dreamed of massacring this people who cheered her at the windows. Ignoble to La Fayette. Ignoble to Mirabeau. Ignoble to anyone who helped her—all because of her hatred of gratitude. She understood nothing. A fool, and a proud fool. Detestable pride.

The press. Farouk done for: all his residences surrounded; given a few hours to clear out; his photographs torn up. One realizes that the regency is a stage toward another regime. The notion of royalty is not rejected in five minutes. Louis XVI kept his right to form ministries and his right of veto for a very long time.

The more letters I open, the more I realize that my advocates and partisans are secret. This is why France is unaware of them, and abandons me. They gave me the Legion of Honor* to make up for a certain neglect. They promise me the Académie and vote for idiots. No doubt it is my glory to live in this shadow of fame, and I must abide by it. I have always preferred friendship to admiration. It is to this vast public of friends that I owe myself and my career. I must accommodate my moral being to it.

. . . .

July 29 · 1952

The Matisse chapel in Venice. It is disastrous that Matisse should justify the idiots who say: "My daughter could do as well." I am constantly shown bad decorative work which is better and which is not worth much. There is such a distance between the magic of the Matisse line and the disconcerting, almost caricatural poverty of his drawings of the Saint and the Virgin, that the eye stammers, the mind stumbles. Impossible to belie the tourists who come in and shrug. That is the real drama of this chapel. Except for its steeple, one door, and a few stained-glass windows, the whole thing is a failure. Which does not keep some persons from swooning over it—the same ones who see nothing in my own frescoes.

In Proust's work, neither child nor dog nor cat is ever mentioned.

Another strange thing: at the Guermantes' final luncheon party, there is only hair gone white—wigs. There is not a single bald man.

---

*In September 1949.

I said there were no children in Proust's work. For I cannot count as children (on the Champs-Élysées) characters who send baskets of orchids and who take caffeine. It is odd that Gilberte can still be "playing" on the Champs-Élysées when she already has all the mannerisms, the vocabulary, and the seductiveness of a grown woman. Gilberte seen at home, at the Swanns', is no longer a little girl who goes to the Champs-Élysées. One might see her, instead, at concerts or at exhibitions (where she goes, moreover), which jars with the Champs-Élysées and wooden horses and waffles.

Marcel's nights. His sudden coldness to Paul Morand, who had written a sort of poem about him in which occurred the words "From what mysterious *routs* have you returned, Marcel?" in which it was not the word *routs* that had caused the difficulty, but the fact that Morand used the French spelling *raout*, so that the word *rat* was discernible. Of course, such a thing had never occurred to Morand, and I suppose he was still unaware of what I had learned from Gabriel's (Jupien's) dreadful indiscretion—the latter's establishment in the rue de l'Arcade being financed by Proust—just as he writes that Jupien's place was financed by Charlus.

The rat killed in a trap was complicated by a photograph of Proust's mother. And if you reread Proust carefully, as I have just done, you keep coming back to the theme he projects onto others: the profaned mother. Transformed into a father in the scene with Mlle Vinteuil, the profaned mother is restored to her original condition when Charlus says that Bloch might interest him if he were to brutalize his mother. It recurs in Saint-Loup and his mother, Mme de Marsantes, when he replies so insolently to her loving concern, at Mme de Villeparisis's. And above all (the rat perversion), when I discover a terrible little sentence hidden in the account of a dream: "that my parents were imprisoned in a rat trap." Perhaps this dream was at the source of this sexual complication, and Proust imagined that the boy being looked for at Les Halles was killing his father and mother in his presence, transformed into rats and imprisoned in a trap.

Tell about Mme Greffulhe and d'Annunzio.

Tell what is missing in Proust: the authentic kindness of Stanislas de Castellane and the lunch at the chef's. His parvenu quality.

Proust, who had a thousand reasons not to be anti-Semitic, manages to seem so in his book.

Tell about the scene at Montesquiou's (like that of the hat), and note the failed *genre artiste* of fashionable people (fans, poems—Montesquiou, duchesse de Rohan, etc.) which makes them into outsiders, though they dream of knowing us even more than we would ever think of such things in regard to them.

The charming duc de Guiche (of slightly Semitic type) transformed into the duc de Grammont. Francine tells me about his son's incredible kindness to her at Cannes, during the Occupation.

I explain to her the (remarkably accurate) Proustian mechanism: kind to the point where he tries to prove he is not anti-Semitic, that he is free of prejudice, that he is not like his milieu—even saying: "Of course, we have Jewish blood in our veins."

Mme de Beaulincourt. I was a boy, and I went with my family—like the bourgeois at Mme de Villeparisis's. She wasn't painting flowers but making artificial ones out of silk. Later Boni and Stanislas de Castellane would say to me: "I used to see you as a child at my aunt Beaulincourt's."

One comes to wonder if Marcel—aside from the scenes of rats and the mother's photograph in the rue de l'Arcade and later in the rue de Madrid (Albert)—ever experienced much more than vague fumblings. This is what he seems to express in his strange idyll with Albertine—about whom one wonders throughout whether she has been the narrator's mistress or not. This is because he transposes his fooling around with boys into normal relationships, and this fits poorly—begins to take on the qualities of love only in his fine divagations on jealousy on which Marcel, shut up in his room, fed his solitude and his obscurity.

Adhéaume de Chevigné weeps on the stairs of the rue d'Anjou the night of Marie-Thérèse's marriage to Croisset—her second marriage to a Jew—since he adored his daughter and was jealous of all her suitors.

After the Frechdorf exile, Laure de Chevigné married off her daughter to Bischoffsheim—Marie-Laure's father. Jewish blood mixed with the Sade line. But, ultimately, the perfect kindness, grace, and good education of Francis de Croisset managed to conquer all obstacles, and his name (an American lady once asked him in my presence if he had changed his name) assumed all the power of a real name.* He was a first-class husband, and his wife never knew a thing about his countless escapades, which involved both sexes.

I was one of the family (through Mme de Chevigné) until the day Marie-Laure said she was going to marry me. From that minute Mme de Chevigné assumed that I was responsible for such a notion—that I was actually trying to marry Marie-Laure and that our family was trying to attach itself to theirs. My mother was furious and told me: "How many times have I told you not to spend time with a woman who doesn't pay her help!"

When Marie-Laure, who was quickly married off to Charles,† told Charles that she would marry him but that she would never love anyone but me, it became clear that the problem was not of

---

*Francis Wiener, known as Francis de Croisset (1877–1937).

†Vicomte Charles de Noailles (1891–1981). He married Marie-Laure Bischoffsheim in 1923. Charles and Marie-Laure de Noailles commissioned Buñuel's and Dali's second film, *L'Âge d'or* and Cocteau's first, *Le Sang d'un poète* (1930). They were the dedicatees of the play Cocteau wrote in 1932, *La Machine infernale*. Painters and musicians were the beneficiaries of their generosity. A writer, Marie-Laure de Noailles (1902–1970) published, from 1937 on, a number of stories, poems, narratives (under the name Marie-Laure and the pseudonym Erila Ferrari). Also a painter, she exhibited her canvases in Paris and in New York.

our making, and the whole family made as much of me as they had before the drama.

Further developments were to cause me a thousand vexations of every kind—especially when Marie-Laure learned through Bérard that I was living with Natalie Paley-Lelong.* Bérard was doing her portrait; he later explained to me that he had told her this piece of gossip in order to make her face more expressive. He made it so expressive that she broke everything in the house—dragged Charles to Paris and came to my place in the rue Vignon to break everything all over again, in Charles's presence! Then Marie-Laure declared she would become Natalie's best friend and come between us "like a gorgon's head," which is what happened.†

She is responsible for Natalie's miscarriage; she turned N against me when I was living with the Markeviches in Switzerland.‡ Marie-Laure thought I was in love with Markevich, that we were living together, and carried this grim melodrama to the point of a sensational visit to the Hôtel de la Madeleine, where I slapped her in Natalie's presence.

When I consider, now that so much time has passed, the period when I was living in the world of society, I realize the danger incessantly incurred in an idle and, fortunately, unimaginative mil-

---

*Princess Natalie Paley, born 1905 in Paris, of the morganatic remarriage of the Grand Duke Paul Aleksandrovich of Russia, brother of Czar Aleksandr III, to Olga Karnovich, who received the title of Princess Paley by an imperial Russian decree in 1915. In 1927 Princess Natalie married the couturier Lucien Lelong and posed for some of the finest fashion photographs of the period (George Hoyningen-Huene, Cecil Beaton, etc.). An enthusiast of the cinema, she met Cocteau at a showing of *Le Sang d'un poète*. Their liaison lasted several months in 1932. Cocteau's poem *"Cherchez Apollon"* (1931–32, first published in *Allégories*, 1941) is dedicated to her. Becoming an actress, she starred in several films of the 1930s with Charles Boyer, Maurice Chevalier, and Harry Baur. She later lived in the United States.

†In Cocteau's *Fin du Potomak* (1940), Marie-Laure de Noailles appears under the name of Vicountess Medusa, and Natalie Paley under that of Princess Fafner.

‡The composer and later orchestra conductor Igor Markevich (1912–1983).

ieu. More imagination in that world with neither heart nor purpose would make it more terrible than the Surrealists were when they telephoned my mother at midnight to tell her I had just committed suicide in a bar.

Fortunately I came in half an hour later. I found Mme de Chevigné with my mother, whom the phone call had wakened in the middle of the night. The news had been telephoned to Mme de Noailles who telephoned to Mme de Chevigné, then to my mother, after my return—and to Gide and to Picasso. Gide, less credulous than the others, came only the next day; he did not believe the anonymous call. On the other hand, Picasso came around at once. He was outraged and was to say to the Surrealists (who declared that they had not played this nasty trick): "If it wasn't you, it was you all the same." Actually this wretched farce was the invention of some petty journalists who considered themselves Surrealists and who confessed their behavior to Yvonne George one night in her dressing room as "a good trick they had played on me." Yvonne George kicked them out and told me the story.*

Oddly enough, it is everything that disgusts me and outrages me about my legend which inspires Mauriac's jealousy. When I was eighteen, one day at the Daudets' near Tours,† where we were staying without the family, I had read aloud one of those stupid poems in which I got up on my high horse and which I imagined to be sublime. Mauriac had just published *Les Mains jointes*. He exclaimed: "I've made up my mind. I'll launch my next book like Poulain chocolates." Whence the nickname Poulain, which is how we always referred to him.

---

*Yvonne George (1896–1930), a popular singer whom Cocteau admired. In 1924 she created the role of the nurse in his adaptation of *Romeo and Juliet*.

†At the Château de La Roche, at Chargé (Indre-et-Loire).

. . . .

JULY 29 · 1952

Storm this morning. The rain leaping on the tiles. I can breathe. I'm beginning the poems for Parisot's book.*

An actor's attitude: Jeannot finds *L'Otage* hateful and asks the producer not to put on this *gibberish*. He does not realize that an actor lives in the immediate and that the immediate has made Claudel taboo. Too noble for the theater.

The darkness to which I have doomed myself is not that of the stage.

Within a Budding Grove. Proust's intolerable snobbery. Even when he makes fun of it.

A greediness for the least details holds Proust down—keeps him from heading out to the open sea. He circulates from one flower to the next, and makes his honey that way.

Letter from Jeannot. Pabst delighted with the new scene. It's being filmed. I write him that if he refuses to act in *L'Otage*, he will have the whole Catholic clique on his back, as an actor refusing to act in Voltaire's tragedies would once have had the whole Encyclopedist clique on his. I advise him to be careful; an actor is doomed to the immediate.

Letter from Jean Genet (Milan). He makes no mention of Sartre's book.

Three days apart, dimples were added to my figures in the hallway; I had managed to scratch them out. This morning, there are nails on the centaur's hand and black embellishments in the red *S*'s of Saint Sospir. Since there is hardly a supernatural reason for such little tricks, I have wondered whose work they can be. Francine, when I show her the nails, opts for the new little maid,

---

**Appogiatures*. A collection of prose poems dedicated to Henri Parisot, one of Cocteau's publishers.

replacing Anna. The black is from an eye pencil, so it must be a woman. I suppose it is the same nasty mechanism that produces scribbles on the walls of Knossos, on the statues of Versailles, or puts lipstick on busts. It comes from a total incomprehension of lovely things, which includes lack of respect and a childish malice.

The death of Eva Perón. In Argentina the crowds are overwhelming; women are crushed to death. Others die of grief. Countless victims. The general keeping watch over the bier dies of a heart attack. In a month, they will say she works miracles. She is "canonized" by the people who already consider her a saint. We are a long way from the creature who, on the Côte d'Azur, disgusted the employees by demanding that the beach be cleared for her and that she be served at all hours of the day or night. Her disease has made her holy. Too bad that people become so decent in disaster. It would be perferable for them to be so in felicity. One would like to see a young man or a young woman take orders in a moment of supreme happiness. Alas, they do so only in the wake of some great disappointment.

Eva Perón always received and visited the poor wearing all her magnificent jewels. Because she had been poor, she knew what attracts the poor. Nowhere is there an instance of such a success. She wanted it. She had tried dance, cinema, and quickly realized that one does not become a lasting idol in studios or bars.

. . . .

JULY 30

Freed of all the dogmas of art (and having perhaps lost the vivacity which is attached to their ostracism), I surrender myself without the slightest resistance to the music of *Tristan* as to that of *Don Giovanni*, as to that of *Le Sacre du printemps*, as to the least song by Piaf which rends my heart.

Nothing seems more agreeable to me than this transition from active to passive, to that permeable object which we ultimately become, after having been an object refractory to certain emanations. In short, I enjoy growing old and no longer being the victim of positions which change so quickly, no longer counting up my old age and that of old anarchies which it is absurd to persist in defending when no one is attacking them.

Rereading *Within a Budding Grove*. One cannot imagine Proust dressed as a child. One thinks of him as always having been a little gentleman in a vest, a hat, and carrying a cane. The way he describes himself waiting for Elstir, who is talking to the *jeunes filles*.

If these girls had ever existed, they would have found him quite ridiculous, laughable with his "pretty vest," "his prettiest cane."

. . . .

AUGUST 1

Unconscious of age. I read in *Paris Match* that Radiguet would be fifty. It is the age he dreamed of reaching, detesting the absurd glamour attributed to youth. But it is impossible for me to imagine him a man of fifty because death stops the hands of the clock and freezes individuals at the moment when we have lost them.

For me, Raymond is fourteen, or twenty. It is impossible for me to form his appearance according to the trajectory which it would have followed and which was perhaps forbidden.

I force myself to reread Proust in no particular order and to take up his different periods in reverse order. His logic gains something from this antichronological method. It is his own, and I feel all the closer to him for it.

Farouk in Capri. He plays the part of a fallen king who will be recalled to power after the governmental miscalculations. Perhaps he is unaware that Egypt despises him; perhaps he imagines that royal prerogatives are infallible among a people of very simple religion with kings embalmed in every cellar.

(Canon Drioton is requested not to return to Egypt: the revenge of the other Egyptologists Varille and Lubicz.)

Proust's two great creations are Françoise and Charlus. Only they have a countenance which cannot be found in any other book. Their race cannot say, like the society people in Balzac (and in Proust): "He is talking about a world in which he was not received."

One charming thing in Proust is the avowal of his bad taste (apropos of Mme Elstir's gowns), particularly apparent in the description of Elstir's canvases, in the emphasis on certain artists' names and even on certain paintings of his own, which (like Mme Swann's promenade down the Champs-Élysées) strongly recalls certain works by Béraud. Proust's account of painting is much more suggestive of Béraud, Besnard, and Boldini than of Renoir, Vuillard, Bonnard, Manet, Degas, and Lautrec, and he never reaches the style of minor masters like Guys or Berthe Morisot, for instance.

One sometimes supposes, rereading Proust, whose work is a kind of monument of the bourgeoisie, that it might be the work not of a snob but of an aristocrat who by some miracle has escaped a milieu whose stupidity he scorns while recognizing the ghostly presence of its ancient enchantments, of its heraldic charms to which aristocrats attach no meaning of this nature, drawing from it only the hauteur of a defunct superiority.

. . . .

AUGUST 2

A certain weariness, reading Proust, in constantly discovering the same mechanisms. At Doncières he forgets the Guermantes' glamour and takes up the theme by granting a certain glamour to the "mysterious" houses of Doncières. Rachel, onstage, has glamour; she loses it in the wings, etc. And floral comparisons accompany each of these little transformations. I wonder if the "Proustians" read line by line or skip. One is alarmed, physically speaking, for his apparently remarkable translators. The very idea of their task overwhelms us with fatigue. (For example, to translate the pages on military maneuvers, after the pages about the restaurant where we once again meet the angels who serve and double the *young Israelites* of the Hôtel de Balbec.)

After my letters, Jeannot decides not to send the management his refusal to act in *L'Otage*.

A bundle of letters arrives from Paris; uncomfortable about being interrupted in my work.

. . . .

AUGUST 4 · 1952

Continue rereading Proust. His magnificent intelligence is particularly fond of describing stupidity. Which is ultimately exhausting. (First dinner at the Guermantes'.)

I have reached the Saint-Loup passage where Proust describes (he must have written it upon returning to the boulevard Haussmann) the scene at Larue's when I brought him a coat, running over the banquettes and the tables. ("As over the snow—Jean leaps over the table like Nijinsky—it was in Larue's purpurine salon"—etc.*)

How disagreeable it is when Proust speaks of friendship, to which he grants no value, when we kept showering him with ours. This explains why, once adopted and idolized by the *NRF* [*Nouvelle Revue française*], he abandoned his old friends to caress new ones.

Thanks to Proust's composites, it still amuses me to imagine Greffulhe becoming the husband of Mme de Chevigné, who found him "stupid as a *goose*." What attracted Proust attracted me as

*Lines from a poem Proust wrote for Cocteau. A complete version occurs in *Opium*.

well in my youth. People in society thought I was mad to keep seeing Greffulhe and to delight in this creature, of whom the duc de Guermantes is the exact portrait. He was regarded as a bore, to such a degree that one day, when I had had lunch with his old mistress in her apartment in the rue Alfred-de-Vigny and was leaving the building, I found him in the concierge's lodge reading aloud (to the concierge and his wife) *Le Cimetière d'Eylau*.

And Mme Greffulhe has become Princesse de Guermantes and wife of that prince to whom I can give no known name.

I have known all the people Proust made his characters out of, and I recognize them in passing the way I recognize at first glance the objects which were the origin of a canvas Picasso shows me. Only I hadn't even imagined they existed before knowing them and therefore hadn't amassed any quantity of dreams about them. Furthermore, my brilliant nonsense of the period suited them better than what I could tell them today. Princess d'Arenberg (whom I have not seen since my society days) recently asked Goudeket, who had invited her and said I would be there, "Is he still as amusing as he used to be?" Proust's *recherche* is captivating, but it is certainly that of a *temps perdu*.

All in all, Proust's considerable work (and perhaps in a minute of sleep we dream a dream as long and as detailed as this work) can be summed up—except for Proust's own genius, instilled throughout—as a lesson in how to live in society, a "manual of youthful and honest civility." There are few pages where Proust doesn't indulge himself in noting differences of caste and milieu.

The misuse of the particle did not keep Balzac from writing inspired descriptions of a world which declared it had never received him.

A thousand times I must have heard Mme de Chevigné tell me: "Marcel is so annoying. He has never set foot anywhere. He talks about things he doesn't know." And she added: "The other day he asked me if I had kept a straw hat with gentians. It's only Mother Daudet who keeps her old hats. I told him so straight to his face."

What amazes me is Marcel's rage and despair because Mme de Chevigné refused to read him, which is like insisting that the toads express enthusiasm for Jean Rostand's studies of their love life.

Astonishment of the *NRF* when I had their editors invited to Mme de Chevigné's at 10 rue d'Anjou. They wanted to know the model for the duchesse de Guermantes (this was after Proust's death), and when Gallimard asked Mme de Chevigné what kind of man Haas (Swann) was, she answered to their great surprise (and mine), pointing at me: "He was Jean. He was Jean, exactly." Of course, there was no connection, but someone outside the world of that society, and who had penetrated it, seemed to them to be of an analogous race, something like a hermit crab, "very witty."

One can explain, for instance, the sudden transition from Marcel's interminable snobberies to the splendid piece about the duchess's red shoes by a thing I witnessed several times in the boulevard Haussmann: a victim of certain mistreatments, or of simple rudenesses so frequent among the aristocrats, and which Proust's imagination amplified enormously, he flung himself into the dark corners of his room and onto paper. Then he wrote the way he stamped on Charlus's hat. He took revenge and made up for that long loving overture of his toward the world of society. It made a kind of brutal break, the shifting of one light to another. And to tell the truth, it is those episodes of revenge that are the best.

Lucien Daudet once played a stupid trick: from the booth at Le Boeuf sur le Toit, he phoned to the duc de Guiche, imitating Marcel's voice and telling Guiche that he was terribly upset at having irritated Mme Greffulhe (the duke's mother-in-law) by his book. Lucien could imitate Proust's voice amazingly. Guiche was half-asleep and couldn't quite make out what Lucien was saying, and he kept sighing: "No, no, Marcel, old fellow, you're all wrong, someone must have been feeding you a line." This little trick must have had consequences, perhaps in the direction I have described. Even so, the trick being all the more incredible since it was highly unlikely that Mme Greffulhe had read Proust or could have understood a single line. She was the one who telegraphed to the Roman amphitheater at Orange, where they were putting on operas: "Reserve Stage Box." Greffulhe was horrible to her and to Mme de Tinan, her sister. He insisted on having lunch at noon; if the women came home late, he shouted to the servants: "Don't serve these sluts anything! Let them starve to death." They were obliged to warm leftovers on a burner in their room. "My wife," Greffulhe used to tell me, "is the Venus de Milo." When I asked him if all his friends at the Jockey Club were as witty as they were said to be, he answered: "Not witty, we weren't at all witty, we were *quick*."

Reading Proust. Sudden collapse in the first eighty pages of *The Captive* (which I've just read). Rehash of themes. Proust imitating himself—and badly. Temperature chart. Extreme fatigue. He manages to lose track of his own characters, forgetting that Morel speaks of "violating" and "dropping" to beguile Charlus, who likes hearing such language, beginning to address the reader, to apologize (Prix Goncourt), sending absurd compliments to Mme Léon Daudet (Pampilia—her signature in *L'Action française*) and to Fortuny, that idiot, showing that his love for Albertine is merely an obsession, that he does not really love her and that for him to possess is to imprison. (Fortuny produced the most hideous fabrics imaginable. I once saw de Max play Orestes in a Fortuny bathrobe covered with hydrangeas. The Fortuny manner fits in very well with Elstir-Bergotte, etc. It is Marcel's own aesthetic in the Madeleine Lemaire-Anatole France period. Besides, Bergotte *is* Anatole France.)

The first half of *The Captive* is literally intolerable. This love *sans* love, this jealousy whose absurdity reaches the point of making Proust say he prefers knowing Albertine is at the Trois Quartiers rather than at the Bon Marché because the store is smaller (he means that she will flirt with fewer people, will cruise fewer people), all this doesn't stand up. Besides, this Paris of Proust in which young people no longer need to find work, since there are only milkmaids, women butchers, women coach drivers, women cyclists, women telegraph operators—this naïve continuity in fraud *engenders boredom*. What is interesting is to see Proust project onto Charlus what he conceals and to take as his own the false duel—when he sends an absurd letter to Albertine at the Trocadéro. (Proust does not realize how obvious this is.) This book is a mountain of absurdities, interspersed with absurd purple patches on linguistics—street noises, etc.

How does it happen that Proust, *methodically* jealous, fails to be jealous of people *Albertine encounters in her sleep*? Far from it: this vegetal sleep calms him and affords him the excuse for another purple patch, a poor one. Luckily for me, he missed the theme of *Plain-Chant*—more Proustian than his paragraphs on Albertine's sleep.*

Book. Dictated as far as the story of the cabbages.† I dictate slowly because my syntax isn't familiar to Bonello's secretary, who is used to taking down testimony.

Then I must dictate the Greece diary and the rest: the sketches for *The Apocalypse*; the poems for Parisot. (Don't forget that the last two chapters of the book are not legible as they stand—to be entirely rewritten.)

Amid all these shaky glories, and this rereading of Proust with an eye which will eventually be everyone else's as well, it is Sartre

*Cocteau wrote the poems in *Plain-Chant* when he was staying with Raymond Radiguet at the Villa Croix-Fleurie in Pramousquier, in October 1923.

†"Of Criminal Innocence," in *Journal d'un inconnu*.

who triumphs by writing *close to the idea*. The older I get, the happier I am that I always avoided a style which superimposes itself upon the object. That is what ruins writing.

The example of Claudel, which Claudelians (and his actors) find sublime. "And the great incontestable stars." What do the stars prove? Gide was right to be distressed by *Le Soulier de satin*, which continues to triumph, even among audiences of miners in the East. Claudel was right, after all, when he told me: "I'm in fashion now, and I'm taking advantage of it."

In the second half of *The Captive*, Proust, having decided he was sufficiently protected, recovers his true rhythm, regains control of his orchestra. The thread of his narrative is now as clear as it was tangled, and from now on he holds on to it. From beginning to end, the Charlus-Verdurin drama follows its splendid trajectory. You can tell Proust is much more at home in Charlus's realm, which he knows so well, than in Albertine's, which he invents without knowing it and which pertains to love, a subject he simply fails to understand. Like friendship, love eludes him; he confuses it with a kind of police court disease, analogous to asthma or to the intelligence service.

The writing itself clears, becoming incisive, distinct, radiant; it *runs*.

. . . .

AUGUST 5 · 1952

Letter from Jean Genet. He feels our life systems have no point in common and, unless certain circumstances permit us to reestablish a serious friendship, refuses to exchange the merest civilities with me and proposes breaking off our relationship altogether.

This letter has raised a great many problems for me. I have thought it over. Wondered where he was right and where wrong.

The letter emphasizes a solitude which is the result of my poor navigation through life, and my supposing that it was only honest to admit as much, so that I have finally been stranded on a desert island, where no one perceives my signals.

Genet says I refused the dedication of *Funeral Rites*, whose title [*Pompes funèbres*] I had suggested to him.* He is mistaken: I withdrew in favor of his dedication to Jean Decarnin. We are inclined to believe that friendships are immutable and survive in a kind of somnolence. But we forget what others are thinking and that their solution develops in a direction which is not the same as our own. Whence certain surprises which distress us, but which shouldn't altogether astonish us.

I have answered Genet that my services to him were inconsiderable alongside the moral example he had set for me and that I wanted him to give his *reasons* for breaking with me. (In his letter, he had said: "You will find me ungrateful. I have owed you a great deal. I owe you nothing more," etc.) I wonder if he will answer or persist in his attitude.

He had said (in that letter): "You have surrendered yourself to commercial cinema." To which I answered that it was precisely my mistake *not* to have concerned myself with the commercial cinema and never to have made a sou—which would at least be an excuse for wasting one's time in that world.

This letter reminds me that at sixty I have remained as I was at nineteen and that the same kinds of events occur in a life quite different from the one I was living then. We suppose we have changed completely, but the soul's physique changes as our face does; only it becomes less wrinkled, and we are greatly deceived as to its alterations.

---

*In 1947; that same year Paul Morihien published Genet's fourth novel, *Querelle of Brest*, with twenty-four drawings by Jean Cocteau.

. . . .

AUGUST 6 · 1952

After the amazing Verdurin evening, confusion sets in again with Albertine. (Proust astutely admits having come under Charlus's influence in the mechanics of his jealousy.)

Dictated the book up to and including the chapter on the justification of injustice.

Corrected certain passages on Stravinsky, Picasso. No longer clear as to what this book is worth, for in passing through a secretary who doesn't know what I'm talking about, it becomes, typed up, another book. It will have to appear in print for me to figure it out.

Saw Chanel, who tells me about her Swiss residency: she no longer pays taxes in France, only a Swiss fine. But for those of us who are not so rich as she, the advantage would be offset by the cost of life in Switzerland. The money would disappear just as fast as it does in taxes.

I remember as an exceptional occasion—for Proust never went out except at night—Proust calling for me up in the rue d'Anjou one *morning*, in the Albaret fiacre, to go see the Mantegna *Saint Sebastian* at the Louvre. He had the look of an electric light bulb left on during the day—or of a telephone ringing in an empty apartment. In the Louvre, people no longer looked at the pictures but at him, with astonishment.

Don't buy gold, says M. Pinay. Only a minister is corruptible, and gold is not.

I am frequently amazed to be understood better abroad than in France, whereas in France I am misunderstood as France is misunderstood abroad. It is likely, paradoxical as it seems, that I am, thereby, the typical Frenchman (foreigners are interested, in France, only in the individual).

. . . .

AUGUST 8 · 1952

Poor, poor Marcel. Poor sick man with his lunatic gaze. He knew nothing of love, only the obsessive torments of his lies and his jealousy. He used them as he did the rituals of the rue de l'Arcade. He transcended them there. I knew his "captive": a stupid bellboy whom he locked up in a room somewhere and encouraged to paint. He made Walter Berry buy his canvases. As Françoise loathed Albertine, so Céleste loathed that boy—and there was some dreadful story of gold rings missing. Only such a boy would have been capable of speaking the wretched phrase Marcel puts in Albertine's mouth (*casser le pot*). Marcel's naïveté. He doesn't realize that a woman, and even less a *jeune fille*, cannot utter such a phrase. On the other hand, it is exactly in the style of his bellboy, who would complain because no one ever opened the windows, so that the break came when he decided to make so much noise opening them. (This scene actually occurs in the book.) He would say to me: "It's deadly in here." I have forgotten if he ran away or if Céleste showed him the door.

The Fugitive. I will write nothing else about Proust. I leave off, saddened by this bad dream, by this nocturnal marmalade, by this cloud of antiasthma powder. All these cruel insects, this whole termite colony are too much for me. I recognize the visible signs when I think of the work in the rue Madame (*NRF*): Marcel's text covered several desks, swarmed in the office like ants. People were deciphering, clipping, classifying, matching up. Even when it all matched up, the anthill remained. Marcel's genius seems to be the genius of the species: that is, of termites or bees. You are tempted to put on a mask or to use insecticide. You feel your soul shriveling inside you. You are frightened.

Incredible thing. In Antibes there is a Picasso show and a Fernand

Léger show. Huge posters announcing them. On the main square, another poster in front of a huge circus tent: "A unique war trophy. Only one of its kind in the world." And inside? Hitler's Mercedes.

Nothing more admirable than the passage on progress, in one of Baudelaire's notes in *Fusées*. He understood everything, anticipated everything. It could have been written this morning.

. . . .

AUGUST 10

Most likely Seghers's letter asking to publish a long poem has started something I didn't anticipate. Against all expectations, ninety-two strophes have appeared.*

Etiquette. The queen says: "Louis the Sixteenth was taken to the guillotine in a carriage. Why are you taking me there in a cart?"

The workers drag Eva Perón's coffin on a caisson.

The Augean Stables win hands down at Deauville.

I am constantly asked for articles about Raymond Radiguet. I helped him when he was a boy. *He is fifty years old.* He can take care of himself.

A journalist once asked Radiguet: "Have you any vices?" "Yes," he answered, "every morning I pull on my pants." (Often repeated since, but it was Raymond who said it. He was fifteen at the time.)

I wasn't going to speak about Proust anymore. But it is still important to tip one's hat to the second part of *The Fugitive*, when Marcel gradually discovers her lies.

The satisfaction of what is called vice is always "fresh" in that it is a departure, equivalent to what a Sunday picnic at the roadside represents for certain people.

Mme X: "Last night I dreamed I was questioned by a psychoan-

Le Chiffre sept (Seghers, 1952).

alyst." "Well," I told her, "that's the most economical way I know of being analyzed."

Some young people in Vienna write to say that they are organizing a theater and want to call it the Théâtre Jean-Cocteau. Unfortunately they add: "It will be the Kingdom of Fantasy." I am forced to answer that I detest fantasy; they can use my name only if their program coincides with my own.

. . . .

AUGUST 11 · 1952

Horrible murder of a British family camping in Lurs.* Four days ago. Yesterday a family was picnicking at just the place where they found Mme D's body.

No more to be said. More has been said. It's like the Dreyfus affair—Caran d'Ache's cartoon. I shall speak one last, very last time about Proust. End of *The Fugitive* (Venice). It is *nothing*, and since Proust was not nothing, you wonder what is happening (was he very sick?).

I have only now come to understand the attitude of Proust's best friend, Lucien Daudet, about his work. "Marcel," he used to say to me, "is like Anna de Noailles. He has no heart. The people he 'loves' he forgets all about in five minutes." Unless he torments them like flies or they afford him an excuse to torment himself. According to the rites in the rue de l'Arcade and the rue de Madrid, now avowable and respectable. The flies children torment, the toads they inflate with a straw, etc. . . . This was the case of Albertine. It was quite useless to burden us with her for a thousand pages (before and after her death) in order to pocket, almost

*The British biochemist Sir Jack Drummond, his wife, and his daughter were murdered on August 5, in Lurs, on the banks of the Durance, not far from the farm of the Dominici family. Jean Giono wrote a short book on the trial which ensued: *Notes sur l'affaire Dominici*, 1955.

without reading it, the telegram (which he believes) in which she admits to him, in Venice, that she is not dead. He doesn't even mention it to his mother and abandons the theme of Albertine's lies, of which this would be the biggest of all.

What counts much more for him are the weddings of Saint-Loup and Cambremer, who become pederasts on the spot. His universe in which *not one young man works* (even the butchers' boys become *butchers' girls*). In which all the characters (except himself, of course) are homosexuals or whores. That absurd display of mistresses, women, *jeunes filles* he castigates his homosexuals for displaying.

"No," Lucien used to say to me (*and he really loved Marcel*), "no, my dear Jean, Marcel is inspired. But he is a cruel bug. Someday you'll understand." I didn't believe Lucien. I had been amazed, though, when fame came to him, to see Marcel drop all his old friends and take up exclusively with the *NRF* group, with critics (including that swine Souday among others) to whom he gave huge dinners at the Ritz.

Proust inaugurated the heartless epoch which Baudelaire heralds in his notes (*Fusées*).

Have you noticed that Proust as a child and adolescent never has teachers? He attends no school. That his bourgeois family imposes no classes, no teachers upon him. His intoxication when his article appears in *Le Figaro*—an intoxication which we encounter again after his "discovery" by Gide, who refused to read him before I compelled him to do so.

Diaghilev had invited Souday to the last private rehearsal of *Petrouchka*. There were five of us there; at the end Souday stood up and said, "M. de Diaghilev, I am far too old to sit in a theater merely to hear someone bang a drum."

Nothing is sadder, more depressing than ceasing to love a work. Alas, I am not like Proust, and I shall not forget his the way Marcel forgets his grandmother. This work will haunt me like a dead woman.

Proust once wrote for me on the flyleaf of one of his books: "In Sweden, people are writing dissertations about me, and your neighbor (Laure de Chevigné) refuses to read me." This was enough for him to abandon Mme de Guermantes, finding her a fool. Fabre did not require the insects to read him. But if Proust reads the insects, he naturally expects them to return the favor.

Sartre's book on Genet is a Sorbonne course. I can imagine the students' faces if this had actually been the case: students who giggle when one speaks of a "pregnant woman."

New letter from Genet. He's coming to the Côte d'Azur.

. . . .

AUGUST 12 · 1952

Copied out the poem *Le Chiffre sept* (or *Soirée d'adieux*).

Began copying out the short poems for Parisot: "Flying Saucers."* Continued dictating the chapter "Of Friendship." Still need to work out the chapter on "*Oedipus Rex*" and the one "Of Distances." Then begin dictating the journal (*Past Tense*). Then *The Apocalypse* for Hindemith.

A good lesson: a former Follies girl, Eva Perón, dies venerated by her people as if she were a saint, and King Farouk, long accustomed to privilege, rouses his people to such loathing that they drive him out of the country.

Tonight began dictating the chapter "*Oedipus Rex*."

While I am writing (it is eleven-thirty), I hear talking and shouting out at sea. It is the promenades boat. It is the fashion for a man with a megaphone to give curt orders to do this or that,

---

*One of the poems in *Appogiatures* retains this title.

for him to be obeyed, and for anyone who makes a mistake to receive a dressing-down. Pleasure of our epoch to receive orders and to obey them. (Not to think. Not to argue.) This game, called "General Orders," is becoming a *succès fou* up and down the coast.

. . . .

AUGUST 14 · 1952

I've finished polishing the prose poems for Parisot. There will be twenty-six of them, unless the mechanism keeps working, though I hope it doesn't, for ultimately this kind of writing—made so illustrious by Baudelaire and Max Jacob—is exhausting.

A touching letter from Seghers in answer to mine announcing the birth of ninety-nine strophes (now a hundred). Certainly the first publisher to *ask* a poet for a poem. On the other hand, Millecam sends an amazing sentence that Gallimard had written him in rejecting his book: "Your book requires a certain attention." But Millecam's book about me, *L'Étoile de Jean Cocteau*, will be published by Éditions du Rocher, in Monaco. I've received the contracts, which I've sent on to him. It is a favorable arrangement, since he can get his money without the *fisc* [treasury] taking it away from him.

Terrible spell of hot weather. Arabs are again starting to blast and dig below the terrace. But the prefect has given orders, and the very discreet explosions no longer shake the house.

I shall only correct the copies of three sets of the *Journal d'un inconnu* once the whole thing is done. I can't face redoing the chapter "Of Distances" by hand. Too many confusing notes—too many repetitions. I'll try to dictate the notes and construct the chapter from the typed version.

Yes, it's true, Proust embarrasses and disgusts me, and not Sartre, in his terrible book on Genet. There is a clinician's high-mindedness in Sartre, a love of the subject he is dealing with, a directness.

One is alarmed but not *embarrassed*. There is something else: a sort of takeover of the literary site, a will to diminish everything around. A serious piece of insanity, making Genet into a sort of antihero. For Genet is far (in his person) from corresponding to this book's rectitude, to its implacable advance. He will have to run away or conform to it. In his last letter, he doesn't breathe a word about it.

The proof that Genet's impurity is a purity—insofar as purity is a substance and not, as is supposed, certain sentiments or actions—is that Genet's thief-lovers have always remained friends of an admirable loyalty: Nico, Java, Lucien, not to mention our poor Jean Decarnin, who had a gaze of astonishing nobility and was utterly devoted to Genet, doing him countless favors. I add Sartre's book, which had to be earned. It would be curious, transforming the moral mass of individuals and their spiritual microbes into visible objects. There would be surprises (though not for me), and the object Mauriac would cut a pathetic figure next to the object Genet.

Spent the night thinking of a faun's head for a mosaic in the niche. I found it by remembering the neck of Picasso's pregnant goat. Tomorrow the mosaicist begins work.

. . . .

AUGUST 15

This morning, copied out three new prose poems for Parisot's book.

From the studio terrace, I hear a lady on the beach shrieking: "Oh! It's salty!" No doubt many people think: earth-water-sky—and that's an end to it.

The mosaicist didn't turn up. The style of the coast. Now the studio is filled with tracing paper and the charcoal is fading.

Dictated the notes made on the plane, on the boat, for the

chapter "Of Distances." This chapter is of crucial importance but will, of course, serve no purpose—but someday . . .

Eight o'clock. Only one star to be seen in the sky. Why? Incredible.

What is more hateful than Jules Laforgue and free verse? True freedom must be won within the rules. To escape prison under everyone's nose.

Mass at Saint-Jean: very close to *Don Camillo*. Saint-Jean is a Communist town; the church filled with people, and with flowers. Young people in sports clothes taking communion. The Communist fanfare, "To the Fields," rang out during the elevation of the Host.

Dark was the Virgin's face when she gave birth to the divine Child. Dark and very young. Mary was Ethiopian in origin, wife of that Joseph who had taken her as his wife because she showed strength at her tasks. Because she was "of color," Jesus renounced her, creating racism, in anticipated response to the Jews' ingratitude.

A woman, a Follies girl at that, has rediscovered what kings and dictators know nothing about; Eva Perón will be canonized, and people will ask for her images in order to suppress her husband's politics. So goes the world.

Americans ought to ponder these words of Montaigne: "Lucius Marcius, legate of the Romans in the war against Perseus, king of Macedonia, wishing to gain the time he still needed to get his army fully ready, made some propositions toward an agreement, which lulled the king into granting a truce for a few days and thereby furnished his enemy with opportunity and leisure to arm. As a result, the king incurred his final ruin."

Fernand Gregh, after a lunch at Jacques-Émile Blanche's, said to Maeterlinck and Degas: "Forgive me for taking you out of your way through the rue Raynouard, but I'd like to show you something very interesting." In the rue Raynouard he pointed to a window and announced: "That's the window of my study."

. . . .

AUGUST 16

Olivier Larronde* and Jean-Pierre Lacloche† to dinner. Fine poet though he is, Olivier is doubtless the only one who never publishes or even circulates his poems. Example of an invisibility protecting itself.

Wrote this morning the chapter "On a Journey to Greece," to follow the chapter "On an Oratorio," which I will make an appendix to the book. Put in the note on Évariste Galois, killed by the pedagogues at twenty.

Shut in for three days. Three days of vacation while the roads are clogged with a handsome crowd, but a dangerous one *from several points of view.*

Eva Perón's canonization by the pope and Genet's by Sartre (another pope) are the two mystical events of this summer.

. . . .

AUGUST 16 · 1952

Spoke to Olivier about Évariste Galois, that mathematical genius who died at twenty-one in 1832, the victim of pedagogical stupidity, after having written sixty pages which are still the wonder of the learned world. No one understood a word of what he had written, at the time. He had been expelled from the Polytechnique. He once said: "I am a barbarian because they do not understand." Actually one wonders what posthumous glory is worth in this already posthumous world and if those who succeed in their lifetime are not the real winners . . . If the comfort of the mediocre (Her-

---

*Olivier Larronde (1927–1965), author of three collections of poems, published in 1946, 1959, and 1966.

†Jean-Pierre Lacloche, a friend of Larronde's. Cocteau exhibited portraits of both men.

vieu, Bourget, Porto-Riche, not to mention Béranger) outweighs the admirable disaster of Baudelaire or of Rimbaud. They vanish and pay for their good fortune by oblivion. But what can you do about it? We speak a language which people end by speaking (or understanding) very poorly. It is too late. Évariste Galois did not even have his Verlaine. Alone with figures which devoured him like a Mexican anthill.

My translator, Marie Hoeck, sends me a postcard representing Dali's Christ—according to American newspapers, I said Dali had made more out of this Christ than Judas had . . . An absurd remark I never made, for the excellent reason that I never knew of the picture's existence.

In our punitive age, Eva Perón's death and its attendant events have moved me deeply.

Goodness is not so stupid, since it profits a man, as our arrivistes would say. I know another modern saint, and I live with her. I believe that there is no human being alive so perfect as Francine Weisweiller, except Édouard Dermit, who is altogether beyond reproach. His total purity, his spiritual substance are incredible. My only glory in this world will be to have deserved the friendship of these two supernatural beings.

All of Dali's outrageousness derives from a sickly timidity which he has determined to overcome. He attacks and deifies himself out of fear. At first people mocked him in Barcelona. He managed to overcome the comrades who mocked him by accumulating reasons to be mocked by them. He has made people afraid to be dupes. Now he is followed and imitated by those who mock(ed) him. He is a madman making his obsessions serve his egotism, his lyricism, his mysticism, his *presence*. His wife (Gala) orchestrates everything, the way Garbo's managers used to orchestrate her *absence*. Garbo persists in the old method when she should have changed it and, late in life, become *simple* and *present*.

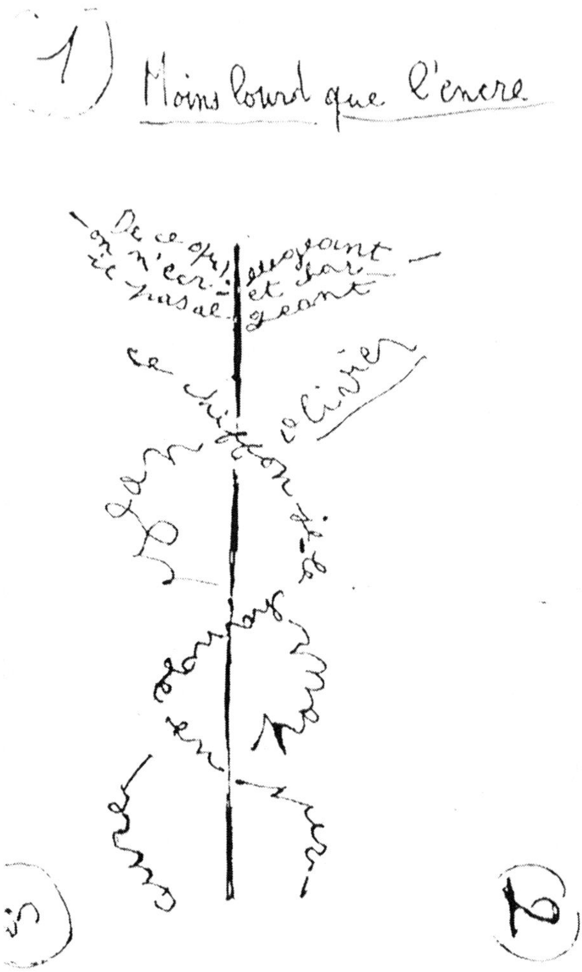

Less heavy than ink
What is not written
to lighten and burden
this scrap I transform into Mercury for Jean Olivier

Mistral. Pains and dizzy spells.

Reread Radiguet? So much more beautiful than the others, because more invisible. The wisdom of Raymond's genius. Wisdom of Édouard's genius as a painter. In a life of nothing but folly, I have attracted only the wise.

How I delivered R.R. of *Devil in the Flesh*. It was at Le Piquey, on the shores of the Arcachon basin. We were living at the Hôtel Chantecler—a sort of log cabin. When I locked Raymond in, he would jump out the window. I copied out his illegible texts, adding mistakes to make him correct them, to make him rewrite.

He combined a Chinese sagacity with an incredible schoolboy laziness. When Grasset asked me to persuade La Sirène to assign him the rights to *Devil in the Flesh*, he gave an advance to Raymond, who was supposed to finish the book at the Hôtel du Cadran Bleu, at Fontainebleau. He returned to Paris, where I was suffering from neuritis, and read me the end of the book, which he had botched. I told him it was unworthy of the rest. He went into a rage (more against himself than against me) and threw his pages into the fire. Later I took him to the Hôtel du Grand Monarque at Chantilly, where I locked him in his room to force him to rewrite the end of his book.

Count d'Orgel's Ball. (Piquey and Pramousquier.) He dictated his illegible pages to Georges Auric, who typed them out on the wooden balcony of the Hôtel Chantecler. Each time a passage inspired Georges to make mistakes, he would seem to be playing his typewriter like a piano, making faces and repeating: "Charming . . . Charming . . ." and Raymond screaming with laughter under a huge straw hat, rolling cigarettes (very clumsily). For he was clumsy and myopic.

Spent the whole morning reworking the poem for Seghers. I have made it rougher, broken it up so that it never seems slick. (Without suppressing certain passages which flow easily and are of a conventional lyricism.) In short, a hateful poem from every point of view—difficult to get hold of: a method in which the invisible excels in order to inspire me, to fortify its defenses.

The prose poems for Parisot are much simpler, with a pseudo-Baudelairean quality; it will probably be said that I am doing imitations. The singularity of these poems must be concealed behind this other method of defense.

A one-eyed Belgian who was the overseer of some blacks in a plantation in the Belgian Congo took out his glass eye and told the men: "I'm going away, but I'm leaving an eye here to watch you." The men believed him and went on working.

Genet telephoned. He will stop by tomorrow.

. . . .

AUGUST 17

The brief episode about Naroumof's hat in *Le Bal du Comte d'Orgel* is far superior to Proust's countless pages about society people.

Genet stole fine editions of books from his friends only to be free to write others just as fine. This is what I told the judges before my public testimony in court. I filled them with the terror of seeming stupid "tomorrow."

To Genet: I think Sartre is annoyed with what I wrote him: his object concealed your substance which he makes use of; his book is more his own portrait than yours. The book contains a long diatribe against "fine minds" who claim that the critic "uses" a work in order to draw his own portrait. But there is not the shadow of a doubt. He has worked you into his thesis and manipulates you in relation to it. I should not be surprised if the book, which sells wonderfully in Germany, is no help to the sale of your own, which it serves, or is supposed to serve, as a preface. We'll have to wait and see.

. . . .

AUGUST 18 · 1952

Thought a good deal about Genet's visit: a stiff, Jansenist Genet, accusing me of having sacrificed my morality to friendship for ten years, telling me he had nothing more to say, that literature disgusts him, that he had burned (torn up) five years' work. All this is full of contradictions. If he didn't care about literature, why burn his texts? He should have sold them for a lot of money and called them posthumous works. Besides, he said he had burned them; then he corrected himself and said he had torn them up. This is because he remembered that this summer there was no fireplace in his room. And friendship should mean more to him than Letters.

I divine another Genet, whom I know well, behind this attitude which, according to him, is very reserved to everyone (except to the rich people whom he deceives and robs). He says that I have written my works in order to conquer people. I *have* conquered them, since they receive me. Now I have rediscovered in myself the child I was before writing, and I spit on them. Etc. I believed it all while he was there. With the night's perspective, I see, as in Sartre's title, the actor behind the saint. Genet's impeccable gray suit: just as we were parting (Doudou took him back to Villefranche), he recovered that sly look of his and that extraordinary kindness. I asked him if he hadn't had to contend with any sort of censorship, such as there had been for the film of *Devil in the Flesh*. He answered that he was not interested in that point of view. Apparently he wants to put in a bad light everyone (except Sartre) who has written and published during his period of silence. He ran into Olivier and Jean-Pierre when he arrived and gave them a horrible greeting. It was so uncomfortable that I had to hurry them away. I used to think he was very close to them. He says that Olivier was acceptable as a very young man, but no longer . . . That he's a sick man. A disordered man. That he is filled with vanity and spite. And he adds: "I cannot bear spite." I ask him if he believes Olivier is Lubicz's illegitimate son. "He's told me he was the illegitimate son of any number of people." Yes, but he looks like Lubicz, which would explain his atavisms. Lubicz and his mother, who are exclusively concerned with occult sciences, have convinced him that he is the Messiah. "There are a lot more than Olivier, these days, who believe that. Shit on them all." To be understood, as in dealing with madmen: *They cannot be the Messiah, since I am.* (New incarnation of Vautrin.)

Listened to *Pelléas* on the radio. *Pelléas* is a pleonasm. One masterpiece on top of another. But in this marriage of preying mantises, the female always devours the male. Debussy's feminine music devours Maeterlinck. Many people imagine that the play is an opera libretto.

Fires toward Biot, Vallauris, Antibes: the smoke we see goes all the way over to Italy. Worried about Picasso. Françoise telephones this morning that it was all to the east—quite far from Vallauris.

The truth? Mme Guy Weisweiller telephones Francine: "Guy is in tears, collapsed in his room. We have nothing left but the house. Not a single tree." Now Picard was at Altana yesterday; not one tree was touched. Everything is intact. And I was stupid enough to write Guy a letter after his wife's call (not to seem to be enjoying good fortune amid other people's disasters).

Renoir. How can you blame Albert Wolff* and the other monkeys for their stupidity when confronted with the first Renoirs. (Or even with the *Moulin de la Galette* and *La Loge*.) Old Gérôme, with

*Albert Wolff (1835–1891), a naturalized Frenchman after 1871, had originally been the Parisian correspondent of a German newspaper and also the secretary of Dumas *père*. Author of six volumes of *Mémoires d'un parisien* and of the theatrical chronicles of *Le Figaro*.

outstretched arms, preventing M. Loubet, president of the republic, from entering the Renoir room: "Don't go in there, *M. le Président*, it is the shame of France." Since these canvases offered them a void formed by the withdrawal of everything painting should not do.

. . . .

AUGUST 20 · 1952

Mozart did *not lay claim to more*. But more *was there*. The mistake is not that Molière takes himself for Sacha Guitry but that Sacha Guitry takes himself for Molière.

Yesterday dictated the end of the notes for the chapter "Of Distances" and the appendix, "Journey to Greece." Added two poems to *Appogiatures*. Wrote the foreword to the new edition of *Opéra* (Arcanes).

Phone call from Frédéric Rossif, who had been sent to Paris for the Matisse film. Matisse has become greedy. F.R. will stop by to see me.

Phrase from *Nice-Matin*: "Barrès, a writer who no longer interests us." According to them, interest resides in the manipulation of immediacy. What counts in a work does not count. They can't even glimpse it. Scrupulously avoid immediacy. Escape the kind of interest critics and journalists take in books.

Thought a lot more about Genet's visit. I have scrutinized my own conscience necessitated by this canonization from below. It is possible that film is, in general, a shameless business, though I believe that neither *Les Parents terribles* nor *Orpheus* is shameless. Moreover, *La Difficulté d'être*, my tapestry, *Oedipus Rex*, and *Léone* do not seem to me to have anything to do with this verdict: "You've done nothing but be a star for ten years."

I keep coming back to that defensive need of Genet's to abolish what others were doing while he was doing nothing. (Did he really destroy five years' work?) What about his resentment of the failure of his own film. He says it was nothing but a pastime, but he didn't consider it any such thing at the time. Yesterday, I didn't even dare ask Java if he had witnessed the destruction of the texts.

Genet's egotism. His face brightened when I offered to take Java to Bordighera by sea. (Java is a deserter.)

The crime at Lurs. What interests me is that the Dominicis have a defense system shot through with lies but whose basic fabric is as firm as that of any truth. If they stick to it, they are impregnable.

Frédéric visits: the Rockefeller Institute is offering two million francs for the film *Santo Sospir*, but requests that I cut everything that concerns Picasso and (at the end) the sentence about the bombs. I refused, of course.

. . . .

AUGUST 21

No more about Proust—but one last remark. Never in his early youth (one is very young when one plays on the Champs-Élysées) is there any question of studies, of school, of teachers. Now this is a rule no one escapes in the French bourgeoisie.

I didn't expect to write the long poem (for Seghers). It is a gift. Goethe was right to say that after a certain age whatever one writes is a gift.

Went to see C. C. at Magnus's. Tonight Olivier and Jean-Pierre describe terrible scenes of a lady on a yacht at Genoa. (Style Henri Bataille.) Contact with that kind of world, even an account of such contact, disturbs me, affords a discomfort prejudicial to my work. Avoid it like the plague.

Sent a new drawing for the cover of the new edition of *Opéra*.

Francine and Édouard have found a little farmhouse in Biot which we are hoping to buy for Édouard's parents when they retire.

Visit from a group of young people. Strange point of view: to make a lot of noise around their work. I explained that noise was defensible if it compromised them without compromising their work. Very difficult to make myself understood.

Dictated the poem. Dictated, by cutting up and pasting what was dictated already, the chapter "Of Distances." I imagine that the whole thing will be done this week. Then all that will be left will be the poems for Parisot and my journal.

I took Java to Italy in the *Orphée II*. There he joined Genet and Lucien (whom I shall take back with me). What Java told me confirms what I think (Sartre): "Jean's toy has been broken. He has been given a new one, but he doesn't know how to use it: too complicated. An electric train. It fills up the whole house, and it is the grown-ups who play with it. Jean has changed since Sartre's book. It seems that he conforms to it and runs away from it at the same time. In Paris, after this book, people treated him like a freak. Even Nico . . . I saw him destroy five years' work, though he did pick up the pieces of a film screenplay and paste them together—he cared a lot about that. I didn't stop him. He would have said, 'What business is it of yours?' Maybe he thought I would intervene. He had just told me he was tearing everything up because I attached no importance to his work. Jean keeps wanting *words* all the time. He attaches no importance to the act of friendship."

. . . .

AUGUST 24

There is nothing more abject, more harmful than this exploitation of heroism in the weeklies and in the press in general. *Match* this week devotes fourteen pages to an underground expedition on which one explorer met death. His comrade decided to photograph him dying at the bottom of a hole. A full page shows his last glance. The article speaks of this *sublime hero* (whom no one asked to do anything—who made this expedition on his own—whereas miners die in the mines several times a day. Besides, the expedition had no scientific purposes whatever). The Carbuccia boy has publicized Alain Bombard's experiments concerning survival at sea; the good doctor's raft proves nothing and interests no one. But he was filmed as he set out. *They should have filmed his return*—or else filmed his death. A journalist's eye is on him: enormous publicity of the void. Naturally—as though on the brink of the prehistoric crevice—we shall see his wife waiting, his father in front of the microphones and the cameras . . .

Monstrous publicity about the miraculous grotto in Rome. An answer to Lourdes. One begins to wonder if the Vatican didn't suggest to Eva Perón that, loss for loss, it was better to become a saint. In a few months' time, she'll be working miracles. Our Middle Ages. Journalistic sentimentality, based on a lack of sensibility. Shamelessness of a vast public accustomed to the worst.

We bought the Biot house yesterday at six. It was raining. Gave the down payment. The drama of the owner's sordid avarice: she was unwilling to throw in the little field in front. We plan to buy a vineyard nearby, which will spare Édouard's father having to work for others.

Orengo came for dinner yesterday.* Millecam has signed his contract. I gave him the little preface. Orengo takes one of my drawings for *Le Bal du Comte d'Orgel*, to see how it will come out in drypoint printing. He wants to publish the drawings with the corresponding Radiguet texts.

Wrote Seghers and Parisot to tell them I was sending the poems.

---

*Charles Orengo (Monaco, 1913–Paris, 1974), founder of Éditions du Rocher during the war; literary director of Librairie Plon, 1949–1960; adviser to Hachette till 1965; and director of Éditions Fayard.

Most people seeing the Santo Sospir frescoes say: "It's lovely," not realizing the calculations which make them so important. The same thing must have been said at Knossos. Curious incapacity to *see* the serious. True, it conceals its skeleton beneath an appearance of charm.

Young painter to Renoir: "*Maître*, what do you think of my picture?" "It's not very good," Renoir says, "but I'll touch it up for you." He works on the picture, which becomes good indeed. The young man tries to sell it but is told that it is a fake Renoir. The young man asks Renoir to retouch the picture so that it no longer looks like a Renoir. Renoir goes to work. But when the young painter tries to sell it, he is told that his picture is worthless. "*Maître*," he asks Renoir, "would you please redo my picture so that it looks like a Renoir and sign it *Renoir*?" Renoir redoes the picture and signs it. The young painter sells it for a lot of money and never forgives Renoir.

Radio singers. No melodic invention. They all moan. Genre of complaint. And the faucet of tepid water runs in every house, all day long. The "Paris" songs are enough to disgust you with Paris forever.

Olivier Larronde says about Sartre's book: "He didn't want to hurt Genet but to perform an exploit on his head: William Tell."

Millecam telephones from the Voile d'Or at Saint-Jean. He has come to see me, will be here at four. I wasn't expecting what he was like: a wraith. His invalid's voice is that of a very young child, even of a girl. His father is Spanish. His mother Provençale. The name is of Belgian or German origin.

Still, you have to be of stronger stuff than the stuff people buy: jazz, radio music, popular novels, bicycle heroes, etc.—in other words, *displease*. No escaping it.

Our substance can please only with the help of a misunderstanding. It is not *what is being worn*.

. . . .

AUGUST 26 · 1952

The final ignominy of the Parisians is to have invented the lie that Stravinsky and I were at cross-purposes in *Oedipus Rex*, that we became enemies to the death, etc. In short, a grotesque *corrida*, indispensable to the swine in the stadium.

Doudou is doing a portrait of Francine painting. Red, adorable, and admirable. One wonders how he rediscovers with such simplicity the strange light of Vermeer . . .

Visit of Parisian journalists and photographers. It will take me three days to get their chatter out of my ears. They have troubled my waters.

Sent the poem to Seghers.

Apparently Mauriac has devoted an enormous leading article to Sartre's book. He calls Genet's *oeuvre* dung. I am reminded of the articles of Albert Wolff, prince of the *Figaro* critics. He had the same kind of perspicacity. Poor Mauriac—insulted in Sartre's book, he could scarcely "answer." But silence is beyond such creatures. They cannot keep from howling straightaway. No perspective—no nobility. Moral filth.

The *inferiority complex* I have developed from the critics' perpetual rejection has made me, in the long run, almost shamefaced when confronting a man who offers no criticism of my work. Millecam, for instance. He has made up for that attitude of student-being-scolded-by-the-monitor which I adopted during Genet's visit the other day.

Letter asking for texts for a film on René Clair—*Naissance d'un film*.* I've asked to see the film, either at Beaulieu or at Nice.

Wrote the article on Ludmilla Pitoëff for *Les Lettres françaises*. I'll dictate it Thursday.

---

*Apparently this short subject was not completed.

Just reread *La Difficulté d'être*. The links are closer than those of my *Journal d'un inconnu*. I repeat myself. I forget that certain things have been said in other books of mine. But I leave them in, considering that readers read badly and forget what they read; repetition of a good thing is good.

Seghers asks me to do a *de luxe* edition of the poem and to add lithographs, as in the Léger book. I have sketched out a few basic drawings.

Letter from schoolboys. I receive a lot of these. Usually they are very personal, and affect a highly complicated style which they imagine will please me.

Generalissimo V. (Argentina) dies the day Eva Perón's coffin is exhibited to the public; he bends down to tie his shoelace and is trampled by the crowd; the crowd is an element which passes over him without seeing him.

Sartre's book on Genet must originally have been a short preface. After a hundred pages, he couldn't stop. This book is the first "court" Sartre seems to pay to poets. He plays his violin. He improvises. He charms *himself*. The theme is dreadful, but he plays. Students adore these exercises in musical virtuosity on the part of their professors. In short, an article like Mauriac's is equivalent to a denunciation. It is the same as informing the police, who were keeping their eyes closed: "This man's work falls under the law's ban. Arrest this bothersome colleague."

Last night, lying in the studio, I was watching Francine and Doudou painting, and I reflected: "How cowardly of you to dare to complain! Here are the two human beings you love most. Nothing happens to be in their minds besides their work and their hope of pleasing you. Francine enjoys herself so seriously, so carefully. Doudou performs wonders without attaching any more importance to them than Francine to what she does." Sometimes I get up and go over to my desk, to correct mistakes that occur to me. Sailboats pass out at sea. These are priceless moments. A calm which many scorn because they do not possess it. A piece of good fortune I shall doubtless have to pay for. Consider my crises as a tax on that fortune.

. . . .

AUGUST 28 · 1952

Letter from Grasset, asking me if Radiguet kept a journal. He has heard that Gallimard is publishing such a thing. Now, Radiguet never wrote a journal. This is either a joke or a fake. Quite in line with my enemies' strategy, after the invention of the quarrel with Stravinsky, to come up with a fake Radiguet journal. I telegraphed Grasset to find out the details. Fake poems by Radiguet have already been published (moreover, utterly unlike his own), preceded by a few nasty lines referring to me.

Received the proofs of Élise Jouhandeau's book.* Strange madness, like certain women one encounters in the street, who seem to live nowhere at all (*The Madwoman of Chaillot*). I will have to say this in the preface, without upsetting Élise.

Went to see Matisse. I find him in bed in the north room. The room is surrounded by paper-cutout frescoes representing blue women diving. Matisse says: "I can't get to the seashore anymore, so I manage here as best I can."

Apropos of the countless canvases hidden in the cellars of Moscow, Matisse says that the Russians have never liked painting. That this is an old state of mind—an old rejection of painters and of images.

Picasso had given a picture to be sold for the benefit of a sanatorium. Then he ran after the people who had come to get it

---

*Cocteau had first known Élisabeth Toulemon (1888?–1971) as the dancer Caryathis, who created Satie's *Belle excentrique* in 1921 and who married the writer Marcel Jouhandeau in 1929. She published the first volume of her memoirs, *Joies et douleurs d'une belle excentrique*, in 1952, with a preface by Jean Cocteau.

from him, saying: "You won't sell it properly—let me sell it, I'll do better for you." And he gave them a check for a million francs.

. . . .

AUGUST 29

Millecam's last day at La Voile d'Or.

Corrected the chapter "On Distances" and arranged the poems for Parisot under the title *Appogiatures.*

Great difficulty making the chapter "On Distances" antiscientific, giving it a certain lightness, freeing it of orthodox pedantry. So that it keeps the savor of heresy, the only one that suits me (that suits poets).

. . . .

AUGUST 30 · 1952

Rain. I have to begin revising the book. But I experience one of those failures of nerve produced by the atmosphere of rejection I have been struggling against for so many years and which I manage to forget when I am working. Once work is done, there is a chance for this kind of depression to invade. An inferiority complex: I wonder whether my denigrators aren't right and if I am deceiving myself as to the value of my undertakings. I have a bad tendency to exaggerate what rejects me and to minimize what is in my favor. This discouragement robs me of the strength indispensable for the completion of my work. Since I believe that this loss of faith is shameful in relation to the two beings who have given me all their trust, I conceal it, and this is yet a further effect which diminishes me.

I misaddressed the poem I sent to Seghers. His letter before the last one had the old address. His last letter corrected it. I telegraphed him to inquire at the post office.

I must somehow, without offering purchase to any sort of pride, rid myself of these depressing weaknesses. I *chose* this struggle and this solitude. It is the defense of the invisible, the theme of my book. But one is always weaker than oneself. A vehicle that doubts . . . That wonders if this role is not absurd in an active world that craves *presence*.

The coast newspapers have doubled their sales since the crime at Lurs. The police are nowhere. But the journalists want to drag the case out and make as much out of it as they can. Knowing nothing, they assume an enigmatic tone: "The police are on the brink of a very important discovery." Which insures tomorrow's sales.

Today at four I have to record at Nice for Radio Lausanne: "German youth today."

Received a letter from Vienna, where the young people insist on calling their theater after me, explaining that the terms which distressed me do not mean the same thing in their language as in ours: *Phantäsie* = imagination, and not caprice.

Last night, dinner at Magnus's, in the former villa of the Grand Duchess Anastasia. Dreadful taste. I remember the grand duchess running after me when I was young, suddenly appearing at my mother's at Maisons-Laffitte, insisting on searching the house where I didn't happen to be, running her cane under the beds. She had written me one day: "I've discovered a little bistro where we won't be bothered." It was La Pérouse.

At last night's dinner, I caused astonishment by saying that except for one dinner party at Daisy Fellowes's, this was the first time I had been out at night since coming to Santo Sospir. "But what do you do?" Nothing. I work. I swim. I sleep. A program which seems incredible to these people, who never stop "doing something."

Letter from Jean Genet: "My dear Jean, the other night there wasn't anything hostile in what I was saying to you. I told you what I thought, but only because you had written me to tell you my opinon. So it was an opinion you heard, nothing else. I live my own life according to certain precepts which I do not ask others to apply, though I should like to admire violently—to the point of envying them—the friends I love. Nonetheless, my dear Jean, if you have any esteem for me, don't worry; I shall always keep the tenderest affection for you."

Letter from Sartre: "Your letters have given me one of the greatest pleasures I could hope for after these two rather arid years I have spent on Genet, and I thank you for sending them to me: who else but you could talk to me about Genet and about my book on him? I think you had already helped him out, long before I ever heard his name.

"I am quite sure that something of myself has gone into the book: I tend to go on a little too long. But you are right, it is the last part which depicts my own obsessions and my own reason for being: the relation to politics, to Marxism, to the Communist party. The dialectic of Good and Evil was written quite cold, and *uniquely* because it is there in Genet.

"You ask me what Genet himself thinks. I believe he is quite pleased. I have never taken this for an objective estimate of my book; whatever one may say about someone in five hundred pages, it is the five hundred pages which remain in his memory, not what is in them. But I am glad that he is pleased, and at least this proves that there is no first-degree error in the thing. No, he was not crushed by the weight of all those words: because I was talking about someone he has buried. After all, *The Thief's Journal* was a farewell. To prison and to literature as well. The two went together. Since he is very 'available,' he has a hundred choices, from a return to theft and prison to a bourgeois existence. Did you know that he's been flirting with the CP? A biographical work on him, especially given his pride, helps him drown the old Adam. It is a stone tied around his neck. He would have been furious if the book had come out in '46 or '47. Today it is his mummy or his statue; in any case, it draws a line, and the *new* Genet is free on the other side of it. Genet will always manage to be free; that is one of the reasons for my admiration of him. What he will do, is another matter. I can't even foresee what it will be. But I am quite inept at anticipations and predictions.

"I too, dear Jean Cocteau, eagerly hope to see you again when I get back to Paris from Italy—will you be in Paris in October? We can talk about all this. But I wanted you to know what a pleasure your letters have given me. Your friend, J.-P. Sartre."

The magazines noisily announce the death of Mme Greffulhe, "the immortal duchesse de Guermantes." Now Mme Greffulhe was the princesse de Guermantes, and Mme de Chevigné the duchess. Eternal inaccuracy of journalists!

. . . .

SEPTEMBER 4

Good visit from the Hindemiths. We talk about the oratorio. But Hindemith's dream (after the oratorio) is to do a modern *opéra-bouffe*, something on the order of *Figaro*. His ideas are specific and very strong. His wife is something on the order of Cosima Wagner. But he listens to her with only one ear—she has a commanding tendency. I promised to dictate my texts and send them to Le Havre. (They are returning to America, where Hindemith teaches at Yale.) Hindemith tells me that he has just heard *Pierrot Lunaire* again. Shoenberg had composed it for cabaret performance, just as Mallarmé had written the *Faun* for Coquelin. The technical singularity having vanished from this subversive work, there remains only a delightful cabaret entertainment; such is the fate of all technique when it supplants internal style.

Received the proofs from Élise. Letter from Marcel Jouhandeau: "Caria was very pleased this morning . . . You can keep the proofs or throw them away—Flammarion doesn't need them. How well I remember a terrible quarrel during which you did my portrait, which Grasset's redhead stole from me so cunningly. . . ."

Seghers got my poem and telegraphs that he finds it "magnificent."

Received the reels for Hans Richter's film.*

. . . .

SEPTEMBER 6

Too much work to write here. Corrected the book, but not the copies. Tiresome work. Finished what I am proposing to Hindemith. Finished the preface for Élise Jouhandeau.

Mme Hindemith told me the following story. After a concert of Hindemith's works in Munich, the audience burst into cheers and came to look for Hindemith in his box. But he was in the wings. Whereupon Furtwängler, who was conducting in another theater and had promised to meet the H.'s afterward, arrives—a few seconds before Hindemith. The public was still applauding in the direction of the box where Mme Hindemith was gesturing to signify: "I don't know where he is." Furtwängler came into the box and, like a circus horse who recognizes the trumpet, walked to the edge of the box and bowed to the audience.

Received the typescript of the German translation of *Bacchus*. It is a real book, with an excellent cover. You could almost print it as it is. This is the working copy for the artists of Düsseldorf and

---

**8 x 8*, an American film made in 1952, with the participation of Hans Arp, Alexander Calder, Jean Cocteau, Marcel Duchamp, Max Ernst, Yves Tanguy, etc.

Berlin.* The translation seems very faithful and solid. A lot of sentences take on a certain power because my translators have rediscovered the original texts, which I had translated into French.

The Lurs case is getting nowhere. It must be a rape of a little girl—a rape *manqué*, for fear of the family which heard cries. Several such rapes this week. Events always occur in series.

Typical Côte d'Azur remark: a restaurant owner in Saint-Tropez declares, "I can't just hang around doing nothing. I'm going to take a nap!"

Spent a good deal of time studying Soutine. The Castaings are wrong.† Soutine is not a great painter. Any more than Chagall. There is a collective hypnosis here and a taste for a certain "subjective" scribbling.

Desjobert had sent me lithographic paper and crayons. I have finished the lithographs for Seghers and sent them off. Cover. Two double pages. One single page. Frontispiece.

There are days when I draw stupidly and days when each of my lines is alive, meaningful. Watch out for the bad days. That is why I keep myself in training by writing unpublishable poems all the time. Keep the hand in practice.

Somerset Maugham has sent back my two books lent to him by Francine, with a very fulsome and very stupid letter. He has the judgments of the public. His success comes from the fact that he writes on the level of the public. Nothing underneath. Nothing behind.

Only a certain race of painters is actually studied. And it is

---

*From Berlin, on August 20, Albert Bebler, director of the Schiller-Theater, informed Jean Cocteau that he had read *Bacchus* and planned to put the play on in the autumn. The role of Zampi would be played by Ernst Deutsch, "whom you know well, and who is the ideal interpreter." He hoped Cocteau would come and direct the play himself—rehearsals at the beginning of October, opening early in November.

†Marcellin Castaing and his wife were admirers of Soutine and had gathered a collection of his works.

about them, and them alone, that books are published. Only they enter the museums. Yet the Prix de Rome goes on. An interminable procession of mistakes and mediocrities does not discourage the students. One wonders why. They must imagine: "It's a matter of snobbery. Later, everything will be seen for what it is." Or some such nonsense. Otherwise they'd stop painting.

. . . .

SEPTEMBER 7

A book from Dr. Albert Leprince, vice-president of the Society of Psychic Studies in Nice. Poor title: *L'Avenir mystérieux et fatal.* In this book, I have found examples that confirm the theories in mine. Certain reflexes provoked by patches of cold on his leg which can suggest that the subject is a visionary of the future. "Past and future are a present which man traverses."

. . . .

SEPTEMBER 9

Vocabulary and ideas of childhood in 1952. Little Carole [Weisweiller] (ten) tells me: "I'm inviting you to a garden party I'm giving in Lurs, on the scene of the crime. There will be gypsy wagons, tents, and athletes who will strangle everyone and beat them up. Machine guns are *old hat.*"

Intelligence is not my strongpoint. It is a transcendent form of stupidity. It complicates everything. Dries everything up. Intelligence is the stag that leads the herd to the slaughterhouse.

Received and corrected the first proofs of *Opéra.* Sent them back to Paris.

Seghers has received the lithographs for *Le Chiffre sept.* Orengo telephones that on Saturday he will bring us the trial plates for *Le Bal du Comte d'Orgel.*

. . . .

SEPTEMBER 11

Unless today's youth lights its fire at the first try, it grows discouraged. I was listening to a kind of potpourri of poems and observations on the radio: Songs of mine (period of *Les Six*). Enough to make you die of shame.

Wire from the Hindemiths: "Chauvigny* marvelous. Perfect background for your words. Emotion and gratitude. Paul and Gertrude."

Drama with J.-L. Barrault. Yesterday I had sent a very strong telegram after reading in the papers that the troupe was not taking *Bacchus* to North America, despite all their promises (no part for Madeleine). Jean-Louis telephones this morning, telling me my telegram is scandalous. I answer that we are even then, since I find his decision scandalous. He insists he never said he would take *Bacchus* to America, etc. This is the climax of a series of disagreeable little incidents which Francine and Doudou sniffed out and which I had refused to believe. I had warned the Barraults that *Bacchus* would cause trouble. I didn't think they would turn against me. I have written a calm letter in which I ask them to settle matters so that I can take the play where I want.

Corrected the three typed copies of *Journal d'un inconnu.*

Received the proofs of the Millecam preface.

Visit from Letellier, who will return to his job in Hamburg and who suspects Alexandre of having rigged the whole Hanover business.

---

*Cocteau had advised the photographer Pierre Jahan to photograph the fantastic capitals of the choir of the Romanesque church of Chauvigny (Vienne).

. . . .

SEPTEMBER 15 · 1952

I receive more and more appeals from young people starting little magazines and coming up against the incredible obstacles France puts in the way of youth.

Visit from a nineteen-year-old who seems quite serious and who is working (on a film) of *Thomas the Impostor*. I'd like to see such a miracle: a young man who makes a film on his own and who manages to translate me without my having anything to do with it. That is why I intend to make contact with his rushes. I had thought that Melville was not so much a young man as a freeshooter whom it would be interesting to set in opposition to the old gang. I made a bad mistake there and had to do all the work myself. I was doing *Orpheus* by day, and *Les Enfants terribles* by night. Melville never set foot in the editing room. I should remember that little experience. But how can you throw up one more wall against this youth which everywhere runs into the same frustrations?

The mosaic has been set. An old Italian workman who looks like Dr. Caligari. It is splendid to see an artisan and his helpers at work; the mosaic is executed in reverse and in patches. Then the ground is cemented, adjusted, and the cubes are broken until there are no empty places left. You see nothing because of the paper pasted over the front. Once his work is done, the paper is moistened, slid off, and the design appears. The mosaic is very fine, very simple, and as we intended, it can be read as black profiles facing each other or as white shapes silhouetted in the middle. I have recomposed the style of the profile masks for the "Oedipus Complex" in *Oedipus Rex*.

Doudou has begun the portrait of Carole Weisweiller. She is in front of some foliage, holding a ball in her right hand. The portrait of Francine in a red smock is resting.

Did the new chapter, "Of Capital Punishment." It will gain me a few more *friends*. Sent off the preface to Jean Effel.

Orengo brings us several remarkable proofs of the plates engraved from my drawings for *Le Bal du Comte d'Orgel*. I have just rewritten the preface.* With the Elzevir letters, the red capitals, and the thirty-six drawings, the *de luxe* edition will make a beautiful book.

Wire from Rosen. Dolin† interested in the ballet *La Dame à la licorne*. I wired back that it would be best to meet in Nice. I cannot go to London for the moment.

Thursday I will shoot my piece of film for Hans Richter. I know Richter's method. He writes some of us, "The others have already signed up," and in that way gets us all. But I don't care—I'm fond of Richter, and I'm delighted to do a favor for Marcel Duchamp.

A thousand little tasks which do not fill up the void. And for me, without work the void is there. I dare not go back to painting. I'd never get away from my canvas, and the texts for the film on René Clair are going to be on my back. On Saturday I'll dictate the new chapter of *Le Journal d'un inconnu*.

The police give up upon the crime at Lurs. But it seems to me that I can see the case as if I were there: The little girl was swimming nude. A young and somewhat crazy relative of the Dominicis sees her and decides to come back. He discovers that the mother and father are pitching a tent. The little girl will sleep in the trailer. He arms himself in case he fails. He fails, for during the night the little girl escapes him and runs, screaming, toward the river. He has to deal with the father and mother, who rush out of the tent. He fires and kills them. Near the river the little girl is screaming.

---

*The original edition, 1924, included a preface by Jean Cocteau.

†The English dancer Anton Dolin had danced in Cocteau's *operette dansée, Le Train bleu*, for Diaghilev in 1924.

Overcome by hysterical fear, he clubs her to death. The Dominicis arrive and advise him to run away. Terrified and fearing that someone will pass by on the road, they drag the corpses away, cover them with the tarpaulin that covered the windows of the trailer. They go home. *They will never talk.* It may be one of the brothers who is the killer, and nothing in the world can get these peasants to admit they are involved in a crime. Besides, such crimes never happen in isolation; they occur in series, and in the same style. The week of the incident at Lurs, there are several murders with rape of little girls.

The English fleet is at Villefranche.

. . . .

SEPTEMBER 16 · 1952

Reread Millecam's book. If it were not for that Algerian looseness which is so characteristic of him—that Arab sloth about revision—the book would be splendid.

Lunch with Marie-Laure—in splendid form. She is living with Marie-Thérèse in Grasse. The family, imagining her accustomed to an extravagant and mysterious life, trembles and goes out of its way not to lag behind.

Letter from Valentine,* who is preparing a book on Satie. She has been told, of course, that I am writing one.

. . . .

SEPTEMBER 17

At Antibes, Picasso is painting a huge fresco of Peace. (For Juan-les-Pins. Éluard's cantata.)

---

*Valentine Hugo, *née* Gross (1887–1968), painter and engraver, a very close friend of Erik Satie and of Jean Cocteau.

Weather uncertain. I have to shoot the film tomorrow morning. If the overcast weather keeps on, this will be impossible, Richter having sent me daylight film.

I think that Millecam's book *L'Étoile de Jean Cocteau* is too vague in relation to my works and too involved in the films—which must correspond to his own desire to make movies. There is a distance between his object of study and the text's philosophical style. This is just the opposite of what happens in Dubourg's book on my theater [*Dramaturgie de Jean Cocteau*], which follows the plots of the plays too closely—keeping the text from gaining any perspective.

It seems that the young have great difficulty in being objective. In making the plastic substance espouse the forms of their spirit. This leads them to search for the beautiful and hampers them in their pursuit of the true (their truth).

The notion of the present, which is a mirage, dominates the actions of childhood. They are where they are. They do what they do. With an incredible strength. Nothing distracts them. The action they are performing devours everything. It is the only one which counts. In my childhood, our postfuneral mourning was merely an excuse to sleep at our cousins' house and to play with them. The death of one of my uncles kept us from going to the circus. This death was regarded only from the angle of that disappointment. Until the funeral itself became, for us, another exceptional performance.

My father's sudden death was first of all a camera which he was to fix the next day and which he did not fix. I couldn't acknowledge his death since he had *promised* me to fix the camera. He broke his promise—and he had never broken his promise before. It was this detail which made his death inadmissible.

What amazes me about Doudou is that the more he works on a canvas, the fresher the picture becomes. His sketches generally lack freshness. It is by dint of working that he achieves freshness.

With all the efforts he makes, he releases his soul in colors and shapes. He must patiently untie any number of threads.

I admit my solitude—there is no other way. But I feel as though I were on a wreck drifting out to sea.

Mail. Hindemith. All set for the subject. Now to find the leading thread. Write to America for specific instructions.

Parisot wants the *Appogiatures*. I shall send them so he can return them to me with his notes. Peyraud will then take them to him in Paris.

Very long letter from Jean-Louis Barrault.

. . . .

SEPTEMBER 18

Lunch at Picasso's, at Vallauris. From two in the afternoon to ten at night he locks himself up with his fresco. No one disturbs him, not even Françoise.

. . . .

SEPTEMBER 19

Picasso is painting a hundred square meters of fresco on composition board for the Chapel of Peace in Vallauris (where the man with the sheep used to be, before being moved to the square). The chapel is behind the (primitive) monument to the dead which we like so much and which is the town disgrace. The studio (huge room on the right) is covered with construction board and lit by fluorescent light. (He says: "I suppose only you and I could take on a project like this.")

PICASSO: I haven't seen Matisse for a year. If I were in Nice, I'd go see him every morning. (Then he adds: "Do you think he'd be so happy to see me?")

J.C.: "What I admire about Matisse is his childish seriousness . . ."

PICASSO: "You're right. Matisse has never fallen into an old man's seriousness—he's fine just the way he is . . ."

Apropos of Édith de Beaumont: "After Édith's death I behaved disgustingly. I didn't answer Étienne's letters. People have to understand what I'm like. They want you to become someone else when you're through painting. My actions are the same as my painting."

Françoise's painting. She uses Picasso's syntax, but with a woman's script, full of grace. This syntax gives her script something solid.

I said to Picasso: "There are two dramas: that of being taboo and that of not being taboo. Everyone says in advance that what you do is magnificent. In advance that what I do is detestable. People see nothing of what you do, nothing of what I do. So it is better to be taboo—it leaves you as much in your solitude as I am in mine."

PICASSO: "It's sad all the same."

J.C.: "My only hope is that I may still be *discovered*. All you have left to hope for is the homage of injustice. To be *rediscovered*."

At the table I note that Picasso no longer takes his medicines. He drinks wine (which he never used to drink)—though very little.

Apropos of Maurice Sachs's posthumous books, which are being published one after the next, I remark to Picasso that I suspect that Yvon Belaval has something to do with this sudden stream. Y. B. wrote me recently: "In Maurice's next book [*sic*] there is this sentence: 'Picasso and Cocteau have spent their lives duping the world.' What should I do?" I told him: "If this nonsense comes from Maurice, leave it. If it comes from you, I advise you to remove it." He wrote me that he was removing it.

Paris and Picasso. In Paris Picasso found Balthus's picture admirable. Now, at Vallauris, he finds it "not bad," as a consequence of all the reproaches made to him for admiring that canvas.

This morning, Picasso, Françoise, and Paulo* leave for Arles, to go to a bullfight.

PICASSO (On Misia's book†): "It's easier to say things than to write them."

PICASSO: "At last we can see each other without escorts."

Phone call from the B.'s to Francine: Come back as soon as possible. Paris used to be a monkey cage—it's becoming a tiger cage. And besides, it's freezing.

. . . .

SEPTEMBER 21

Worked all last night and all Sunday on the self-portrait. Luckily the resemblance was there from the start. The task has been to organize lines and shadows so that the work remains a writer's work.

Match has me saying, under the heading "Vallauris": "Ceramics grateful to the great Picasso." Just like me. What a horror! What the journalists really want is to turn us all against each other.

This portrait stares at me with a terrible intensity. Nothing to do with our gaze in a mirror. It looks to me like another me, a different me, more myself than I am, someone who would write better than I do.

Phone call from Jeannot. Before leaving the Comédie Française, he will do both *Mithridate* and *L'Otage*. The film with Benzi‡ is finished.

---

*Son of Picasso and Olga Picasso.

†Misia Sert, *Misia*, Paris: Gallimard, 1952.

‡*L'Appel du destin*, directed by Georges Lacombe. In this film, Marais played a father for the first time, and his son was played by Roberto Benzi, at the time a young orchestra conductor.

SEPTEMBER 22

The journalists' inaccuracy comes from the bad influence of modern art; *they're afraid of resemblance*.

Worked on the self-portrait. Up to a certain point, I was doing the work. Then the portrait took over. All I had to do was obey.

Letter from Kurt Desch. It is Gustav Gründgens who will play the Cardinal (in Düsseldorf).

The translation was made from the typescript. Desch, to whom I sent the Gallimard copy, now has the promptbook cut and corrected.

I've put the new chapter, "Of Capital Punishment," after the story of the little girl and the cabbages, "Of Criminal Innocence."

It is indispensable to dictate the whole passage on the Greek trip for the *Journal*, but it will take me away from my real work. I shall dictate it at the end of October.

Wrote a dozen new texts for *Appogiatures*.

SEPTEMBER 23

When an ear goes deaf, on account of age or after some infection, hairs begin to grow in it. This is the ear's defense, antennae by which it tries to catch sound, to regain its loss.

An underwater fisherman here on the coast heard the slightest sounds at great distances while he was at work. Once his wife cut the hairs in his ears, he couldn't hear any longer—he had the sensation of being deaf in the water.

The helicopter, the water bicycle, the fiacre in which I so enjoyed seeing Rome.

Nora came for lunch yesterday.* Georges is suffering from an attack of gout and refuses to consult doctors.

*The painter Nora Auric, wife of the composer.

Mario Brun and his photographer came at four to take pictures of the mosaic.

. . . .

SEPTEMBER 26

Francine doesn't know Bernard Faÿ.* She has *never seen* him. Someone goes to the authorities and accuses Francine of having been responsible for Bernard Faÿ's escape. The authorities take action, without making preliminary investigations, and arrive at Santo Sospir. An official interrogates the shopkeeper, the garage attendant. Asks Francine for a written statement, signed by her. Disgraceful behavior.

Finished my self-portrait and the little picture of the sleeping woman with the flying saucer.

. . . .

SEPTEMBER 27 · 1952

Happiness of little girls. Carole says: "I wish I could have a day from seven in the morning to ten at night when I could do whatever I want." I ask her to describe the schedule of such a day. She thinks a minute and answers by describing all the things she usually does. But *en bloc*. The pleasure of gluttony. Childhood detests moderation.

Carole is leaving the coast tonight.

Every photograph of Chaplin published in the papers is very beautiful, noble. You feel that he exists in some sort of solitude, a mystery, an equilibrium which neither American insults nor the London triumph can destroy. Impossible to be more within the actual and within the inactual.

---

*The writer Bernard Faÿ's collaborationist attitude during the Occupation had caused him to be imprisoned during the Liberation. He devoted a chapter to Jean Cocteau in his book *Les Précieux* (Librairie académique Perrin, 1967).

Feeling ill for several days. I attribute it to the British atomic tests and also to finishing work (whether on a book, a poem, or a canvas), which leaves hands and soul adrift.

Telegram from Valentine [Hugo]: "Dear Jean, Did you know we are going to dance the acrobats from "Parade" at the Théâtre de Babylone next Tuesday in unlikely costumes against a gray wall. Kisses."

Valentine respects what is respectable. And how naïve she is. As we know—and shall know again. Helpless against an ignorant age which blurs all distinctions. The *alphabet soup* of our childhood. Amazing, actually, that a few letters still rise to the surface after so much stirring with the ladle.

. . . .

OCTOBER 3

Too much work to take notes. Painting of the *Etruscan Vase* whose edges form profiles. If I exhibit, it will be in Nice, in February. The best date for the gallery, on account of the carnival.

They have managed to make the niche for the new mosaic. It will be laid on Monday. Fine article by Mario Brun in *Nice-Matin* (photograph of the floor mosaic).

Corrected the final proofs of *Opéra* (Arcanes). Put the drawings in order.

Registered letters from Alexandre: threats, blackmail, etc.

. . . .

OCTOBER 4

Received the film of the mosaic. Will project it tonight.

Letter from Grange about my exhibition in Berlin (success). Phone call from Aragon: Éluard back from Saint-Tropez with an attack of angina. Very sick.

. . . .

SATURDAY

Visit from Mme Cuttoli, who wants me to make her a tapestry for America. Picasso is making a large tapestry for another lady. The one for the bedroom is still to be done. Since I have very little time, I have proposed a strip the size of three large canvases side by side.

Mme Cuttoli found Gaston [Palewski] very melancholy and discouraged. He says: "I am going to have to begin everything all over again." Begin what? The general has missed the boat.

Apropos of the texts to "save" Versailles: I realized in Munich, during my show there, what contribution ruins make. In the middle of the hall, they had placed some bronze statues by Rodin that had been torn apart by bombs. Which gave them a power and a strangeness so remarkable that afterward, seeing these same statues intact, I found them weaker. I wonder if all of antiquity would not benefit in our eyes from a disaster which would divinize it, imparting a sacred grandeur.

Orengo came yesterday with the test plates for *Le Bal*. They seem splendid to me. I will add the corresponding phrases from the book, which will make it possible to distribute them properly.

Saw the film of the mosaic. Excellent. I'll wait for the last reel (still at Kodak) to finish the whole thing.

. . . .

OCTOBER 10

We go to Düsseldorf on the fifteenth through the twentieth. Performance of *Bacchus* with Gründgens on the eighteenth at the Düsseldorfer Schauspielhaus.

It is a simple matter to paste a label on the product and to gain from it a certain standing. We saw Italian films benefit and then *malefit* by the label "neorealist." Now these films were made by oriental storytellers. Like the Orient, Italy lives in the street. The caliph, instead of disguising himself as one of his people, disguises himself as a camera. He seeks out the mysterious plots which occur in the streets, in the houses. In *Miracle in Milan*, de Sica carries the oriental tale to extremes.

Lunch yesterday at Mme Cuttoli's, in Antibes. She wants a tapestry and rugs. I sketched the models for the rugs. I will make the cartoon for the tapestry when I come back from Germany. Picasso has visited Matisse, who is very sick. Claude* was the only other person at the table. Went to the Musée Grimaldi—Léger room. *Dead canvases*, painted by a team.

Mme Cuttoli tells me about Polychrome Village: a wretched, inaccessible village in the mountains above Menton. Something about convincing a bank to buy the houses, so that they and the mountain can be painted, to invite artists to live in this horror.

I observe that greed in cats often prevails over instinct. The cat chooses its grass, but it eats the lizards, which are bad for it. If it is thirsty, it will drink bad water. At Milly, many of my cats and dogs have died because they drank ditchwater.

. . . .

OCTOBER 11

Sent Richter his film, after checking the editing with Dr. Ricoux.

Finished the picture of *Castor and Pollux*—intersecting profiles in the egg, with the meandering line of the swan's neck. I'll exhibit in Nice (February 10) and probably at the Grimaldi at Antibes in July.

Visit from Hartoy, and from B., who arrives from Paris. Everything he says reveals the fatigue and bad humor of that city, where

*Picasso's son.

everyone wants to criticize and where there is no enthusiasm left. Parisians find everything "boring."

Letter from Seghers, enclosing his text (the article on my poem). A publisher's article in this style is surprising.

My article "External Use" in Isou's journal (Lausanne-Paris). I had no idea this journal was so involved with politics.*

Letter from Leni Riefenstahl: ". . . I have learned through Jean Marais, to my great joy, that you care for my films. . . . Though I cannot write you in your language, I hope soon to have the pleasure of meeting you in Munich, when we can discuss the possibility of several Franco-German film projects. . . ."

. . . .

October 16 · 1952 · Düsseldorf

We were to leave Nice yesterday morning by an Italian plane at eleven, change planes at Geneva and fly to Zürich, sleep over in Zürich, and leave the next morning for Düsseldorf at eight. But the Italian plane (old model) had some sort of radio accident. By five we were still in the Nice airport, so we missed the connecting flight. Back to Santo Sospir. Started out again this morning at eight-thirty from Nice for Orly, where Alec met us and drove us to Le Bourget, to take the eleven-thirty plane for Düsseldorf. Reached Düsseldorf (Eden Hotel) at three. Gründgens was in rehearsal. He had sent his secretaries and the photographers. I am writing this note at the Eden, where the Rosens were expecting me and where I have seen Gründgens, just finished with his work. Unfortunately it appears that he has changed or cut a good deal. The German language moves more slowly than ours. The play was too long. Besides, if I understand correctly, he is afraid of the

---

*Cocteau's article (". . . it is not youth I have preserved, it is childhood . . .") was published in *Le Soulèvement de la jeunesse* in August 1952, among photographs of Communist demonstrations.

bishop, the Catholic milieu, etc. I shall go to the rehearsal tomorrow at ten-thirty, and see the journalists afterward.

Gründgens is a great actor and a great director. It is possible that he is mistaken (and he asks me to tell him so), but I should be surprised if he does not create a strange and Lutheran atmosphere for *Bacchus*. Indeed, the play is returning to its true idiom. My only fear is that Gründgens will try to "soften" it, to give it "elegance," to impress upon it a suppleness it does not possess. At least, this is what I make out of what he told me at the hotel. If it is true, it will be a pity; it is the "hard" style which would be interesting in Germany, where the French plays that are performed are so rarely violent.

Phone call from the Brekers. I shall see them tonight.

Saw the Brekers, who seem to be living in quarantine. Arno had the eminence which all desired. Unforgivable. Who would have resisted—not having a sou—the offer of everything? None of those who blame him for it. One would have to be Christ to refuse the temptation on the mountain. It is thanks to Breker that Picasso and I were saved from the worst. I shall never forget it.

. . . .

October 17

This morning at ten-thirty, Gründgens will show me the production. I spoke to Breker of his apprehensions. Breker says there is no need to be apprehensive. It is the citizens of Düsseldorf who pay an annual stipend for Gründgens's theater—he can do whatever he wants. Moreover, German theaters are run by intellectuals and not by ladies, as we do it in France. The public goes to the theater as if to church. Not for amusement, but to receive a kind of higher education.

Three o'clock. I have seen the rehearsal. Gründgens is splendid, beyond praise. The production swirls around him as though around a red column. His voice, his glances, his gestures, his whole person exude elegance and grandeur. One *sees* his slightest intentions, and a certain *expectation* before the others speak gives him an extraordinary authority. The young people are full of fire and sometimes quite moving. The company is excellent, poorly costumed, but that doesn't matter. The play gains something by its immersion in the German language.

Gründgens wears armor *à la* Richelieu under his red gown. Each time he sits down or moves rapidly, you sense that he is engaged in a dangerous mission. He has played down the humor of the Bishop's role, out of his dislike of "effects" as well as for fear of "staging" a bishop in Düsseldorf. He believes it is absurd to compromise the play for the sake of a few "effects." After the performance I went up on the stage and suggested a few pieces of business. But the theater was full of photographers, and it was difficult to be heard.

We then had an excellent lunch in the hotel grillroom, and at five I have a press conference upstairs in the lobby. Gründgens wants me to insist on the work's objective aspect: I am not expressing *myself*. It is my *characters* who express themselves.

Telegram from Desch, arriving tomorrow. Tonight we dine with the Rosens.

Seven o'clock. Just out of the press conference. Hard to make oneself understood. But I think I said what will help Gründgens. My theme was: the play is objective. Theirs was: a poet's play is never objective. I answered that the poet is merely the vehicle of the unconscious, which permits him to believe in his objectivity, even if that objectivity is subjective.

At the end they asked me if I made a plan first and then followed it from beginning to end. I answered that I started with a plan and then did not follow it.

Rosen dinner. Around eleven, the film clubs of which I am president were to call for me to say a few words at the end of one of their meetings. They must have come while we were at dinner and decided not to disturb me; I had seen some young people come into the hotel dining room, remain standing, and then leave. But unless an Alexandre drags you around by the lapels, everyone here is very polite and very solicitous about not tiring you or disturbing you.

. . . .

OCTOBER 18

As everywhere else in Germany, Düsseldorf has one brilliantly lighted street, the rest being dark and mournful. The restaurants are full of a German clientele, whereas in Paris the restaurant clientele is foreign. Difficult to understand this strange matter of a fortunate defeat and a miserable victory. Appearances are deceptive. An English boy working in the restaurant here told us: "England is lucky. Privation is universal, and no one has any special privileges." Most likely he is right, and the appearance of luxury in Germany, in France, and even in America derives only from the spectacle of privileges.

Apparently the weather was grim until just before we arrived. Radiant weather—not one cloud in the sky this morning.

This morning Gründgens invites the actors in *Bacchus* to his house; I will probably join them at eleven.

. . . .

SUNDAY MORNING · OCTOBER 19

Gründgens was amazing. The success was amazing. I got to the theater at seven-thirty. Dr. Badenhausen showed us into the little salon just offstage. The management was afraid that the bells for the war dead would ring at eight and disturb the performance.

But the authorities had given orders. At quarter to eight I took my seat at the far left of the house, with Francine and Doudou. There was a lot of applause for me in the house. Then the show began. The whole company was in top form. At the end of the first act I was impressed by the silence, for Gründgens insists that there be no applause before the intermission. The second act was performed, and then, despite this ruling, there was applause for Gründgens after his big scene with Hans. At the end of the act I could hear the applause, great gusts of sound, from the little salon. After the last act there were thirty or thirty-five calls. I had to come back and bow with Gründgens, with the young performers, with the entire company. Since the public would not stop applauding, Gründgens had them lower the fire curtain. But they went on applauding anyway. We had to go through the little door and come back out under the proscenium several times more. As we went through the little door, I murmured to Gründgens: "We're passing through the iron curtain." At eleven we went to the Maison de France. This was pathetic: some German ladies did the honors, for the consul's wife could think only of powdering herself, and the consul of eating. He said to Francine: "Let the others take care of it, so long as I have my sausages." Desch wasn't able to come, suffering from food poisoning. He had sent his colleague. We sent him a telegram signed by all of us.

Before the performance, Gründgens had sent me this message: "My heart is with you—I no longer exist. It is the play alone which will perform the Cardinal's role. Yours, G.G."

As I listened to *Bacchus* in his language, it seemed to me I wrote the play in German. Not for a moment did it seem to be a translated work. Everything showed up the mediocrity of the costumes, and transcended them. A poignant power emanated from the play. The audience never laughed in the wrong places, and always laughed in the right ones. Smiled where smiles were appropriate. Kept silent and listened religiously where silence and attention were in order. In this Catholic and Protestant house, I several times asked myself if Mauriac, in Paris, hadn't been utterly mad.

At the Maison de France, a Frenchwoman said to me: "Yes, but Gründgens is always Gründgens." I answered: "Luckily for us."

He had been concerned about playing a priest; after the performance I advised him to apply to the Vatican. I regret not seeing the results of a performance in a theater full of young people. Yesterday was what is called the "elite" audience, but it is true that this audience—usually a dreadful one—reacted like an audience of young people. The theater staff couldn't get over it.

. . . .

October 20

Yesterday I went to say good-bye to Gründgens at his (rented) house. His real house is in the Russian zone and has been confiscated. He talked to me a good deal about Erika, about Klaus, about the whole Mann family and his drama with them. "They have always looked at the surface," he told me, "without seeing what is underneath." Erika, after the fall of the Reich, wrote a book about her ex-husband [Gründgens] with the same kind of dangerous frivolity that Klaus had been guilty of toward me in New York. Dr. Badenhausen, a friend of Klaus, spirited away the manuscript and brought it to Gründgens. If the book had appeared as it was written, Gründgens would have had to speak to the audience from the stage to defend himself. Ultimately the confusion and nonsense of Klaus and his sisters were indirectly my fault; they imagined they were *Les Enfants terribles*—they even made a play out of my novel which they put on in Berlin before the war. This play was scandalous, and without the slightest connection with the spirit of the book. My children did not know their own poetry, their own glamour; in fact they detested it, opposed it. Those who imagine themselves my children want to *play* horse instead of *being* horses dreaming of turning back into people. Thomas Mann's children mixed my book with their father's "Blood of the Walsungs." All this was very corrupt, stained by drugs and bravado. Poor Klaus ultimately committed suicide at the end of this cul-de-sac of a life. Erika is living in Austria. Their drama is a drama of frivolity.

Gründgens tells me that he was in Reinhardt's company when Reinhardt put on *Orpheus* for a single night. If I understood him correctly, Gründgens, very young at the time, played the role of Death. Reinhardt's wife, Mme de Tiensk, wanted to do a production of *Orpheus—Oedipus—The Human Voice*. But Feist (translator of *La Voix humaine*), insisted on being present at each rehearsal, which exasperated Mme R. and caused the whole project to collapse. Gründgens says that Feist died fifteen days ago. I had been amazed by Feist's silence, since he had flooded me with letters obsessively proclaiming his translator's rights, which no one dreamed of contesting.

Gründgens considers *Bacchus* his greatest theatrical success in several years. Arno Breker told me later that *Bacchus* was a great piece of luck for him, since he was beginning to be the kind of idol people attack.

Gründgens told me: "My legend is as absurd as yours. I avoid it in solitude. And contact with the public does not dissipate that solitude, because I never act without bringing down a moral curtain between the public and myself. I am too afraid of falling into the trap that is constantly being set for us. The success of actors in Germany is a great danger for the young." (I had noticed in the wings that Gründgens kept drawing me away from the young performers each time I congratulated them on their work.) "For Düsseldorf, there is a pro and a con. Berlin wants me, but I am afraid of Berlin; they think democracy is their own invention."

I suppose that Berlin has a longer memory and that they still resent G.'s attitude during the Nazi regime. He is accepted in Düsseldorf because he saved so many Jews.

Gründgens sends me an album of all the photographs taken of me in the theater. These countless pictures remind me once again that you never suspect what it is you are doing and show me in a host of attitudes and positions I never knew I had taken.

G. spoke to me about the translation. At first he found it impossible, full of argot and very limp. He forced the translators to correct it, French text in hand. There was, among others, one incredible thing: when the Cardinal speaks of Copernicus, he adds: "He is stubborn as a mule." Which the translator had changed to "He's stubborn as the pope's slipper (mule)." When it came to *trafficking in indulgences*, the translator referred to the "black market." In short, I owe to G. a certain decorum and the rectification of a false breeziness which the translator must have considered "very French."

But as a matter of fact, I prefer a clumsy exactitude to an "adaptation" like Ronald Duncan's. Gründgens devoted the greatest care to revising the text and to comparing it with the original.

Now we have to wait for the press. I point out to Gründgens that a triumph in the house means nothing. It would be unfair to forget the triumph in the house in Paris, especially on the critics' night—which didn't keep them from ignoring it altogether and beating me black and blue.

We fly to Nice (through Zürich) at eleven. Dr. Badenhausen accompanies us. We are leaving this city where the theater is like mass—where, aside from spiritual nourishment, there is nothing to eat, were the young search, search, and find nothing, where children make rings around you in the street to beg for charity.

Saw the Brekers again. Mimina says: "We don't like talking about the injustice we have suffered—it would embitter us. I won't do it; neither will Arno. They've destroyed everything he's made. Now he must make something new. There's nothing else to do."

. . . .

OCTOBER 20 · 1952

Dr. Badenhausen and Gründgens's son accompanied us to the airport. With Alexandre, it was radio reporters and photographers. How calm this seems by contrast. What a relief! We stop at Frankfurt for a currency check, then at Zürich, for the connecting flight to Geneva.

We reach Zürich. Actually, except for direct flights, air travel is a suburban train, a relay coach. Arrive in Geneva at three. Met by journalists, photographers, and the radio reporters. Described *Bacchus* in Düsseldorf. I write in the Italian plane (Geneva–Nice). In Düsseldorf we had brought the sun with us. It was raining when we left and rains everywhere on our way.

Uncomfortable little plane. We fly through a storm at nine thousand feet. Shaken up, as if in an old jalopy. Stewardess scared to death. Women vomiting. We land at Nice an hour and a half late. Storm. Glad to be on the ground.

. . . .

OCTOBER 21

Wonderful sun. Summer. Weather for swimming. Too warm on the terrace. Francine's ceiling. Perfect work on the part of Lorenzi's men. I'll have the little court where the mosaics are painted brick red around them.

Letter from Mermod (Lausanne) asking for a preface to his new edition of *Carte blanche*.*

---

*Originally published in Paris in 1920.

A note that Aragon called: Éluard better. The Vél d'Hiv will be heated for the sale.* Seghers is making sure the poem will be out. I'll take the plane Saturday morning and be back at the cape by Tuesday.

I send a few lines to the Schauspielhaus for the press, written on the plane between Düsseldorf and Zürich.

. . . .

OCTOBER 24 · 1952

Mario Brun's article on my return from Germany and the success of *Bacchus* there, in *Nice-Matin*. The more time passes, the more suitable it seems to stay here on this coast, with its newspaper, its galleries, as if I were a provincial author. I got to Paris (the CNE sale) because it is absurd to seem to be spiting a city, avoiding it on principle, and because after the Liberation, when an effort was made to do me in (Breker), Aragon and Éluard kept me from being touched. Important never to forget the heart's laws.

Yesterday came a happy, fat lady in bathing costume; she got out of her car filled with dogs and children and threw herself into my arms. Impossible to locate her, to attach a name to her face. I pretended to recognize her, answering one embrace with another.

This morning a few lines from her explain the mystery; it was Marie Powers, the splendid actress from Menotti's *Medium*. Strange that someone in certain circumstances and a setting no longer appropriate to her type can become so unrecognizable . . . I had always seen Marie Powers onstage, or on the screen, or else in evening gown in the wings.

*The sale of the National Committee of Writers, at the Vélodrome d'Hiver in the rue Nélaton, on the afternoon of October 25.

Issue of *Écran français*. Description of the sale. Except for me and five or six other "names," there are only Communist writers. Everyone must have stayed away, despite the patronage of the president of the republic. If I am questioned, my personal politics are simple enough. Aragon did me a favor, and I accept.

Wrote the article for the Tiepolo-Guardi exhibition (*Nouvelles littéraires*). Will send it tonight.

Dinner last night at La Pausa. Coco and Déon are coming here for lunch today.

Tested the brick reds for the little court. Avoid the mistake of the Midi, which consists in painting façades (in Nice, for instance) an already-faded pinkish red.

. . . .

OCTOBER 25

Air France plane (Nice–Paris). Passengers' obsession to keep fiddling with the ventilators—either to focus them on themselves or to spray an icy blast on someone else; it isn't hot in the plane, which doesn't keep the ladies from smothering, fanning themselves, fiddling with the ventilators.

. . . .

OCTOBER 26 · 1952

Paris. Pleasant weather. The house. Véfour. The huge Vél d'Hiv with Picasso's splendid curtain for Romain Rolland's play.* A young man explains to a group: "Don't you see that it represents capitalism being overcome by us, and peace coming to our aid?" Later, Cécile Aubry shrieks: "What's that horror?," glimpsing the curtain

---

**Le 14 Juillet*. Revived at the Théâtre de l'Alhambra on July 14, 1936, with a curtain by Picasso and music by Auric, Honegger, Milhaud, etc.

through the crowd that parts a moment between our stand and the curtain. When the taboo of the name no longer works, poor fools say what they think. And that curtain is a marvel of grace, power, of secret equilibrium and youthful passion.

I signed books steadily for two and a half hours, till seven-thirty. The crowd kept pushing the table and crushing the partition separating the stands from the floor.

To my left was a dreadful young man, a total stranger, who was signing my books on the first page even before handing them back to me. Not knowing if he was authorized to do this, I endured it, but I forbade him to sign the poem *Le Chiffre sept*—which Seghers had just published and which I was seeing for the first time. This morning Aragon telephoned; I told him about this person, whom he thought I had brought with me. In short, a crook or a creep. Of course, it doesn't matter; people have no sense of what an autograph is. They ask you to sign books by other people, to sign anything. Cécile Aubry was signing my books. Only Doudou refused.

Before the sale, I had seen Aragon and told him what I thought of the abstainers who had rushed to the CNE during the de Gaulle period. I made 200,000 francs. All in all, six million were taken in. Éluard is critically ill. He will have to live very carefully—no alcohol. I was somewhat apprehensive about this crowd with its empty pockets—and I was wrong. It is the poor who do without and buy the most. Sometimes there would be a young man who couldn't afford *Le Chiffre sept*. And then Doudou would make someone with more money buy it for him.

The loudspeaker kept playing the Bach concerto for four harpsichords that we used in *Les Enfants terribles*. The racket was incredible. But it seemed to me that there were a lot of stands where no one was buying anything and which were giving us nasty looks. At seven-thirty I cleared out. Aragon went on selling till eight. We were at Milly for dinner. I am home with Louis and Juliette, with Annam who licks my ears, in this house which I adore and which loves me.

Huge package of books and letters.

. . . .

OCTOBER 28

Milly. Visit from the Parisots. I give Parisot the last text for *Appogiatures*: "*Places retenues.*" Visit from Josette Day. She stays for dinner and spends the night. We all leave together the next morning at eleven. Paris. Lunch with Seghers at Véfour. Phone call from Aragon at Véfour. Forty thousand francs pilfered from the 200,000 of my sale; they suspect the fellow who was signing to my left.

Three o'clock, in the rue de Montpensier. The car from the radio station arrives. I record for Seghers and *Le Chiffre sept*: two different recording sessions. And Brasseur records, too.

At four o'clock, with Grasset. I give him the *Journal d'un inconnu*. The contract had been sent to the agent in the rue Pergolèse with the title *L'Homme cet inconnu*, and the office there was quite surprised I had adopted Alexis Carrel's title (*Man the Unknown*).

At six, I record in the Rue François Ier, with Jack Palmer White, for Chaplin. At seven-thirty, Jeannot and Georges* in the rue de Montpensier. Dinner at Véfour, where I run into Lazareff, Bernheim, and Brandel. Talked too much. Tongue *soufflé*—should be the *pièce de résistance* in a restaurant where you meet journalists. Aragon telephones back that the fellow from the sale has a different name from the one on his badge. Since there were a lot of pictures taken around our stand, we'll be able to be on the watch for him.

The fellow from the Vél d'Hiv stopped in at the little bookstore in the rue Montpensier. He said, "I'm always with Cocteau. I went with him to Germany." He was trying to swipe books.

---

*The dancer Georges Reich.

This morning, several appointments. Lunch with Alec and departure from Orly around three. Will be at Santo Sospir this evening.

Saw Colette. Her left leg is bothering her, but her courage makes her seem to be in good form. I promised to send her Madeleine and the cats. In January she'll go to Monte Carlo.

. . . .

OCTOBER 29

Letter from Dr. Badenhausen: the German press continues to respond. He sends me a great pile of articles.

"Opinions" on a solid work have no importance; all that counts is the "movement" it provokes.

Pierre Peyraud telephones that someone in London wants to redo *Beauty and the Beast* in color and asks me to provide not only the script but the art direction. It would mean a small fortune for me, but how unfortunate if the British film didn't measure up to my original. If a British director could *translate* me into the language of images, I would accept. But Bérard is dead. Paquin's inspired seamstresses are dead. And what actor would consent to a makeup job for the Beast that takes five hours? Moreover, there is no question of my "redoing" something I've already done. For our agents and companies, all that counts is money. What counts for me is being alive.

. . . .

OCTOBER 30

Reread the book on Sade. Strange that people who set the soul so high and the body so low should admit all the soul's torments and gloat over them so, when his novels incriminate a man like Sade for a few minor debauches, outrages far less serious than the tortures of the Question and the poisonings of which so many kings have been guilty. Sade (like Wilde) is merely the signboard of license, which has been the mainstay of bordellos in every period, and the whores who protested his mistreatments must have suffered many others . . . Sade's case rests not on his debaucheries but on the magnifying use of them he made.

This morning the workmen are scraping and painting the little courtyard.

I wonder if I will dictate the rest of my *Journal* or wait for our return to the coast. The canvas for the tapestry isn't ready yet, so I am between two stools.

. . . .

OCTOBER 31

The garden is trying to write. Astounding: this morning the grass is growing in the form of huge capital letters, very legible but quite mysterious, like the ones daubed on walls along the highway (political slogans). The grass has been seeded everywhere. What doesn't form letters doesn't grow at all and provides these tall letters or figures with a dark green background. An unknown language.

Seghers has sent me thirty copies of *Le Chiffre sept* for dedications. I'll send them back tomorrow.

Visits yesterday from the Cléments and the Aurenches. They come from the Auberge de la Colombe at Saint-Paul-de-Vence. Aurenche tells me that Prévert is an old child playing tricks. His bad humor: I attribute it to the uneasiness he feels knowing he is a minor talent, though he dreams of being something more. Natural that he should denigrate major talents. I admit that if I were Prévert (inconceivable), I would be sick to death of hearing *Les Feuilles mortes* and *Barbara il pleut sur Brest* on the radio.

Ophüls wants me to write the scenario of a film on Isadora Duncan. An impossible film—necessarily inaccurate and absurd.

I saw too much of Isadora, and was too fond of her, to be part of such sacrilege. Obsession with flaying people still alive; Isadora isn't entirely dead. And what to show of her? And who would play this role of a woman so casual, so robust, dancing from studio to studio, and from bed to bed, from bad taste to worse, all with an extreme, untranslatable grace. (A soft Rodin.) The scarf she trailed behind her, on which some clumsy person was always stepping, which dragged her backward and strangled her in Nice—I borrowed that scarf for the scene with Jocasta and her red scarf in *The Infernal Machine*. My Jocasta is much closer to Isadora than any film could be that merely tried to tell the story of her life. Agents express amazement when I reject fortunes that would ruin me.

Speaking of Pierre Brasseur on the radio, I forgot the main thing: I was the one who gave him his first role—in my adaptation of *Romeo and Juliet*.* He was the page of Marcel Herrand, who played Romeo. Jean Weber also made his debut in the piece, as my page (I was Mercutio). We were all very young.

Sent Desch a lithograph for the cover of *Bacchus*.

The little red courtyard is painted. I see now that we should have painted the inside of the arcades as well. The work will be done after we leave.

To help—in all modesty—our works create themselves.

Chaplin greeted by all the riffraff of the movie world. Happy to be far away.

. . . .

NOVEMBER 1

Tomorrow, *Jour des morts*. All my wonderful dead will be in my room. How could I complain? They protect me, surrounding me

---

*First performed in 1924 and published in 1928.

with their splendid emanations. I live with a woman who is an angel, an adopted son who is another. At Santo Sospir, which is a paradise.

I work at what works in me. The rest I reject. I am (and I don't touch wood) a happy man. Besides, I have no fear of death. Am I doing what I have to do? I have no minute free to do more.

Why is it, I wonder, that I have always had acclaimed failures, catastrophic successes? Because a group of journalists and the famous Parisian elite try to put themselves between the public and myself. This obstacle vanishes abroad. I suppose it will block my path until my death, and even after; for example, Jean-Louis Barrault's mistake of selecting the plays for his American tour according to the judgments of Parisian critics. I had proof of this in Germany. It is true that *Bacchus* requires close attention—difficult in another language.

Has this obstacle influenced my withdrawal from the theater and the cinema? Very likely it has. The certainty of having to fling myself against this wall must paralyze my old craving for the spotlights, the footlights. The obstacle is the same for books, but somehow books trouble this pack less.

Forty years of this pack. Forty years of their pursuit. Forty years of keeping ahead. Forty years of being treated as a beginner . . . Forty years of freedom. For forty years I've been in their hair.

Richter has received the film and sent it to the laboratory to be duplicated. Duchamp offers to compose a speech with the words spoken backward, though without using a mechanical reverser. Direct reversal. It would be funny to reverse this backward method so as to turn the words pronounced backward forward. An unforseeable language.

Summer weather. Not a cloud in the sky. Flowers. The lawns continue their strange typography.

Dictated this morning the preface on the dance for Jean Guéritte. Preface for another book on dance (for *l'Arc-en-ciel*). Mostly about Diaghilev.

Nothing bothers me so much as my attacks of depression when I see only the wrong side of the medal. Make myself do breathing exercises, and abide by those orders which one gives the unconscious—and which it records.

To be happy in the sun and complain: ignoble. H. told me in Düsseldorf: "I don't like beautiful weather; it makes too great a contrast with my solitude and my work. You have to be happy and free to endure the sun."

Telegram from the producers of the René Clair film: they're coming Monday to show me the reel.

Intoxication with the mechanism of cities. L. used to say to me: "You won't be able to take it." Convinced that I am depriving myself. That I am doing myself harm by living in the country.

In France people adore funerals, cemeteries, black clothes. Chrysanthemums on graves.

. . . .

NOVEMBER 2

I notice that ever since the film of *Les Enfants terribles*, the Bach-Vivaldi concerto for four pianos is constantly played on the radio—and it never used to be played at all. This is always one of the benefits of cinema.

I remember that after *Les Enfants terribles*, Francine found a stack of the records in a shop on the Champs-Élysées, and when she asked for the concerto for four pianos, she was told: "You mean the music for *Enfants terribles*." Strange times.

While I am writing these lines, the radio is broadcasting the first movement of the concerto. Then the speaker announces: "You have just heard the concerto for four pianos by Bach-Vivaldi." Digest style.

This week, nothing but Chaplin—but not a word about his film. Only the title and then how much people love him. The laughter and tears the film inspires. His public fame rests on his secret glory. He has transcended judgment. *Verdoux* is a secret glory. This film was resented because Chaplin didn't accompany it to Europe. When Chaplin travels, his secret glory can be smothered under praise.

The truth that our colleagues smother under their praise came out the day before yesterday—out of the mouth of René Clément: "I am amazed. The photography in *Limelight* is worthless. I am never wrong about the photography of a film. I can't make anything out of it." Etc. So speak these gentlemen when they speak in the name of the cinema. "You have only one school. Your own. You are the greatest of the great" and other hollow remarks that avoid talking about the film.

I haven't seen *Limelight*. I suspect it is the crowning glory of the "Laugh Clown Laugh" state of mind, of which Dali has spoken. A twist of the handlebar to the right, after the twist to the left (*Verdoux*). But the soul of Chaplin's films never changes, the gaze of his films, something which transcends taste and technique—the main concern of our filmmakers.

Claudel's visibility, and Giraudoux's, have killed and judged their invisibility. It is significant that *Tête d'or* is never revived, the one play in which Claudel still seemed to protect his invisibility (had not yet found the secret of pleasing).

Letter from Studio-28, after the visit from Frédéric [Rossif]. Charles de Noailles told them that I was the only one who could persuade Marie-Laure to release the negative of *L'Age d'or*. They want to revive it with *Le Sang d'un poète*. (I have written to Marie-Laure.)

Offenbach, a musician of genius. Everything is invented—new, airy, inimitable. Records of *La Belle Hélène*—the wrong voices. And impossible to understand a word. French singers (especially the women) don't understand articulation. Of course, the German language is more elaborately articulated than ours—but one can sing French without being inaudible. When Americans learned the French text of Menotti's *Consul*, none of them knew our language. They learned its mechanism. That kind of work produced an ideal articulation. You understood everything. Hence it is not impossible to make our singers articulate—but no one dreams of doing so.

Jeannot telephones. He will see Chaplin tomorrow at the Artists' Union. I told him to whisper in his ear why I have avoided meeting him in that mob. It seems that at the reception in the rue Ballu, Bernstein interrupted an intimate exchange between Chaplin and René Clair by laying a familiar hand on Charles's shoulder; when Charles looked up in surprise, he said: "I am Henry Bernstein." Total blank.

I have begun taking notes for the text on the film on René Clair, *Naissance d'un film*. The producers are coming tomorrow with the reel. I'll see it at Beaulieu. I've already decided not to follow the images, which produce a pleonasm. I shall talk to the public (through Gérard Philipe) as if I had my back to the screen. I used this method for Emmer's *Saint Ursula* (Carpaccio).* That came off well. I'd like the music of Clair's films to accompany my words.

When I was asked to give Ingrid Bergman her Oscar, it was at the Louvre, under the spotlights, at the feet of the *Victory of Samothrace*. A speech was expected. But since Ingrid didn't understand our language, I found it simpler to say a few words of welcome and to embrace her (which was not easy, since she is so tall). A few days later, it was my task to present Cerdan and Chevalier on the stage of the Opéra. In the wings Chevalier said: "Whatever you do, don't talk about the others." Housekeeper's

---

***La Légende de Sainte Ursule*, 1948. Jean Cocteau wrote the text for this short documentary.

work. If you refuse, you seem a monster. If you accept, people say: "Him again." Better to keep clear of official festivities. (Which doesn't avoid prefaces and memorials. But that is less tiresome than presence.)

An American lady, a friend of Roosevelt's, said to me at Mme Cuttoli's: "Isn't there a little too much fuss about Chaplin? After all, he's only a clown." I answered her: "I hope you are fortunate enough to have many clowns like Chaplin, or like Garbo, or like Einstein." They're not your compatriots, but you owe them what prestige you have.

. . . .

NOVEMBER 3

The producers of the René Clair film came this morning. I'll see it tonight.

Apparently the young people of the Cocteau-Théâtre in Vienna have done nothing much. The Vienna journalists congratulate me on not having come to see their performance. But how can you deny the young their opportunities? Besides, it is not impossible that the journalists are mistaken.

Huge package of letters from Paris. Answered them all. Difficult to refuse trips and lectures. But you can't keep running over the face of the earth. The mere idea overwhelms me with exhaustion and puts my mind in a whirl.

Saw the film—rather disorganized. But it will turn into something if we link it together with words.

. . . .

NOVEMBER 4

May weather. The flowers are deceived. The honeysuckle is sprouting, and the iris. Dictated the text of the film. Went to the Victorine to see the reel—with the music (desynchronized last night at Beaulieu). The music adds a lot. I'll try to record tomorrow and to shoot the scene they want.

Phone call from Jeannot. He's seen Chaplin's film, which he finds admirable. *People are disappointed because it isn't funny.* Jeannot was crying so hard at the actors' reception that at first he couldn't speak to Chaplin. However, he overcame his tears, gave him my message, and Chaplin then told him that he had to go to Scotland first. Then he announced in *Le Monde* that he was going to the Midi to see his friend Jean Cocteau. I'd be very sorry to leave the coast before he got here. The same wild-goose chase as during my last trip to New York.

. . . .

NOVEMBER 5

Supposed to record and shoot this morning at the Victorine, but all I could do was record from ten to noon. Shooting these two wretched scenes lasted from one to five. The Victorine was empty—filled with oranges and flowers.

Rosen telephones again about that film of Ophüls's on Isadora Duncan. I can't seem to make them understand that I'm the last person in the world to undertake such a project.

At the Victorine, I saw the site of the Air France crash. The plane grazed the laboratory roof, clipped off a palm tree at the edge of the studio, crashed into an olive tree in the neighboring field, right at the fence. The head of the lab was sick over it for three months. They lifted the corpses out of a flaming pit (the gasoline). There must have been a terrible moment: when the lab chief thought that some madman was buzzing the roofs.

Don't close the circle. Leave an opening. Descartes and the Encyclopedists closed the circle. Pascal and Rousseau left it open. One must avoid filling in the gaps. Our age has made this mistake.

. . . .

NOVEMBER 6

Sent off the copies of *Le Chiffre sept*. Prologue to great cataclysms.

. . . .

NOVEMBER 7 · 1952

Mauriac awarded the Nobel Prize.

I finish the big tapestry for the Biennale.

Favre Le Bret telephones and asks me to agree to be president of the Cannes jury. Articles on *Bacchus* in Germany still being sent to me by Dr. Badenhausen.

Huge package: Grasset's proofs (for his own book).* He telephones and asks me to read them ("very carefully"). My own book has gone to the printer. Which saves him from having to read it.

I listen to the records of *La Belle Hélène*. Perfect music and words. I knew Hortense Schneider—at Mme de Chevigné's. She was ninety years old. She crooned her way through her part for me and said that the orchestra had complained to Offenbach that she wasn't following them, whereupon Offenbach had shouted from out front: "Then all you have to do is follow Mme Schneider." That was the first time the orchestra had followed a *chanteuse*.

" *'Dis-moi Vénus'*—and I showed a little bit of my leg and made a suggestion of a gesture of a high kick. But just a suggestion, you know. I would say *'Dis-mois Vénus, quel plaisir trouves-ti'*—because I had noticed that in the theater *ti* became *tu* . . ."

It's true that I knew both Empress Eugénie and Hortense Schneider. The young people around me can't get over it. For them it's as if I had known Marie-Antoinette and Jean-Jacques Rousseau.

---

*Bernard Grasset, *Textes choisis*, edited by Henri Massis, with a portrait of the author by Jean Cocteau (Paris: 1952).

Have just seen the film of the paintings in Kodachrome. Doudou's picture *is* the house—the likeness more intense, truer than if we had filmed it directly. I'll have these films put end to end and show them during the Nice exhibition.

. . . .

NOVEMBER 8 · 1952

Finishing the cartoon of the tapestry. Back to Paris next week.

Begun reading the Grasset proofs. After all, he thinks, and what he thinks he writes well. Of course, he doesn't mention either *Les Enfants terribles* or *La Machine infernale*, but I should have expected that. And this doesn't bother him in the least, when he telephones: "I've sent you my proofs because you are one of the three people who matter to me."

Prepared the catalog for the Nice exhibition—with a short preface.*

I worked morning, noon, and night on the panel for the tapestry. I have become bodiless—abandoned by my real self, which is struggling to emerge, to take its place on the canvas. No sense of time. It was nine in the morning; it is nine at night. I have noticed nothing. Besides, I close the shutters and work by electric light. Without any points of reference. All of it lasts a moment. And the phonograph keeps playing over and over the same record from *Don Giovanni* where the recitatives come hurrying one after the other—where these fanatics exchange secrets at the top of their lungs, punctuated by the harpsichord.

Hindemith is right to say that the recitative is a sublimated theater. I keep thinking about that opera he wants me to write for him.

---

*This exhibition was held during the month of November 1952 at the Gallery Jean de Cailleux, rue du Faubourg-Saint-Honoré.

Two long-playing records which I just leave on the machine to play over and over: *Don Giovanni* and *La Belle Hélène*. A melodic genius links these otherwise unrelated works.

Those fine minds I scandalize so have taken their time, I believe, in coming to understand Mozart's tragic quality. At one time they granted no more importance to *Don Giovanni* than they now grant *La Belle Hélène*. Art should inspire an erection in the soul. All the rest is literature. It doesn't matter what excites me; it is always invention and figures. The exact and the discovered. Research bores me to death. The soul doesn't respond.

. . . .

SUNDAY · NOVEMBER 9

Storms, tidal waves, earthquakes. Houses collapse in the north. Waves ten yards high submerge the southern coasts. Man doesn't find this to be enough; he dreams of H-bombs, of manufacturing cataclysms.

Back to *La Belle Hélène*, which I tire of no more than of *Don Giovanni*. Because I set invention (what you find before you look) above technique and aesthetics. Spiritual quality is expressed by the operetta as much as by the opera. Mozart and Offenbach (strange as the pairing of these two names may seem) must have had charming and cruel souls, filled with grace and vitality. Even in Offenbach there is a certain sadness, a certain sense of the tragic. The chorus "*Pars pour la Crète*" is funny but savage. Poor Menelaus is as pitiable as Leporello. The same is true of Gounod's *Faust*, which I rank above many respected works, and which, in its oneiric freedom, joins *Pelléas*.

In our period, the last inventors of melodic line function in a minor zone. Maurice Yvain—whose line abandons him whenever he aims higher—Charles Trenet—and sometimes Marguérite Monnot, Piaf's collaborator. They find something . . . No one else.

The rest all substitute a sort of plaintive and pessimistic cantilena for the optimistic rhythm of an "air." When we awarded the Prix du Disque, we had a terrible time finding a melody likely to pass from mouth to mouth—to be whistled in the street.

Le Sacre du printemps can be whistled in the street. I've heard it under my window at the Palais-Royal. Later I learned that the whistler, a mason, used to be a stagehand at the Théâtre des Champs-Élysées.

This strange pairing of Mozart and Offenbach reminds me of another. For the caricaturists Sem and Cappiello,* by the profound truth, the intensity, the elegance of their line, if they do not achieve the vitality of a Lautrec, greatly exceed a host of *serious* painters.

France makes me laugh when she protests against certain Nazi ceremonies—which take place in Germany. Is she doing anything different, with her anti-Semitism and Rebatet's two fat volumes† honoring the (SS-type) false Resistance and the Vichy personnel?

Human memory. It has already been forgotten that in a ridiculous poem entitled "As You Wish, General" (World War I), Claudel says: "And Goethe and Nietzsche, with their vomit of shadows, whose very name wakens horror. . . ." And the ode to Marshal Pétain that has become the ode to General de Gaulle? . . . There must be limits.

Poor Mauriac. At his death he will have had it all. Except it.

Reread Millecam's book in detail. He analyzes the invisible by means of the invisible. He does not manage to change my invisibility into an object. If you don't follow me, you cannot follow him.

---

*The influence of Georges Goursat, known as Sem (1863–1934), and of Leonetto Cappiello (1875–1942) is apparent in Cocteau's early drawings. See his preface to *L. Cappiello* by Jacques Viénot (Paris: 1946).

†Lucien Rebatet, *Les Deux Étandards* (Paris: 1952), two volumes.

This is the case with all interesting critical works. (Rivière on Rimbaud.)

Millecam's exegesis of *L'Ange Heurtebise** doesn't stand up. But no exegesis does. Like the man who said of Picasso's curtain: "It's Capitalism smothering the world and Peace coming to the rescue." Why not? A work is always susceptible of a thousand different allegories. It is the pretext for each reader to use it according to his talents. As for *L'Ange Heurtebise*, Millecam adapts it to his own person and attributes his own feelings to me. No doubt he will be quite amazed by the chapter of *Journal d'un inconnu* where I describe the birth of this poem. He will say: "Cocteau doesn't understand himself, so I will assume the responsibility of understanding him."

Wind fallen. Cloudless sky. I linger at Santo Sospir. I should go back to Milly, but I am taking advantage of the flowers until some general blows the whole thing up.

America. Stevenson, swept into the political mainstream, may not realize the unexpected weight of failure. An occult influence is stronger than an official power. His minority is no such thing; he can do a great deal, much more than Ike and Mamie, neutralized by success.

Chaplin's triumph. True glory, acclaimed and acknowledged, is the rarest thing. It can occur only in the realm of the cinema. I was thinking of his remark "I wish I could cut the dance with the rolls out of my film." At his first Parisian dinner (Tour d'Argent) the people at the next table asked him to do *the roll dance*, as was to be expected. He refused quite politely. "It's an old gag, too old," he said to those boors.

Sartre had asked me to sign the Congress of Vienna manifesto, against the cold war. This morning I saw my signature in *Les Lettres*

---

*Poem, with a photograph of the angel by Man Ray (Paris: 1925). Reprinted in *Opéra*.

françaises. As Sartre's signature proves, this manifesto is not a Communist one, but in a spirit of freedom two Communists have been invited to sign it: Éluard and Aragon.

. . . .

NOVEMBER 10 · 1952

Letter from Baden-Baden and a very nicely done program for *The Infernal Machine*. The letter from the Institut Français considers the production remarkable and the sets of "great intensity." There remains the translation; if it is the old one, it is detestable (the one revised by Maria Fein).

Gründgens performed in Wiesbaden. The demand for tickets has obliged the company to give an additional matinee.

Still no answer from New York about the film or from Gélin about his cover. And I took so much trouble to keep neither Gélin nor Richter waiting.

Letter from Tours. The printer Arrault says he is sending copies of *Opéra*, "in which *our good typographers and printers* have done their very best." The word he uses for *typographers* is *typos*.

Incredible weather. Warmer every day, and more beautiful. This morning, a family was picnicking on the *rond-point* of the cape, outdoors.

. . . .

NOVEMBER 12

Received the copies of *Opéra*. Impeccable work. Bad cover: stale, fancy.

Charles de Noailles, to whom I had written about Buñuel's *Age d'Or*, answers that he fears a Catholic cabal. He had told Rossif: "Speak to Cocteau. Only he can convince my wife." Marie-Laure tells me: "Speak to Charles." Charles tells me: "It's my daughter Laure's affair." Etc.

Telegram from Danièle Delorme: "Daniel* in a serious accident." No details.

Recorded a text about Darius Milhaud at Radio Nice for Italy.

Sent the poster for the Nice exhibition to Mario Brun this morning.

Still no news of the duplicate film from New York. Incredible.

. . . .

NOVEMBER 13

This year, a poetry offensive. *Le Chiffre sept*. New edition of *Opéra-Appogiatures*. Let the rest sleep. *Journal d'un inconnu* should be the center of the mechanism. Success or failure, no matter. Line of work. Follow that.

Telegram from Richter: "Film delightful. Letter follows. Marcel [Duchamp]. Richter." The incredible slowness of New York. The duplicate won't be ready until next week.

Jeannot telephones. He has heard nothing about the accident referred to in Danièle Delorme's wire.

Telephone call from the prefecture: authorization granted. They had thought we wanted to build on the boundary line. Francine and Doudou went to Biot with the contractor and the workmen.

Admirable Francine. One sees such things only in *L'Auberge de l'Ange-Gardien*.† Who else would buy a house and a vineyard? Who else would see to its being totally furnished in order to insure a family's happiness? Only she—without ever wanting such a thing to be known—as if this miracle were entirely the responsibility of Doudou's father.

Just reread the proofs of *Carte blanche*, which Mermod is re-

---

*The actor Daniel Gélin, husband of the actress Danièle Delorme.

†A novel by the countess de Ségur (1864).

publishing in Switzerland. I wasn't, as it happens, the least embarrassed by this work from 1920, except to notice that I frequently repeat myself. But it is indispensable to repeat oneself in order to be understood. Everything has shifted, changed, blurred. Picasso has become Dionysian. A vast tropical disorder is growing out of our modest flower pot. But I was right to announce that a great house was being built. Yesterday, on the radio, there was no need for me to change anything in speaking of Darius; all the old things I had said about him were still true. In short, I happen to discern no break in the line, no assertion I am ashamed of.

I wrote a long letter to the Hindemiths, listening for the hundredth time to the recitative of *Don Giovanni*. I'd like to find a recitative style to frame the "airs" Hindemith wants from me. Maybe go back to the notion of the modern *Faust* I was supposed to write with Kurt Weill . . .

In a letter from Jules Romains (whom I had written, congratulating him on his speech about our confusion of values): ". . . I need not tell you that in reminding the Institut de France of its duties of renewal and 'essential' recruitment, I was thinking of men like yourself."

I keep thinking about that modern Faust in the form of an opera (airs and recitatives). Hindemith's wife is hypnotized by Don Quixote. A hateful subject for singing and the theater. As has been proved: each time anyone touches this masterpiece, a catastrophe results.

. . . .

SATURDAY · NOVEMBER 15

Back to Milly. Splendid weather. Provence lovelier than Greece. Detours and fog around Auxerre slow us down. We embrace Point* at five. Milly at midnight.

---

*Chef of the restaurant La Pyramide, in Vienne.

. . . .

SUNDAY · [NOVEMBER 16]

Jean-Pierre Peyraud for lunch. Considerable success of *The Eagle Has Two Heads* (play) in Liège. Case of *Beauty and the Beast*: I consider the possibility of taking everything in hand, if I am given a free hand.

. . . .

MONDAY · NOVEMBER 17

Back to Paris Tuesday.

. . . .

NOVEMBER 18

Saw *Limelight*. Not tears: fear. Chaplin pleads without being accused. He believes he is the defendant. He is, as all poets are. But the film is bitter—which is unpardonable, given his fame and his fortune. One day he said to me: "How many kicks in the behind I had to receive to make certain serious things understood." No doubt he wanted us not to laugh at his films, but to pity him. He has a childlike fury of humanitarianism (like Einstein). In *Limelight*, he pours out a great rancor upon the public. From which there results an embarrassment, an uneasiness. The theater was almost empty. The film is being shown in four huge houses. But Chaplin's glory has transcended his success.

In short it's America's fault: Chaplin is pleading his cause in America and against America. Elsewhere, where he is loved, this no longer holds.

The clown's name: Calvero (Calvary)—the calvary of a clown. I remember his telling me about a film he wanted to make: the crucifixion in a bar. No one realizes what is going on. A drop of blood falls from Jesus onto the shoulder of a dancer, who flicks it off. Only a dog howls at the moment of death. (Very Belgian. Very Swiss.) Charles wants to be a thinker, and thinks only in terms of action. He gives up "gags" because he wants to be only a thinker. To explain. To prove. To prove that he gives women their start and that they abandon him (that he sacrifices himself for them).

Éluard died at nine this morning.

At Éluard's. Someone else on his bed. A huge alabaster puppet.* Dominique† brave and simple. All the horrible stir around the haughty indifference of the dead.

Wrote a few lines for the press. Will broadcast tomorrow morning.

Saw Small this morning: I think I will entrust him with all the translations of my plays. I can't go on letting mself be betrayed left and right. Give the plays to Small and the books to James Lord. (At least *Journal d'un inconnu*. Unless I put everything in Small's hands.) He has made an excellent impression on me.

Snowing. We'll go to Milly Tuesday night. Back on Saturday for Éluard's funeral.

. . . .

NOVEMBER 21

In Paris, back in mud up to the eyes. Éluard's death transformed into a political demonstration. I have quickly returned to the country. I'll attend the funeral tomorrow. (Luckily the police have forbidden the procession.) We'll meet at one-thirty in front of the cemetery. That charming little spring of pure water being disguised as Victor Hugo.

---

*See Cocteau's poem *"Quel est cet étranger . . . (Portrait de Paul Éluard sur son lit de mort),"* in *Clair-obscur*.

†Éluard's wife.

Marcenac, in Paul's bedroom: "I'm beginning to realize who you are." He says this, but in my ear.

Any praise of me would make them *all* sick. But they are not sick when it comes to calling on me for prefaces, articles, broadcasts, etc.

At Picasso's. The radio. He talks. Claude Roy talks. I myself had talked in the studio in the avenue Recteur-Poincaré. Obvious that the proceedings disgust Picasso as much as they do me. And I am asked to be president of the "Friends of Charles Chaplin." And other presidencies, which always cause more trouble than they are worth.

. . . .

NOVEMBER 22

Thiébaut asks me for a chapter of the book for *La Revue de Paris*. Already gave one to *La Table Ronde* and one to the *NRF* (Paulhan). Grasset may feel I'm giving the book away. I've said as much in my answer to Thiébaut.

Bellmer writes me for the frontispiece of *Appogiatures*.*

Received and read the missing parts of the Peter Doyle–Walt Whitman text. Either it's true and of incredible interest. Or else it's false and this Davoust is a sort of Douanier Rousseau of eroticism. I'll give the thing to Parisot to figure out. Very suspect but very curious. [Added later: "The piece was apocryphal."†]

Six o'clock. Back from the funeral. No rain. Grim. In the grandstand, to the right of Dominique and Aragon. On the bier, tricolor and the mask molded on Paul, in his lifetime. Huge photograph in the style of the Stalingrad ceremonies. Political speeches. Aragon's violent diatribe against the police (who had forbidden the proces-

---

**Appogiatures* was published with, as a frontispiece, a drawing of Cocteau by Modigliani. A drawing by Hans Bellmer illustrated the poem "*Pieds d'Omphale.*"

†See Jean Cocteau, "Translation of a text from Peter Doyle to Walt Whitman" in *Le Livre blanc*, followed by fourteen unpublished erotic texts, introduction by Milorad (Paris: Éditions Persona, 1981).

sion). "I would forbid it," he said, "for Sartre and for Mauriac." In short, the police have saved everyone from having to make a terrible winter's walk. Hideous Père Lachaise: a huge garbage can. As we're walking out, Vercors stops me: it's Balzac's little grave.

Casanova, the Communist deputy, says in his speech: "China is in mourning." On one of the big wreaths: "The Vietminh to its beloved poet."

Letter from Gertrude Hindemith . . . Extreme difficulty reaching an agreement with them on the subject for an opera.

. . . .

NOVEMBER 29 · *Milly*

It has been impossible to write a single word. Since nine in the morning, the doorbell has been ringing, and people have been waiting, sitting on the stairs. Everyone wants something. I escaped to Milly. The result of all these little tasks is that I can't correct the proofs of my book, and my real work is interrupted. For instance, I have just written: the page for Sartre for the Congress of Vienna. The page for Colette's birthday (*Vogue*). The page for my presidency of the Friends of Charles Chaplin. The preface for the exhibition of children's painting. The fifteen minutes for the BBC French broadcast. Answered the letters forwarded from Santo Sospir.

Style of telegrams, 1952: " 'Orpheus is your host. Communion with you next Saturday—Ajaccio Ciné Club."

The crates have arrived from Germany; we can't get them out of customs because that blessed Alexandre has the senders' slips and insurance papers. *The Infernal Machine* is being performed at Baden-Baden in an infernal translation, with sets which they are trying to tell me have determined the work's success. *Les Monstres sacrés* is being done in London with no indication that it is an old entertainment written to distract Yvonne de Bray from the agonies of 1940. At Berlin on December 12, a festival is being organized for *Orpheus*, "because this film has never left the major houses of Germany since its first showing" (I've sent this letter to Lulu W. as hardly corresponding to the distributor's accounts).

Chaos. Chaos. My little agent tries to make order, but the mountain of chaos appears ever larger. I have held up all English-language translations and entrusted my translations to M. Small, a very decent fellow with a great textual intelligence. For forty years now I've managed to survive on a name, on legends, without anything solid to sustain them.

. . . .

NOVEMBER 30

Finished correcting the first proofs of *Journal d'un inconnu*.

I have a cold. Rain. Workroom ceiling leaking.

Parisot telephones that the missing proofs for *Appogiatures* have been found. Ask him to add to Bellmer's plate my drawing by Modigliani and a wash drawing by Bérard.*

. . . .

DECEMBER 1 · 1952

Lunch with Sartre. He asks me for a letter for the liberation of Henri Martin. When Martin distributed his texts in Indochina, he did not yet belong to any party, any group. His solitude represents the spirit of freedom of France. We cannot respond to it by imprisonment.

Mauriac's frenzy to force his way into a family of minds where he does not belong. Articles on Sartre, on Genet, on Éluard, on Pichette, on me, all prove his rancor at not being one of us. By "us," I mean even enemies concerned with the same things.

---

*This was not published.

Corrected the first proofs of *Appogiatures*. Sent Modigliani's drawing and Bérard's to Parisot.

I suppose we'll manage to get the crates out of customs on Thursday. We'll open them at Francine's, in the presence of the insurance people. Customs says there's a difference of eighty kilos from the sending weight. Perhaps they have forgotten the painted bricks.

Paris is a funny town. Publishers know perfectly well what their colleagues are doing. Moreover, Grasset has announced everywhere that his Cahiers Verts are publishing *Journal d'un inconnu*. Letter from Gaston Gallimard: "I hear you have written a *Journal d'inconnu*, which I certainly expect you will let us publish. Etc."

Saw *Mithridate*. Considerable success, one which exceeds the level of the performance. *Only Jeannot is a prince*. He played his role with extreme reserve. The paternal friendship Yonnel (Mithridates) feels for him was perceptible and came over the footlights. The entire gallery shouted: "Marais! Marais!" at each call. Which in the newspaper *Aube* became: "Jean Marais was booed."

At the Café Régence, after the performance, the director tells me he's going to revive *La Voix humaine*, with Louise Comte and Casarès alternating. I had promised the role to Louise Comte. But Casarès would be marvelous in it. When I promised the role to Louise, Maria was not yet a member of the company.

Yonnel takes me aside in the wings and begs me to persuade Jeannot not to leave the Comédie Française. But aside from the face that he's ruining himself financially, I need him to revive *La Machine infernale*.

. . . .

DECEMBER 2

Visit from Jean Genet. Very uncomfortable. This is no longer the Genet who attacks. It is the Genet who asks for advice. The advice is simple: write. If he doesn't write, he doesn't eliminate. He poisons himself.

"You and Sartre have turned me into an idol. I am someone else. And this someone else has to find something to say." He talks about going to Morocco.

. . . .

DECEMBER 4

Letter from the mayor of Joinville. The Saint-Maurice studios are to be closed (consequences of the Leduc maneuvers). Fake ruin in order to sell to the Americans.

Whatever you do, you're in a crossfire. A day will come—and it's coming closer—when it will be impossible to remain in the middle. This is what I realize in Sartre's case. (He has refused to have *Les Mains sales* put on in Vienna during the congress.)

Portrait of Grasset. Very difficult. Blurred face. Bad lighting in the rue des Saints-Pères. Fluorescents and old yellow bulbs. Better finish at home tomorrow.

Thiébaut telephones from *La Revue de Paris*: Wants authorization to cut three or four sentences from my chapter.

Dinner at Hersent's. He's been stuck with all the *art brut* leavings. I remember the cellars of Léonce Rosenberg, where all the sub-Cubists used to be stacked—Herbin, Metzinger, etc. H.'s walls are covered with bandages, mustard, grimaces, onion soup. Certain New York museums look like this. Too bad, for if Claude is *le bourgeois gentilhomme*, as Balthus claims—he's still a fine fellow.

. . . .

DECEMBER 5

Auric informs me of a scandalous silence in the press with regard to Jean Desbordes, tortured and killed in the rue de la Pompe without opening his mouth. He is referred to as the "pharmacist Desbordes." Jean had *married* a pharmacist. And now, when every last-minute Resistance worker is overwhelmed with praise, a shadow is cast over the death of this splendid boy, just as a shadow had been cast over his works.

Took the proofs of *Appogiatures* to Milly. Orengo has managed to buy my books from Paul Morihien. He plans to pulp the three thousand copies of *La Difficulté d'être* and do a new edition without the countless misprints of the original.

Text for the BBC approved. I send it to Small for him to translate. It will be read in both languages.

Four o'clock. Just finished the portrait of Grasset in the rue de Montpensier. I couldn't manage it in the rue des Saints-Pères. I found him at my place, in his absence. I've actually pretended to redo it, adding only the lines of the shadows.

Paul Morihien has just had me sign the paper authorizing him to sell the books.

Beautiful letter from Edith Sitwell, thanking me for dedicating a poem to her. Letter from Gaston Gallimard: lunch next week at Véfour. Letter from Marcel Duchamp, arranging the sound for the film.

. . . .

DECEMBER 8 · 1952

The Orengo operation is complete. The books will go from the rue de Beaujolais to the rue Garancière.*

Millecam surprised by the silence surrounding his book on me. The silence is a normal thing. But it is difficult, I admit, to get

*Books published by Éditions du Rocher were at the time distributed by Librairie Plon, 8 rue Garancière. Charles Orengo was the literary director of Librairie Plon during the fifties.

used to that alternating rhythm of racket and silence. I still feel the discomfort and the shock of it.

Yesterday found all the notebooks of my *Journal** which were at Paul Morihien's. Leafing through them, I realize once again how much you must accumulate in order to obtain ever so little. The terrible labor concentrated in a single drop, whose scent immediately evaporates. I put the notebooks in a drawer. Overwhelmed with fatigue just reading them.

Letter from Düsseldorf. Gründgens is sick—which upsets the *Bacchus* tour.

Yesterday I had a kind of fit about plays not revived, books poorly distributed, translations not made. I must surmount these disgusting weaknesses at all costs. Today, Monday, I shall stay alone in the country. I must reflect and get hold of myself. Too much happiness in the right-hand pan of the scale is paid for in the left one. It is important to acknowledge this and to fight against depressing emanations.

I am dying slowly and at top speed. I scorn this earth and accumulate actions and objects. I tremble for those I love. My own death is indifferent to me, except as it inspires fear in them. I struggle slothfully. I am the site of incomprehensible contradictions. My intelligence terrifies me.

Finished the preface Grasset wants for René Bertrand's book. In it I say: "You treat me as a scientist. I treat you as a poet. Here is something to reduce the conspiracy of noise to silence. Our students 'dry up.' Our duty is too difficult . . . Our silence collaborates with the silence of the cosmos, with the silent mechanism of the stars."

Even if I do not understand what I am, that is what I must be. My only safeguard.

Amid a thousand notes which I find helter-skelter in my cup-

**Journal sous l'Occupation, 1942–1945* (forthcoming).

boards (I have just come across the first version of *The Infernal Machine*, which I thought was lost), I set aside this note which proves that for a long time I had been thinking about a journal which would not be strictly speaking a journal at all. "I'd like never to have to worry about taking notes, but in the evenings just to write down some brief remark, a phrase which I dropped in conversation, or which someone else said to me. I should think there would be fewer losses in a man's mind if he did something of the kind and remembered only what struck him most. If I had been so rash as to keep a journal, aside from the fact that it would involve too many people in my affairs, no one would believe how many different things happen to me every minute of the day—and incredible things, since I myself wonder if this is even possible and if the people around me aren't crazy. One or two notes a day would avoid the jumble so difficult to understand and inadmissible for those to whom few surprising things happen and who, far from rejecting them, long for them and hope they will happen."

Rereading these lines, I realize that I often exceed this rule and that I still record too many details. My life has changed. Once it was a fall, and I bounced from step to step. Now what confuses me derives from the multiplicity of the forms of expression I adopt. But my life in itself is calm, exempt from that conflagration which was incessantly lit in my rooms and which I fled, carrying away the fire. If you open an old trunk, you are horrified because it disgorges forgotten dramas, photographs of faces you no longer recognize, letters you don't remember ever having received, dead friendships. I think of those drawings of mine scattered all over the world, of those texts strewn left and right, which would fill several volumes.

On the same day I am shown an article in the *Observer* declaring that I have become famous without ever writing and an article from Berlin entitled "Universality of Jean Cocteau." Probably the British journalist has never read anything by me and therefore assumes I have written nothing. Probably the German journalist has read a little by me but divined the animal's skeleton according to the few bones which have come into his hands.

Leafing through the notebooks of my *Journal*, I come across this curious and significant (undated) letter from Jean Anouilh, which reveals the source of *The Thieves' Carnival*, of *Eurydice*, of *Antigone*: ". . . Of course you are one of the essential spectators of my *Antigone*, and I didn't know you had come. The sensibility of those of us who were twenty between 1925 and 1930 owes you Greece and the games of death. I owe you something else essential, the sense of play. One fine day at the age of 16 or 17, I emerged from my Batailles (so to speak) and stumbled over *The Wedding on the Eiffel Tower*; it was love at first sight. With the seriousness with which I do everything, I began studying this comedy-ballet to discover how such a thing could be done. And that was the beginning of an essential turn of my career. . . . Afterward, I read *Orpheus*. 'I'll tell you all this better.' . . ."

During the Occupation, Jünger once said to me: "If newspapers are ever published on a postage stamp, there will still be room enough to insult you."

. . . .

DECEMBER 10

Lunch at the Élysée, *en famille*. The president's extraordinary freedom of speech. He told me about the struggle he had to get Colette her cross (of the Legion of Honor). One wonders why, having given her the cravat, they should refuse to go any further. Nothing more absurd than such nuances. "She performed stark naked on the stage of the music hall." I was able to speak as freely as I would at home. Good people who dream of a long rest in the country.

. . . .

DECEMBER 13

Letter to Maurice Bessy: ". . . the definitive word as to my view of *Limelight*. Charles's genius is not in question. But when one has become the crowd's idol by playing the role of a bum, the crowd will not tolerate one's playing a bum's role.

The noise around a name permits them to impose silence around a work.

Laurence Olivier asks the Comédie Française to send only Marais's *Brittanicus* to London. Long faces of those ladies and gentlemen.

Telegram after telegram from London. Translation and translators eliminated. No question of protecting me, but of protecting themselves. Poor answer from Miss Hoeck in the *Observer*, after the article about me. Abusive ladies. My agent adopts the formula: protect M. Cocteau against himself.

Doudou. His virtues have the same power as others' defects.

Genet organizes around those he loves a kind of abstract beauty which excites their ethical sexuality. He kneads them. He torments them until they prove themselves worthy of him. Then he abandons them, and they become the strange escort of knights ready to defend him against any attack whatever.

Received the thick book in which my study on Apollinaire is published.*

Badenhausen writes that our young "Bacchus" has had an automobile accident. He is in the hospital. The theater has called in an actor who performed the part in Oldenburg.

A masterpiece testifies to a form of spiritual depravity. If it were transformed into an action, society would punish it. Which is, moreover, what usually happens.

**Les Écrivains célèbres*, vol. III, edited by Raymond Queneau (Paris: 1953).

I have passed through the wall of noise. I have passed through the wall of silence. I am disintegrating.

Honi soit qui bien y pense.

On the radio, Astruc talks about his film, which has just won the Prix Delluc. He cites past winners, forgetting only me, of course (I won it for *Beauty and the Beast*).

I have been asked for a little note in *Les Lettres françaises*, in *Ce soir*, and in *Les Nouvelles littéraires* to say that the "pharmacist Desbordes" is none other than Jean Desbordes.

. . . .

SATURDAY · *Milly*

Letter from Genet about *Le Chiffre sept*: ". . . I have just read *Le Chiffre sept*, and you can understand my delight in realizing that you have remained the poet you always were. The whole movement of the thing is magnificent, but what I love above all is the simplicity of tone and the pathos of the theme. The passage from the sea to the madwoman is perhaps the finest part. Well, I am very happy and I send you this little letter to tell you so, and to tell you of my very great affection. . . ."

I was thinking this over last night. My enemies (who express themselves by pen or by silence) have considerable justification. I turned my coat between twenty-five and thirty. True. But only to put it *right side out*. They cannot understand this. Especially since I realized my errors long before I was capable of furnishing valid proofs of my conversion, of my transition from a facile life to a profound one.

Giraudoux used to say to me: "You are our lightning rod. When someone thinks of falling on us, he falls on you."

I'm rather fond of the publishers who are so concerned to pick our nits—Grasset, for instance, or Thiébaut at *La Revue de Paris*.

They open our eyes to our oversights, our confused sentences. They do us the greatest favors. Thiébaut keeps telephoning (again this morning) to warn me about this or that suspect term in the chapter "Of Distances."

At Mme Cuttoli's. Claude Valéry tells me that his father wrote down, between four and six every morning, whatever came into his head. Result: cupboards full of note books whose publication is impossible because it would fill fifty volumes and cost a fortune.*

Names. *Borgia* is a tragic name. *Goethe* a huge, serious name. Etc. *Jules Romains* could never convince his public under the name *Farigoule*. *Jean Cocteau* possesses a sort of comic lightness. This has a lot to do with people's fear of linking it with "serious" studies of fiction, poetry, drama, cinema, etc.

. . . .

SUNDAY–MONDAY

Wrote the preface to *The Thousand and One Nights*. Extended the BBC text. Back to Paris this morning. Exhaustion of buying bears, monkeys, rabbits for the children. I don't remember if I've told the story of the toys and Frédéric Pagnol. Michel Simon brought a box of toys to the Pagnols. Frédéric opened it and shouted with delight. Marcel: "You might say thank you." Frédéric: "Oh? I thought they were presents."

. . . .

CHRISTMAS · 1952

The more hairs fall out, the more antennae grow in.

---

*Valéry's notebooks have been published in two editions: one in twenty-nine volumes, by the Centre National de Recherches Scientifiques, 1957–1971; the other in two volumes by the Bibliothèque de La Pléiade, edited by Judith Robinson, 1973–1974.

Journalist: What would you like to see hanging on your Christmas tree?

J.C.: Journalists.

A mountain of difficulties of every kind. Twenty years of negligence and vagueness. Pierre and Orengo have met and are trying to establish a little order . . . But there is too much chaos, and everywhere. This attempt to set things right disturbs the countless profiteers accustomed to pilfering me, exploiting me unhindered.

Reread Sartre's wonderful text on Mallarmé in volume III of *Les Écrivains célèbres* (where I published my Apollinaire). I think that because of his secret desire to be a poet, Sartre is the only man capable of discussing poets, and if I were to ask anyone to write the preface to a monograph on me, it would certainly be Sartre, who it is fashionable to say despises poets and doesn't understand a thing about them.

Christmas at Milly. The tree. Children. Francine gives me a painting by Renoir, a beauty. I hang it in my bedroom. I give her the manuscript of *Le Chiffre sept*. (The Renoir represents a cart and a woman under three trees. Slate sky. Pink ground.)

. . . .

DECEMBER 26 · 1952

Alone in Milly. Francine and Doudou in town. They come back tonight. Nothing is harder for me than living in the country without work to do and without yet having got into the habit of it.

Doubts about Small as a translator. Don't forget that my style is not Anouilh's, or Puget's, or anyone else's. Translators do not realize that something else exists besides the meaning and that the weight of each word forms the equilibrium of a sentence.

I'd like to reach an agreement with Orengo, so that his services would extend beyond the publication and republication of my books. I'd like him to exercise control over everything I produce—keep my work from fraying out—rewind the spool. Pierre is first-class as far as checking a contract or a sale goes; unfortunately he knows nothing about the mechanism of letters. For twenty years now the spool has been paying out the thread, anyhow and anywhere. One wonders by what miracle my name has remained on people's lips. (No doubt because of the films.) Now a writer's basis is his books, and my written work is a floating derelict. L.W. couldn't care less; she was concerned (however inadequately) only with the films.

Today, the day after Christmas (the tree is still on my workroom table), I should try to see a little more clearly. By dint of emptying old trunks, rereading old texts, rediscovering old drawings, I realize that my real life as an artist began *very late*, and that the attacks of a milieu in which I divined a certain truth (the truth) had many justifications. Instead of going to school until I was twenty, I *began* at twenty, with the wrong luggage visible on my back. How long was the period in which I tried to make up for lost time! Even at the moment of *Parade* and the sojourn in Rome with Picasso (1917), my inner and outer styles were not beyond reproach. It was with *Le Secret professionnel* (1922) and *Thomas the Impostor* (1923) that I began. *Le Grand Écart* (1923) belongs to a confused zone between what had entangled me and what would allow me to find my way out of the maze. All the works which precede my meeting with Radiguet give me the impression of the clumsy efforts of someone trying to grope his way out of a snare, with no particular method or patience. *Orpheus* (the play, 1926), *Essai de critique indirecte* (1932), *La Difficulté d'être* (1947)—and not forgetting *The Infernal Machine* (1934)—are works in which I had found my way, but I should like to follow it farther. In the *Journal d'un inconnu* there are snarls I am incapable of disentangling. Perhaps one publishes too quickly.

Should one put away the manuscript—wait? Perhaps then our mistakes would stare us in the face.

What matters is the hard, simple style—one that doesn't leak, one that sticks. Such a style never shows its age. Its only risk is to become unreadable for the distracted, as has happened with Montaigne (by dint of precision and point).

. . . .

DECEMBER 27

Frequently, reading a book, I come across some offensive remark aimed at me. Apparently authors act by contagion, or else I attract such iron filings like a magnet. Many of these little wounds are delivered to me from a frivolous past which has assumed, in order to reach those authors, the slow speed of starlight: what age and work have made of me *has not yet reached them*. Nothing is more dangerous than a "start." Your entire career is influenced by it, even if a tremendous effort takes you beyond the initial circumstances. You will never be thanked for such efforts, and any transformation you work upon yourself will in fact be regarded as a deception. A brilliant debut followed by a collapse or else a good average—that is what prevails.

Universally suspect: that is my lot. And I should have so loved to be believed, to inspire confidence. Naïvely I had hoped my work would ultimately conquer bad faith—but bad faith is invincible. I have already supplied it weapons against me, and it profits by them. It will always profit by them, even after my death. Bad faith has the power of publicity. *Do not take me seriously*: that has been pounded into their heads.

My name has outstripped my work. Now my work must catch up with it.

When too much injustice overwhelms me, I listen to the recitatives from *Don Giovanni*. In them I always find calm and solace.

. . . .

DECEMBER 28

Mass at Milly. The old priest very proud of his heating system—which doesn't work. Very proud of his organ—which plays out of tune. A few old ladies and some awkward young people. The scandal is that such sublime teachings and such serious ceremonies should have fallen so low (confusion of goodness and stupidity).

The older I get, the more I believe that it is only goodness which counts—but a goodness which does not extinguish mind, a goodness which functions as wickedness functions, a tenderness as blind as hate.

It is certain that my behavior is incomprehensible and that if I were to change it, I should throw the spiritual mechanism out of joint. The old priest must have wondered why I was at mass this morning, since I do not customarily attend. If I were to play the role of chatelain, I would go to mass every day. If I were to play the role of atheist, I would never go. But I play no role and regard myself as neither chatelain nor atheist. This morning I experienced a kind of inner order (or counsel) to go to mass. I am in the habit of obeying this sort of impulse without attempting to understand it. I suppose that this order (or counsel) corresponds to the profound necessity I experience to follow not "a line" but "my line." Which disconcerts the French symbolized by Molière, whose miser is continually miserly and whose jealous lover is continually jealous. Whereas living consists only of contradictions in being, of accidental levels which fuel the machine. This morning there were only broken machines around me in church, machines still running only because of a slight incline . . . I have often noticed this among the Communists, though it is easy to be fooled because the incline is steeper; the broken machine rolls faster.

I confess not having understood a word of the pope's Christmas message. The pope is against both individualism and disindividualization-by-dictatorship.

"If you oppose the death penalty, what would you do with criminals?" I would form them into a legion, a splendid resource for nourishing the legal crime of war.

Our drama is not to have acknowledged that the mystery was within us, to have located it outside. The gods. God. Our virtues: God. Our defects: the devil. Henceforth the *know thyself* had no further meaning. It is the taboo of primitive peoples, born of their fear and feared by them after having externalized it. "Man has made God in his image" is no joke but the sad truth . . .

I think, therefore I am. One could say: I think, therefore perhaps I am not, since thinking allows me *to believe that I am*.

In Bergson, as I recall, every philosophical system can be simplified, then simplified further, and further still, until it becomes a point. And this point is what the philosopher was not able to say.

The particular will always (ultimately) conquer the "general."

My old general Clapier used to say: "A general must never yield—not even to the evidence."

Translator's Note

IN THIS FIRST of several volumes of late journals, we enter with Cocteau upon the last decade of his life. Nor will it come as a surprise, to those of us who have followed him (at a distance) through the most metamorphic career in Western culture since Merlin, yet the most single-minded poetic vocation since Orpheus, that Cocteau here repeats himself—indeed cannibalizes himself. The last two volumes of prose,* half journal and half essay, excellent in their Montaigne-like sagacity, draw upon the life registered in these journals, the complex and harried existence of a man who could *stage* anything.

Perhaps it is of some use, certainly it is of great pride, to his translator that 1953 was the year I myself met Jean Cocteau. It must have been during one of the very few days the poet allowed himself in Paris, and I recall my pilgrimage as an effort to resolve,

**La Difficulté d'être* and *Journal d'un inconnu.*

by application to a master, the conflict between concentration and dispersion. At the end of what I might call in the full sense of the word an *audience*, I remember how the poet gave me some advice which it turns out he gave to a great many others as well—perhaps because it was such good counsel in his own case. Dryly, wryly, as he spread his famous hands between us, Cocteau said: "What other people reproach you for, cultivate—it is yourself." I see now that there was an answer—or at least, a response—in the impatient poet's words, and I have translated his journals in order to keep faith with his . . . faith, the faith of a poet in his unpersuadable calling.

The specific merit of these journals is, of course, the *energy* of the life displayed, excruciated, fallen upon the thorns of its own creative impulse. Beyond the discontents of the sixty-year-old *grande vedette*, beyond the ill-tempered sniping at Gide, at Proust, even at Genet, there is a fundamental action in these journals which makes them Exhibit A in the alphabet of our exemplary dedications: *poein*, "to make." Indeed, in accounting for the works which constitute no more than episodes of his career, Cocteau assigns to them a series of variations on the notion of *poetry*: *poésie de roman*, *poésie critique*, *poésie de théâtre*, *poésie graphique*, *poésie cinématographique*, etc. We are to understand that once a Cocteau produces novels, criticism, plays, drawings, films, they cease being these things and become part of *poetry*, which, like electricity, is not so much a thing as the way things behave once they are made by a human being. (Of course, this is not the same as saying that they become merely Jean Cocteau, though that is always—dangerously—the next step.) The splendor of this distracted existence is the generosity of an inveterately creative impulse. On almost every page Cocteau responds to his own necessities (". . . finished the new poem . . .") and to the demands of others (". . . sent off the introduction to Apollinaire . . ."). Drawings, films, poems (and the management of their appearance in the world), an endless stream of objects and texts, of *works and plays* are secreted by the poet as the cocoon within which he will stave off death (even if at times it is no more than silence that he defeats). The charm and the *lesson* of this journal are there, in the dedication to work, even in these late years, the work of recuperating his own past. . . .

In this particular volume Cocteau undertakes a new *mise-en-scène* for the opera-oratorio *Oedipus Rex*, upon which Stravinsky invited Cocteau to collaborate back in 1925 (". . . because I greatly admired his *Antigone*. . . . Cocteau's stagecraft is excellent. He has a sense of values and an eye and feeling for detail which always become of primary importance with him. This applies alike to the movements of the actors, the setting, the costumes, and indeed all the accessories . . ."). In a sense, this final staging is the completion of a cycle which had made many demands: in 1928 Cocteau published his French text for the opera-oratorio (originally performed in Latin) and six years later came to terms with the myth of Oedipus, or rather the cycle of myths that extends, as Cocteau himself points out, from the hero's "Siegfried-like youth, consumed with curiosity and ambition . . . to the transfiguration of this playing-card king," who triumphs over his conflict by submitting to it, who emerges from his tragedy by sinking *through* it, who passes from "the livid, mythical light of quicksilver" out into sunlight—blind, ignorant, and guided by his daughter, Antigone, who speaks with the voice of his mother and wife, Jocasta. The terms Cocteau came to are generally regarded as his finest work for the stage, a masterpiece of the modern theater, *The Infernal Machine*, a crowning expression of that truly Parisian gift for an encompassing style in which all of Cocteau's long career flourished (floundered?) at times so flagrantly as to seem—who has not resisted *all* those seductions, but who has not yielded to *some* of them?—frivolous, but always with the true *lacrimae rerum* note. Appropriate, then, that in these late journals Cocteau should return to *Oedipus*, to himself. For it is not only an exploitation of his *patrimony* that Cocteau stages anew for his old master and friend, a symbolic murder of his father (as classical literature is received and devoured as the ancestor of French literature), but the other great inheritance, the other great theme of descent that he *realizes* here: the theme of the Possession of the Mothers. All of modern French literature is under this sign, of course; that is why so many of the greatest works of the twentieth century are by homosexuals: Gide, Proust, Cocteau, Jouhandeau, Genet. Deposing Daddy, marrying Mommy: that is the great occidental undertaking, and in Cocteau's Oedipus cycle, from *Antigone* to the final *tableaux* for Stravinsky's great music, all the instruments concur, all the influences converge to create beyond the incest taboo as beyond the stigma of sexual heterodoxy, a dazzling emblem of parricide and piety as we have traditionally known it in our cultures. Now that Jocasta is internalized into no more than a voice, speaking only when her daughter and granddaughter, Antigone, speaks, now that Oedipus is mutilated, the marital conflict is at an end, and the pair are simply—simply!—mother and son, or father and daughter, again. Purified, they pass, with Antigone, into what Cocteau's voice (he narrated the work with Stravinsky conducting, in Paris and in Germany, in the course of these journals) properly calls *gloire classique*.

The reader will be interested to find Cocteau projecting these roles onto the odd family he has reconstituted for himself: his adopted (younger than himself) mother, Francine Weisweiller; his adopted son, Édouard Dermit. There is an extraordinary psychodrama taking place in the course of these often vexed, vehement, vociferous pages, a reworking of the Sophoclean recognition scene at Colonus (Santo Sospir—Paris was his Athens), a domestication of the sublime—an inclusion within the household bonds of life of precisely what had loomed as inaccessible, ecstatic, aloof.

In this volume we find Cocteau accommodating his life to myth with all the insolent familiarity of a rightful heir. *Spectateurs, vous allez entendre. . . .*

—RICHARD HOWARD

Works by Jean Cocteau

Poetry

POÉSIE, 1916–1923 (Le Cap de Bonne-Espérance.—Ode à Picasso.—Poésies.—Vocabulaire.—Plain-Chant.—Discours du grand sommeil)
ESCALES, with André Lhote
LA ROSE DE FRANÇOIS
CRI ÉCRIT
PRIÈRE MUTILÉE
L'ANGE HEURTEBISE
OPÉRA, ŒUVRES POÉTIQUES, 1925–1927
MORCEAUX CHOISIS, POÈMES
MYTHOLOGIE, with Giorgio De Chirico
ÉNIGME
POÈMES ÉCRITS EN ALLEMAND
POÈMES (Léone.—Allégories.—La Crucifixion.—Neiges.—Un Ami dort)
LA NAPPE DU CATALAN, with Georges Hugnet
LE CHIFFRE SEPT
DENTELLE D'ÉTERNITÉ
APPOGIATURES

CLAIR-OBSCUR
POÈMES, 1916–1955
PARAPROSODIES
CÉRÉMONIAL ESPAGNOL DU PHÉNIX
LA PARTIE D'ÉCHECS
LE REQUIEM
FAIRE-PART

Poetry of the Novel

LE POTOMAK
LE GRAND ÉCART
THOMAS L'IMPOSTEUR
LE LIVRE BLANC
LES ENFANTS TERRIBLES
LA FIN DU POTOMAK
DEUX TRAVESTIS

Critical Poetry

LE RAPPEL À L'ORDRE (Le Coq et l'Arlequin.—Carte blanche.—Visites à Barrès.—Le Secret professionnel.—D'un ordre considéré comme une anarchie.—Autour de Thomas l'imposteur.—Picasso)
LETTRE À JACQUES MARITAIN
UNE ENTREVUE SUR LA CRITIQUE
OPIUM, Journal d'une désintoxication
ESSAI DE CRITIQUE INDIRECTE (Le Mystère laïc.—Des beaux-arts considérés comme un assassinat)
PORTRAITS-SOUVENIR
MON PREMIER VOYAGE. Tour du monde en 80 jours
LE GRECO
LA BELLE ET LA BÊTE, Journal d'un film
LE FOYER DES ARTISTES
LA DIFFICULTÉ D'ÊTRE
LETTRE AUX AMÉRICAINS

WORKS BY JEAN COCTEAU

REINES DE FRANCE
DUFY
MAALESH, Journal d'une tourneè de théâtre
MODIGLIANI
JEAN MARAIS
GIDE VIVANT
JOURNAL D'UN INCONNU
DÉMARCHE D'UN POÈTE
DISCOURS DE RÉCEPTION À L'ACADÉMIE FRANÇAISE
COLETTE
LE DISCOURS D'OXFORD
ENTRETIENS SUR LE MUSÉE DE DRESDE, with Louis Aragon
LA CORRIDA DU PREMIER MAI
POÉSIE CRITIQUE I and II
PICASSO, 1916–1961, illustrated by Picasso
LE CORDON OMBILICAL
LA COMTESSE DE NOAILLES, OUI ET NON
PORTRAIT-SOUVENIR. Interview with Roger Stéphane
ENTRETIENS AVEC ANDRÉ FRAIGNEAU
JEAN COCTEAU PAR JEAN COCTEAU. Interview with William Fifield
POÉSIE DE JOURNALISME, 1935–1938

POETRY OF THE THEATER

LE GENDARME INCOMPRIS, with Raymond Radiguet
PAUL ET VIRGINIE, with Raymond Radiguet
THÉÂTRE I: Antigone.—Les Mariés de la tour Eiffel.—Les Chevaliers de la Table Ronde.—Les Parents terribles
THÉÂTRE II: Les Monstres sacrés.—La Machine à écrire.—Renaud et Armide.—L'Aigle à deux têtes
ORPHÉE
ŒDIPE ROI—ROMÉO ET JULIETTE
LA VOIX HUMAINE
LA MACHINE INFERNALE
THÉÂTRE DE POCHE
NOUVEAU THÉÂTRE DE POCHE
BACCHUS
L'IMPROMPTU DU PALAIS-ROYAL

Graphic Poetry

DESSINS
LE MYSTÈRE DE JEAN L'OISELEUR
MAISON DE SANTÉ
25 DESSINS D'UN DORMEUR
SOIXANTE DESSINS POUR LES ENFANTS TERRIBLES
DESSINS EN MARGE DU TEXTE DES CHEVALIERS DE LA TABLE RONDE
DRÔLE DE MÉNAGE
LA CHAPELLE SAINT-PIERRE, VILLEFRANCHE-SUR-MER
LA SALLE DES MARIAGES, HOTEL DE VILLE DE MENTON
LA CHAPELLE SAINT-PIERRE
GONDOLE DES MORTS
SAINT-BLAISE-DES-SIMPLES

Books Illustrated by Cocteau

LE POTOMAK
LE SECRET PROFESSIONNEL
LE GRAND ÉCART
THOMAS L'IMPOSTEUR
LE LIVRE BLANC
OPIUM
LA MACHINE INFERNALE
PORTRAITS-SOUVENIR
RENAUD ET ARMIDE
ORPHÉE
PORTRAIT DE MOUNET-SULLY
LÉONE
DEUX TRAVESTIS
LES ENFANTS TERRIBLES
LE LIVRE BLANC
ANTHOLOGIE POÉTIQUE
LA NAPPE DU CATALAN
OPÉRA
DÉMARCHE D'UN POÈTE
CARTE BLANCHE
LE GRAND ÉCART—LA VOIX HUMAINE

WORKS BY JEAN COCTEAU

LA CORRIDA DU PREMIER MAI
THÉÂTRE I ET II
LE SANG D'UN POÈTE
NOUVEAU THÉÂTRE DE POCHE
LE CORDON OMBILICAL
QUERELLE DE BREST, by Jean Genet
LA COURSE DES ROIS, by Thierry Maulnier
LE BAL DU COMTE D'ORGEL, by Raymond Radiguet
SOUS LE MANTEAU DE FEU, by Geneviève Laporte
DOUZE POÈMES, by Paul Valéry
JEAN COCTEAU TOURNE SON DERNIER FILM, by Roger Pillaudin
MONTAGNES MARINES, by André Verdet
TAUREAUX, by Jean-Marie Magnan

Cinematographic Poetry

LE SANG D'UN POÈTE
LE BARON FANTÔME, dialogue for the film by Serge de Poligny
L'ÉTERNEL RETOUR, with Jean Delannoy
LES DAMES DU BOIS DE BOULOGNE, dialogue for the film by Bresson
LA BELLE ET LA BÊTE
RUY BLAS, with Pierre Billon
L'AIGLE À DEUX TÊTES
LES PARENTS TERRIBLES
LA VOIX HUMAINE, with Roberto Rosselini
LES NOCES DE SABLE, commentary for the film by André Zwobada
ORPHÉE
LES ENFANTS TERRIBLES, with Jean-Pierre Melville
LE ROSSIGNOL DE L'EMPEREUR DE CHINE, commentary for the film by Jiri Trnka
LA VILLA SANTO SOSPIR
LE TESTAMENT D'ORPHÉE
LA PRINCESSE DE CLÈVES, dialogue for the film by Jean Delannoy
DU CINÉMATOGRAPHE
ENTRETIENS SUR LE CINÉMATOGRAPHE

Works with Musicians

PARADE, ballet (Éric Satie)
HUIT POÈMES (Georges Auric)
CHANSONS BASQUES (Louis Durey)
LE PRINTEMPS AU FOND DE LA MER (Louis Durey)
COCARDES (Francis Poulenc)
LE BŒUF SUR LE TOIT (Darius Milhaud)
TROIS POÈMES (Darius Milhaud)
DEUX POÈMES (Jean Wiéner)
LES MARIÉS DE LA TOUR EIFFEL (Groupe des Six)
SIX POÉSIES (Arthur Honegger)
LE TRAIN BLEU, ballet (Darius Milhaud)
SIX POÈMES (Maxime Jacob)
ŒDIPUS REX (Igor Stravinski)
LE PAUVRE MATELOT (Darius Milhaud)
ANTIGONE (Arthur Honegger)
CANTATE (Igor Markevich)
CHANSONS DE MARINS (Henri Sauguet)
LES TAMBOURS QUI PARLENT (Florent Schmitt)
LE JEUNE HOMME ET LA MORT, ballet (Johann Sebastian Bach—Ottorino Respighi)
PHÈDRE, ballet (Georges Auric)
LA DAME À LA LICORNE, ballet (Jacques Chailley)
LA VOIX HUMAINE (Francis Poulenc)
LE POÈTE ET SA MUSE, ballet (Gian-Carlo Menotti)
LA DAME DE MONTE-CARLO (Francis Poulenc)
PATMOS (Yves Claoué)
ŒDIPE ROI (Maurice Thiriet)

Index